FILIPINO IMAGES

Culture of the Public World

New Day Publishers

REPRINTED 2005

Published by
NEW DAY PUBLISHERS
11 Lands Street, VASRA /
P.O. Box 1167, 1100 Quezon City
Philippines
Tel. (632) 928-8046 / 927-5982
E-mail: newdayorders@edsamail.com.ph

Copy Editor: **Elena Damaso**
Cover Art: **Achilles Saligumba**
Formatter: **Harold J.C. Alvarez**

The National Library of the Philippines CIP Data

Recommended entry:

Mulder, Niels.
Filipino images : culture of public world / by
Niels Mulder - Quezon City : New Day Pub., c1999
1 v

1. Culture. 2. Social evolution. I. Title.

HM 101 306.09599 1999 P99000160
ISBN 971-10-1038-0

Background

In Southeast Asia, I have been studying urban middle-class culture ever since I came there in 1965. At that time, I went to Thailand. Later on, Java (Indonesia) became a field of interest. In 1983, I arrived in the Philippines and hoped to find a place comparable to Chiangmai and Yogyakarta. Ironically, I chanced upon Lucena City, a town with little historical depth and no traditions of its own. Meanwhile, I must have spent some 28 months in the islands, and much of that time in and around the city of my choice.

Much the same as most foreigners, I noted the country's "western" facade: the currency of English in the press, the law, and when speaking to me; the (Filipinos') casual "openness" to strangers. As an anthropologist, I knew I was in for trouble. Things, nowhere, are what they appear to be. Westernization, whatever that is in public life, may conveniently cover how things really are and how people really think. Naturally, and soon enough, I would find out.

When, in time, I came with my first interpretations, or rather ideas about life in the society I observed, it was as if I were making allies and adversaries. One colleague was adamant in dissociating himself from my work. A well-known social critic blew his top and refused to talk to me. Then, those remaining friendly with me had their objections, too. They liked the title of my preliminary paper, "All Filipinos Go To Heaven," but protested what they perceived as negativism. Even the observation that Filipinos demonstrate great intimacy with the saints and the Trinity drew ire: "You are making fun of us." My dearest friend remarked: "All white people look down on us." I was included.

One thing this indignation made crystal clear, foreigners are irritating. If they say something friendly, it must be mistrusted. If they say something neutral, it must be negative. If they say something honest, it must be damning, "They do not take us seriously." This is not to say that Filipinos who take their fellow Filipinos seriously would not be critical. They are painfully carping of their society, "I recommend you take a puff. That pastry is good here. It is just like Filipinos, puffed up and full of hot air." I am probably not supposed to remember such remarks, and certainly not to concur with them.

All this did not keep me from publishing my ideas as they matured. I brought them together in *Inside Philippine Society.* When launched, the book was introduced as:

> I was shocked with what NM was saying in his new book. He was saying things about the Philippines and Filipinos that were the opposite of what I knew. I didn't like it. That was during my first reading. Now I have read the book two times more, this time *between the lines*. If I read him correctly, he is saying we Filipinos don't know pretty much about ourselves. And I accept that, wholeheartedly.

The once thoroughly angered critic reacted to it, too, "What I like about it is the fact that it is a very compassionate rendering of my society." All the same, I had been impressed by the vast quantity of adverse opinion that greeted my, and other foreigners' work. When I discussed this predicament with a well-respected American Jesuit, he knew the situation inside-out, "In this place, you can't win."

Too many foreigners have come to Philippine shores. Too long was the period of colonization. Too deeply penetrating were the elements of alien culture. Filipino being was subverted, and the time of *being* on their own has been so short. The time to discover themselves and to build a self-confident nation was, so far, simply not there, and all the time they feel–rightly or wrongly–to be surrounded by arrogant powers who think they know better. Small wonder Filipinos are oversensitive to foreign opinion. They could do without it, and yet, of all Asian countries, the Philippines is probably most exposed to the "globalizing world," and thus may feel that cultural colonization continues unabatedly. This indeed is very vexing.

Not to add insult to injury, I should, perhaps, shut up, just watch, and keep my ideas to myself. Another option was to collect the ideas Filipinos advance about their own being and society. What are the ideas about themselves they circulate among themselves? After all the criticism I had been exposed to, after my and their frustration, this seemed to be an eminently interesting project. This was how I decided to collect *Filipino Images*. The images I chose to amass are those circulating in the wider society, those that contribute to the making of public opinion.

I think I could not have done this work without my previously gained familiarity with the Filipino way of life, at least, as I learned to appreciate it during my regular stays in Lucena. There, I got to know many people who helped me to gain some understanding. I've also been so fortunate as to meet a few persons who have been persistently patient with, and good to me. Vinya Alcala, and Poly Belen and her family by themselves make me come back as often as I can. During the period of gathering the data on the culture of the public world, I met many knowledgeable people in Metro Manila. Over the past few years, though, I have grown weary of the capital, and my contacts there declined. Even so, I still want to express my appreciation to Fernando "Butch" Zialcita for his continual interest and support.

Niels Mulder

Preface

The text of this book could have been structured in a variety of ways. What the reader is presented with now is a step-by-step introduction to Filipino culture that moves from the most accessible to the less-easy-to-come-by aspects of life. We begin with the urban environment, the image somebody who is newly arriving can see for himself. This is not to say that such a newcomer understands everything that catches the eye, but it is first impressions that, upon longer acquaintance, may gain more, or diminish in, significance. A townscape, after all, is an environment fraught with messages, a good reading of which can tell us a lot about the life going on there and the spirit that inspires it. This is what our grand tour of Lucena City aims at.

We are interested in more than just buildings and locations, monuments and churches; we want to discover what these, and banners, flags, pollution, and parades convey. Granted, these are images as they come to the outsider; they could also be seen by locals, but most often locals are not aware of them. Residents are used to it all; they take it for granted, thus, my drawing of attention to certain things frequently evoked amazement, as well as irritation.

Still I think that an environment, even if not consciously noted, impresses the mind in the same way "hidden persuaders" do. I, therefore, also maintain that it tells about mentality.

The second step in our discovery tour brings us to the newspaper. As the Philippine broadsheets are published in English, they are quite accessible. While we shall also review the vernacular tabloids, we shall be mainly concerned with the more prestigious press. The question remains all the time, as to what images do the press impress on the mind?

How do people in the public debate describe their society? What are the aspects they highlight? To find this out, we shall begin with first impressions resulting from an intensive reading of one of the biggest dailies published. Like the image of the townscape, we speculate about what a newcomer may note in this newspaper. Then the account moves on to the inventory of three broadsheets and three tabloids, all issued on the same day, in order to inspect the run-of-the-mill reporting. Most of the fun is in the chapter's third part when we spend attention to certain recurrent topics. These will be illustrated by extensive quotations which, in their turn, frequently require short introductions or commentary to be able to place them in context.

By their very nature, newspapers refer to how life is lived and how it is thought about. To be understood, they appeal to common culture and shared experience. One of the important sources of the latter two lies in the national school system. There, a fund of general knowledge is created that later serves as a pool of prevalent ideas that sometimes acquire the status of truism or truth.

Really, schoolbooks should be read by anybody who aspires to have more than superficial acquaintance. These are very important parts of national culture, and particularly useful to get to know how life is officially thought about and represented. To arrive at this knowledge, however, one needs to be able to read the social studies textbooks in the local language, that is, in this case, Filipino. Many adults seem to be reluctant to consult such literature.

Over the years I have learned that school texts are exceptionally useful. The Southeast Asian social studies curriculum may be poor if viewed from the vantage point of social science, but it is rich in values education, ranging from basic behavior to civics. It invariably lectures on the great merit of government and how students will benefit from respect for authority. It explains the basics of public administration, together with the rights and duties of the subject, or citizen. Very importantly, it offers the standard ideas on history which one most often hears uncritically repeated.

Altogether, it is a powerful ideological mixture that serves, at least, self-justification and identification towards outsiders. It also offers some ideas about the society students live in that regularly contrast, as they must, with the tenets of nationalism and doctrine. After all, social life anywhere has its shortcomings and problems, and Philippine society offers no exception. Still more pregnant, and in some contrast with Thai and Indonesian school texts, the present state of society appears as extremely unruly, and far from the hoped-for harmony of national community and the aspirations expressed in the Constitution. These last two topics, again as taught at school, are the subject matters of Chapter 4 and the appended Excursion Two.

The Philippine social studies mixture of realism and idealism is not to everybody's liking. According to certain nationalist circles, especially those concentrated at the social sciences faculty of the University of the Philippines (U.P.) at Diliman, Quezon City, the teaching about their own history and being is colonial and insulting. It is comparative, too, meaning that it explains the country and its people to a real or imagined public of outsiders.

In order to counteract this tendency, they have developed a perspective from within, depicting Filipinos in their own right while writing history as an internal evolution of Philippine society. This is, of course, a worthy and very important endeavor that should be applauded. The approach also has its flaws, a measure of dogmatism and self-congratulation seemingly being part and parcel of it. Yet, its influence cannot be denied, and surfaces in academic disputes, newspaper columns, and novels alike. It is, therefore, more than justifiable to investigate history written from this nationalist point of view, and to expose the resulting image. Chapter 5 attempts to accomplish this.

The next chapter evokes images nationalists may find despairing. The interest of fiction is that authors are entirely free to write as their imagination commands. Yet, if they want to convey a message, they must operate within the margins of what their readership can recognize, reject, or identify with. This is precisely what ambitious authors want to do. Often, they are highly critical of their own society which they want to expose. But others, too, who set out to depict a friendlier environment leave so many traces in their work of conditions they would, deep down, rather not expose, that almost every novel set in contemporary society can be a source of social information.

For our purposes it is unfortunate that only few contemporary novels are set in Philippine society today. Many writers appear to appreciate other periods. In view of this relative paucity, I also had to take recourse to two collections of short stories that, by their nature, evoke atmosphere more than concrete circumstance or complex relationships. Yet, since they largely agree with the overall picture, they add power to it.

In the last chapter, we shall try to explain the images collected, firstly, by putting them into context and, then, by juxtaposing the Filipino culture of the public world with those of Thailand and Indonesia. In the Filipino case, the context will be historically argued with a focus on the evolution of the national elite and the western origin of Filipino high culture. This resulted in the pregnant cultural opposition between the privileged and the poor.

Over the past 30 years, however, numerous new people have come up who constitute the middle classes. In terms of culture of the public world, it is important to understand their newness. They have arisen in response to economic change. They concentrate in urban areas. Their social imagination is severely retarded. They generate little positive culture of the public world–which they equate with politics–and often seek security in familial moralism and religion. This results in a bifurcation between politics and morality, between public and private spheres.

Historically there are important differences between the Philippines, and Thailand and Indonesia. In the Philippines the early culture of the public world sprouted from a class of people with vested interests. In Thailand and Indonesia we cannot underestimate the role of the (idealistic) intelligentsia. Even so, in recent years, say the era of national (economic) development, of urbanization and migration, the cultures of the public world tend to become rather similar through the dominance of economic and career considerations, consumer culture, mass media, and massive general education. Carried by the new middle classes, and with the fading of original optimism, the current culture of the public world in the Southeast Asian region receives less impulses from civil society than is required for its wholesome development.

Introduction

"But Sir, it is their democratic right." After so many years, this answer has indeed proven to be foreboding.

It was said to me when, as a guest of the hotel, I inquired about the devastating noise at the swimming pool below my room. Now I know that going for a swim is being on excursion, a day of fun and snacks and beer and, of course, the good old ghetto blaster. Around the pool, people cluster at tables the management provides. There they put their things, their food and drinks, and the inevitable sound machine. They feed the apparatus their favorite tapes, or switch on the radio, and ascertain to themselves that the blast is to capacity. They must, if they want to be sure to hear their own music and not that of the neighbors' who have similarly installed themselves nearby.

To an outsider it may be a debilitating experience. The Philippines is a clamorous place, without "music," nothing goes. On the bus, in the jeep, at the restaurant, the shop, the mall, the bookstore, the noise is compulsive and compulsory. Often it is loud.

At many a party or eatery, it is very difficult to communicate, let alone to converse. Do people like it that way? No, most of them don't; they are accustomed to it. How is the majority to impose its will or taste on the few who enforce clamorous customs and exercise their democratic right? After all, public space is everybody's, and it may be hazardous to claim equal right and civil consideration.

My early experience with public space in the Philippines evoked certain questions. Not only because it was different from the various environments I knew from Europe, but it also was at remarkable variance with Indonesia and Thailand. This, to an anthropologist, is, of course, not so amazing. History and culture play their parts in shaping the public worlds people live with, and the ways they understand the same. It may be that we live in a globalizing world; it does not homogenize the shape of public space.

It may be that the twenty-first century is the "century of democracy"; it will not make for uniform public worlds. In this day and age of ever-intensifying international contacts, it may be crucially necessary to understand difference and variation among people and nations. It is naive to think that democracy means equality. It is ignorant to opine that European history, so diverse in itself, is to be repeated any place else.

It is fair to say that contemporary public worlds are constituted by comparable components. Urban centers clearly belong to it. So does an advanced level of general education; then, mass media, middle classes, mobility and migration. Such public worlds really become modern through a measure of citizens' participation, which fills them with more or less influential "public opinion." Democracy, therefore, seems to logically belong to a modern public world, but then, somehow, this conclusion stops here. There are no two countries where democracy means the same thing. Public education varies from place to place. The media bear a recognizable national stamp. Many members of the middle classes are not even interested in active citizenship!

Public worlds come in many shapes and guises. They have different histories, too. They arise when the task of government specializes, when the state gradually sets itself apart from the society. In Philippine school history, this is said to have happened well before the Spaniards arrived. Then the *barangay* (village/community), composed of some 20 up to 100 or 150 families, is supposed to have been headed by a ruling *datu* who held all power, but who listened to the advice of a Council of Elders, and who was assisted by the nobility, the so-called *maharlika*.

Such a complex structure may have been in place in the Manila area where a 7,000-strong population was concentrated at the time of Legazpi's arrival in 1571. It seems unlikely, though, that the smaller barangay had that measure of political organization. This much is clear, however, government was centered on a chief, and his "first family" or clan enjoyed more privileges and power than the others.

A really recognizable state, its "public" sphere situated at a great distance from the natives, comes into place as a result of the Spanish conquest. Less through its soldiers and more through its missionaries, this state deeply influenced the original society. Naturally, it also needed the active support of the former petty rulers. By co-opting the ruling families as a privileged intermediary class, these became the early precursors of the present oligarchy.

It had to wait until well into the second century of Spanish dominion that a world market-oriented economy begins to develop. While the tobacco monopoly remains in the hands of the colonial government, other export crops begin to be cultivated by Spanish Filipinos, ruling families, and Christianized Chinese mestizos. While these disparate elements blended and fused, and became the very recognizable ancestors of the current ruling elite, we should note that a system of production arose, well-divorced from the earlier practice of subsistence farming. Juxtaposed with the sphere of the state, another public realm came into existence, namely, the economy.

Native entrepreneurship flourished, and certain families became very rich. Their wealth spurred the demand for culture, for education and when, after almost three centuries of colonization, modern European schooling became available, it resulted in a "class" of highly-educated people loath of colonial discrimination. They demanded representation, reform, equality and, naturally, a say in political affairs. These people are known as the *ilustrados,* the intelligentsia. For our purposes, it is important to observe that next to the spheres of state and economy, an active civil society had arisen that aspired to play its part in the public world. Henceforward, a modern public world would develop, consisting of the institutions of the state, the economy, and civil society. Henceforward, public opinion mattered.

This is very much the state of affairs we meet with today. The native entrepreneurs and their ilustrado offspring have evolved into a political class that seemingly owns the state. They, together with many Chinese and other foreigners, have a firm purchase on the economy. Next to these establishments, we find the civil society. It is a product typical of modernity, and thus an essentially twentieth-century occurrence in most of Asia. Especially during the past 30 years, this civil society, and with it the modern public world, has rapidly expanded. So, although the early manifestations of a modern public world became visible in a more distant past, its rapid expansion, involving ever wider segments of the population, is new. These days, most people are not only directly affected by the conditions of state and economy, but also want to have a say in public affairs.

From the evolutionary perspective developed above, it may be clear that the modern public world is a fairly recent phenomenon in the Philippines, as well as in many other countries. Let us only think about such contemporary developments as massive migration; heavy urbanization; nationwide education; mass media; the rising middle classes; the monetization of life and, particularly, the basic changes in the system of production in a formerly agricultural economy. The cities are largely new; so are the people who dwell there. Most of them do work very unlike their parents or grandparents. They are well-informed, et cetera.

Their newness, and the novel situation they find themselves in, poses most interesting problems. They have no tradition to help them in finding their way. Their backgrounds refer to a less fluid past, and most have been educated with rules to go by that are difficult to apply, at least to the public world. This is, naturally, also affecting their private existence where the "securities" of the past, marriage for one, have been eroded by new practice, such as divorce and the emancipation of women. Everything in the modern world seems to be moving fast. Many people despair that they are losing their hold on life. Religion, in all its forms and guises, flourishes.

It is fair to say that there is almost no culture, no tradition of the public world to follow. In its present manifestations, this realm is, therefore, confusing. Culture, a system of ordering ideas, needs to be made. Thus, what we witness in most of urban, and increasingly in rural Southeast Asia is culture-in-the-making, the outcome of which is still totally unpredictable. People are exposed to modern consumer culture; to electronic media; to predatory politics; to ever-widening mental horizons; to new professions; to new ways of living; to urban anonymity, and it is questionable whether or not all this augurs a twenty-first century of democracy. Why would that be the case?

In the Philippines, a Constitution has been written to spell out what the culture of the public realm is hoped to become. Of course, present practice is different. This fundamental law contains ambitions and aspirations, ideals and dreams that may never be realized. While we shall find references to the 1987 Constitution in this work, we shall particularly address the current culture of the public world. The question we ask ourselves is how people think, and learn to think, about their wider society; about life beyond the family and immediate community. What are their ideas? How do they imagine the wider society? What are their images of it? As such, this study is an inquiry into the origins of public opinion.

In the preceding Background, I have indicated how I came to the idea of collecting images that people hold themselves of their society. These will tell us much about how people think their environment is to be constructed. Such an approach is cultural, is anthropological, which means that we do not depart from the structural, the sociological question of how things really, "objectively" are, but that we focus on mental images, on products of the mind. Therefore, apart from my impressions and interpretations of the urban environment, we shall primarily be concerned with written sources, such as school textbooks, the press, novels, and suchlike. From these it will be clear what kind of opinions people negotiate among themselves about their wider social life.

The fashion in which a public world is constituted is, without doubt, much more complex and comprehensive. It is not limited to thinking about it. Part of the modern public world is practice, experience, such as going to the movies, being stuck in the traffic, having to transact at a government office, watching television, voting at the polls, being at school, working in the office, and all manner of other activities. Part of that world is visible, such as the townscape, buildings, advertising. It is audible and olfactory, too.

A very important part of the culture of the public world has to do with consumption, with lifestyles, fashion, sports and entertainment. In this book, the substance of this economy-driven consumer culture will be largely neglected, even as it receives plentiful attention in the press and, especially, in all types of weeklies that tell people how to dress and where to go, how to live and what to eat.

From these considerations, it is immediately clear that we cannot aspire to do anything exhaustive. *The* image of the public world simply does not exist, and whatever is seen depends on the eyes of the beholder. There are images–myriads of them. What we shall focus on in this work are certain sources of public opinion, which need to be given some context too. The images people hold relate to more than their experience with things public. They also, and importantly, relate to the whole of their existence, which includes their private lives. Often the images they hold of things public have been constructed according to the logic of private life; often things public are seen in the starkest possible contrast with family ideals. Therefore, to a certain extent, one explains the other.

By presenting a scope of images that may be mutually contradictory or complementary, it is hoped that readers can develop their own images of how life is seen among the urban middle classes in the Philippines. In order to achieve some coherence, some observations have been inserted as commentary in the main body of the text. Later, in the book's closure, it will be attempted to explain the images and opinions reviewed.

As just observed, such images cannot be exhaustive, even if the subject matter concerns the broad field of public opinion. Among members of the nation's intelligentsia and social activists, many alternative scenarios are created about how to shape Philippine society, about how it should be. The people concerned are often vociferous. They try to influence public opinion. With the exception of the nationalist discourse, the many points of view they represent have not been directly set forth; it is especially by way of columnists and novelists that such–often progressive–points of view have been brought to the fore.

Contents

List of Abbreviations

Bulletin - *Manila Bulletin*

DECS - Department of Education, Culture and Sports

EDSA - Epifanio de los Santos Avenue (place of anti-Marcos protest, 1986)

MS - *Manila Standard*

NDF - National Democratic Front

NPA - New People's Army

OCW - Overseas Contract Worker

OFW - Overseas Filipino Worker

PDI - *Philippine Daily Inquirer*

PGNC- Philippine Government and the New Constitution

TMT - *The Manila Times*

TPJ - *The Philippine Journal*

TPS/The Star - *The Philippine Star*

1
Reading the Townscape

A CITY is a setting freighted with all sorts of symbols that say something about life going on within its confines and environs. The most obvious of these are monumental, such as buildings of government, churches, statues of memorable citizens, schools, hospitals, impressive commercial structures and hotels, and as a provincial capital, Lucena is well provided with all of these. Old buildings are virtually nonexistent because of the rather recent founding of this town in the second half of the nineteenth century when the government of the then province of Tayabas, now Quezon, was relocated near the coast. This probably explains the absence of a plaza which is the hallmark of the older, Spanish colonial towns that encircle the city on three sides.

These older settlements of Sariaya, Tayabas, and Pagbilao have clearly marked plazas, dominated by big churches and the town hall. Such squares are places to erect monuments built through civic initiatives, and these always include a Rizal statue. The plaza at Sariaya is the most "classic" in that the other two sides are taken by the conspicuous facades of big, now-abandoned villas of the principal families. Fortunately, these impressive dwellings have been kept in good repair by their nonresident owners, and some of them have recently been restored to their former glory.

It is, therefore, appalling that the drive towards self-glorification has, first of all, resulted in a proliferation of "monuments" on the free space of the plaza proper, often referred to as the *parke,* and that now a third of its space has been occupied by a big, high and unseemly basketball stadium which destroys the view of the plaza as a whole. So, after partly having been sacrificed to the ever-crowded and noisy national highway from Manila to the South, the plaza, as a priceless historical monument, has lost its last semblance of integrity. It is only few people who get furious about this.

Sariaya has more to offer the tourist than this disrespectful demonstration of disdain for history and identity. Especially to the south of the plaza, late colonial-style houses still abound. With this style I mean those heavy stone structures that serve as a dark first floor, on top of which we find the living quarters, built in brightly painted wood, with its sliding doors. The windows are evenly divided into small squares–each square filled with a *kapis* shell–that serve as small, frosted glass-like window panes which filter down the brightness of the day to a quiet, fairy-tale-like light.

But who is interested in fairy tales these days? Many of these graceful and precious reminders of the past are sacrificed to make place for, mostly insipid, concrete modernity. In the Lucena I got to know in 1983, several of these houses still existed. Now their number has dwindled to four, of which it must be said that they are well-preserved by their owners who obviously take pride in them; but seen as a public heritage they are not; there is no law protecting urban beauty.

In the absence of a plaza, Lucena City has a public park at the far end of Quezon Avenue. It consists of three sections, a shady part (with trees) in front of the office of the provincial governor that serves as a recreation ground with some facilities for children; a not-so-shady part where few people venture, with stone paths and weird monuments set in lawns, right in front of the massive provincial Capitol building; a far-off section dominated by an impressive Quezon shrine that sees a crowd on Quezon Day, every 19th of August, when a great display of imperative civic ritual attracts everyone capable of wearing a uniform, from Knights of Columbus to bank employees and teachers.

At the short sides of the park area we find, at its shady side, a neglected private garden and, beyond the monument with its grandiloquent inscription, the dilapidated station and tracks of the Philippine National Railway where, indeed, two trains a day, in both directions, pass during the night on the Manila-Bicol run. Opposite the *Kapitolyo* we find a huge "chapel" of the Iglesia ni Cristo, a much more modest place of worship of the United Church of Christ and a few "biggish" villas.

The real center of town, where the hustle and bustle is, is along some quarter kilometer of Quezon Avenue. There, one is in the commercial heart with many banks and shops, most of the more prestigious restaurants and meeting places, several movie halls advertising gory films, a few beer parlors offering Filipino dishes and *pulutan* (appetizer), and a considerable number of fast-food outlets selling soft drinks and everything from spaghetti or hamburgers to ice cream or *dimsum*.

Since the late 1980s, when people began to invest, and buy, again, these symbols of modernity have burgeoned. So now, in between Big Mak at the one end and the new eight-storey shopping mall with its McDonald's outlet, we find at least 18 "plastic" food places, of which the local giant, Jollibee, with 3 air-conditioned floors, and right opposite the cathedral, holds pride of place.

The cathedral is at the center of a vast complex of school and affiliated buildings. It is separated from the fumes and noises of Quezon Avenue by a spacious front yard in which, these days, and next to other meetings, frequent Catholic Charismatic rallies are held. To the rear of the ecclesiastical complex stands, near and yet somewhat peripheral to the downtown area, the *munisipyo*, or town hall. In spite of its modern facade, the building is dingy like other public places. In a way, the munisipyo encloses, on its front porch, a miniature plaza where we find the inevitable Rizal statue, funded by the women of Lucena in 1912, and the flagpole displaying the national banner, day and night. Because good old Rizal has to weather shine and rain, fumes and dust, he needs to be cleaned and manicured from time to time, and this is just what happened when he was recently given a fresh coat of paint resulting in conspicuously shiny fingernails.

Especially since being partly ravaged by a fire some years ago, business at the town hall proper is rather restricted. One needs to go there to buy postage and to mail a letter; one also finds a few licensing offices, et cetera. The second floor accommodates the rather spacious municipal library, good to consult daily newspapers and, of course, many sorts of, mainly dated, books. Here one often meets groups of schoolchildren in search of information. Interesting is the admonition, "Do not let it be you who people will point out as having disturbed the silence in this library." It is a rather incongruous warning in a room where the librarians themselves switch on the television, and where one or two among them have their quietly tuned transistor radios on their desks.

Anyway, much or most of the municipal business is now conducted at the large annex at Better Living Subdivision, some three kilometers further up the road at the busily developing outskirts of town. In spite of having been in use for a few years only, it is striking how rapidly government buildings can convert to an uninspiring atmosphere and drab look.

Next to Quezon Avenue, the commercial district comprises three further parallel streets between it and Dumacaa River. It is there that people announce social activities on banners above the street, from homecomings to Charismatic rallies, and from processions to sporting events. In the absence of a regular local press, a fine way to know what is on in town.

In the district, we find 4 cinemas showing violent Filipino action films, and most of the 85 financial institutions, 22 of them being banks whose doors are protected by at least 2 security guards with their shotguns. The visitor is reminded that he should deposit his firearms with them before proceeding to the counter. Located on the high bank along the river is everybody's fresh food center, the ever-busy market. This and other downtown shops attract impressive crowds that, most of the time, reach the area by public utility vehicles. This keeps a lively transportation sector, such as jeepneys and tricycles, in business, but also fills the streets with "fattish" diesel fumes and the characteristic smell of noisy two-stroke engines.

The economic regeneration after the disastrous Marcos years is clearly visible. In spite of expelling buses, and moving the interlocal jeepney terminals well out of the center, and rerouting the flow of traffic downtown through one-way streets, the area is clogged these days, and traffic is slow at almost every hour of the day. Besides, a lot of construction is going on.

If two to three floors were, until recently, the norm, now five to eight storeys appear fashionable among the Chinese businessmen putting up these signs of the inexorable march of progress. This means that there is more floor space available on the very intensively-utilized few hectares that comprise the downtown area. This, in its turn, attracts more traffic and demonstrates the futility of town planning as long as any property owner is allowed to put up buildings that fit his fancy. Anyway, while not so long ago some unbuilt-up, or vacant, stretches of the peripheral downtown area were taken up by makeshift, very noisy night spots of doubtful–although well-connected–legality, now more permanent structures arise, on top of which we may find several, duly licensed beer gardens. A lot of money seems to be made, and spent, at present, that is, at least, until the current financial crisis began to bite.

During my first visit, in 1983, the town had a reputation for night life: a fine place to have fun, attracting people from as far as San Pablo, a good hour's drive away. There are quite a few reputed restaurants serving rather mediocre food in generally smelly and noisy, to very noisy, dining halls. There are discos, beer parlors with live music, movie halls, and a few of those dimly-lit watering holes that attract their customers by staging bawdy shows in which 15 to 16-year-old girls undress themselves.

Aside from these, one may find a generous supply of "chicks" at motels and in the "health temples" where a massage is included in the service. Of late, this branch of business is spectacularly booming, and the GROs (Guest Relations Officers, the latest euphemism for hospitality girls) are hopefully doing well enough not to need to become a *Japayuki*, such as the female Filipino entertainer is known in the land of the rising sun.

Yet, the biggest industry in town is not entertainment but education. Every school day, approximately 40,000 pupils and students are on their way to elementary, secondary, and college institutions; 12,000 alone peopling the Quezon National High School, and some 7,000 the private Manuel S. Enverga University Foundation, established to serve "God and Country." So, on ordinary days all sorts of school uniforms abound in the streets, while holidays make for rather calm conditions, even if business and market are (open) as usual. From the sheer number of students to the total urban population of some 60,000, it can readily be deduced that many hail from the wide environs of the city.

Apart from banking and commerce, education and entertainment, Lucena offers many other services. This is evident in an abundance of private hospitals and clinics that are reputed to give better service than the poorly staffed, poorly equipped provincial Quezon Memorial Hospital, in front of which one finds two funeral parlors. Lucena is a center for conventions, too; it boasts of many rather big hotels, most of them located on the National Highway going to Manila. When the Jehovah's Witnesses organize their yearly meetings, not a single bed remains unoccupied, and although many are accommodated in the compound and buildings of the national high school on the occasion of regional sports meets, the hotels are also filled to capacity.

Like the rest of the Philippines, religion is conspicuously present in town. Its symbols are ubiquitous. Santo Niño images adorn pay-desks and night clubs.

Religious posters decorate many a wall. Churches still dominate the urban skyline. On certain calendar days, processions are a mandatory part of community life, with the yearly fiesta, Christmas, and the Lenten season as highlights. The Mass attracts crowds, and Europeans may be amazed at seeing so many people going to church.

It is not just the Roman Catholic places of worship that are well-attended. Protestant sects and the loud Charismatics have spread in all corners. The conspicuous structures of the Iglesia ni Cristo, that very successful native rival in the religious market, have become standard features of urban and village architecture. Many jeepneys sport religious names, such as "Mother of Perpetual Help," or "Repent . . . Jesus Comes." People making the sign of the cross when passing a church are a common sight.

At the edge of town, where the urban area is still giving way to a more rustic appearance, the bishop resides in what is known as his palace. Over recent years, the vast compound has been filled with ever more and ever bigger buildings, the diocese obviously not being short of money. A little down the road the Episcopal compound is challenged by the newest "chapel" of the Church's fierce competitor, the Iglesia ni Cristo. It stands adjacent to the Fresh Air Hotel that contains several chapels for prayer and meditation. The hotel is a popular venue for religiously-inspired retreats and marriage-revival weekends. Going down the road to town, the building of a night club, once a place of sin, has been converted into a center for singing and clapping Charismatics. In brief, religion appears well and alive, and forms very much part of the townscape.

Less conspicuous than churches, but perhaps no less important, is the habit that strikes the eye as "build yourself a monument." At their entrance, certain neighborhood associations are given to display the names of their board members, while not failing to remember former presidents and other officials. Others attempt to perpetuate their names by inscribing them on their projects, such as a piece of fence, a public garbage can, or a civic hall. Graduating students like to donate something to their *alma mater*, a billboard or so, that announces the names of the generous givers.

Small monuments of all sorts, put up by Rotarians, Jaycees or Kiwanis, greet the visitor on his way; popular among these are concrete waiting sheds. The main purpose of this civic activity is to proclaim name and excellence. This is the more so in the case of politicians. They build roofs to wait under, police boxes, the "First Pedestrian Overpass in Southern Tagalog," bridges, markets, and so on, to declare their merit as provincial governor, senator, congressman, or mayor; in doing so, national politics assume a marked parochial flavor, which is not so strange, because it is in such communities that the vote must be cultivated.

In the Philippines, politics is a matter of personalities and rhetoric, not of platform and ideology. It focuses on persons, not on the nation. The attempts at nation building that originated with politicians are in the laws that decree that school days must begin with flag-raising, anthem-singing, and reciting the Pledge to the Nation; that students must read Rizal's novels, study the Constitution, and undergo some military drill. Similarly, flag and anthem rituals stand at the beginning of office days, club meetings, scouting activities and, occasion permitting, these are complemented with a religious invocation. Depending on one's agenda, a person may have to go three or four times a day through this routine that supposedly brings the nation to life. Yet, as long as people acquiesce in having the American flag depicted on their one-hundred-peso bill,[1] these nation-building activities do not seem to be very effective.

One of the first ceremonial occasions I witnessed in Lucena was a beauty contest at the local university college. Over the years, it became clear that to be beauty queen or club's muse is a coveted prize. The quest for prominence surfaces in civic and religious processions, in the selection of Miss Kindergarten, on the society pages of the newspapers and, importantly, in graduation ceremonies that mark, with picture and diploma, the distinctions earned. Subsequently, these certificates will be displayed at the walls; in doctor's and law offices, their demonstration should inspire confidence, and justify the fee. To be distinguished, to stand out among one's fellows, is apparently important, and it is not just politicians who are given to this. As a result, people are addressed and referred to by title, being Doctor, Attorney, Mayor, Councilman, Engineer, and suchlike.

The final distinction one can earn, is the grave in which one will be buried. In this way, cemeteries are turned into contests between opulent tombs for the remains of the more prominent families. Several chapels over graves, some even two-storeys high, provide better housing for the dead than can be hoped for by ordinary people. To keep the latter out, these are kept under lock and key. This habit even appears to affect certain members of the Iglesia ni Cristo who, in spite of the image of austerity and simplicity it cultivates, sometimes build oversized graves in the characteristic design of its "chapels." On All Saints' Day, these graveyards come very much to life when people join their deceased relatives in a kind of a family reunion. Then simple graves as well as immodest tombs turn into picnic places, with some "eternal gardens" even providing music to guarantee a pleasant atmosphere.

Music forms very much part of life. In going for an outing to the beach, a good quantity of beer and ice is as essential as the *karaoke* machine. Weird is the office where one does not hear a radio. At the swimming pool at the Fresh Air Hotel, plugs are provided to connect the good old ghetto blaster. Inconsiderate of neighbors, the switching on of a loud radio seems to be as much a right as smoking wherever one pleases. This spills over to jeepneys when drivers apparently expect their music to drown out the sounds of the road. In restaurants and beer gardens, compulsive rhythmic noise is as unavoidable as on most buses. Loudest of all are certain passenger tricycles whose very *raison d'être* seems to be their proud drivers' broadcasting of a deafening drone.

Flanked on three sides by subdivisions (clusters of houses with small gardens where professionals and the better-off live) is a rather big military compound. Even so, the military presence in Lucena is not remarkable. The years 1987 and 1988 were the exception. Then, the New People's Army (NPA) made its presence felt, and the area around nearby Mt. Banahaw was dotted with military camps, checkpoints and roadblocks. In those days, the local commander, a member of our tennis club, came to play his games escorted by two soldiers in full combat gear, armed with assault rifles; they had to stand guard over him at two corners of the court. It did not make me feel at ease, similar to the presence of armed soldiers in beer parlors, or on patrol in the streets.

Nowadays, the military is inconspicuous again, and one seldom sees official uniforms in the city apart from some policemen on traffic duty during rush hours. The "military" dress one most often sees is that worn by secondary-school students on their civilian army training. Then they perform some drill exercises, at which the boys with their wooden imitation rifles and the slight girls on their big boots make an endearing rather than a martial impression.

Similarly, the other institutions of government, though visible, form less part of life, and do not stand out. The massive Kapitolyo stands in a peripheral location, near the low-profile office of the provincial governor. Other bureaus are in ordinary, house-like buildings. Often, political activity is concentrated in the subdivisions, centering on individual power-brokers at whose doorsteps one can note a steady stream of visitors. On occasion, politicking becomes very visible when politicos are grandstanding in campaigns, or at opening ceremonies of all sorts. They are keen on publicizing themselves.

On the streets downtown, sidewalk vendors abound. There, they are obviously not allowed to peddle their wares at will. Closer to the main market, however, the streetscape grows more jumbled and becomes somewhat smelly and untidy. In a way this contrasts with the image most people project of themselves.

Almost everybody starts the day in clean clothing. Attire tends to be simple, sports or t-shirt, very often complemented with blue jeans. Many people exhibit slogans or cartoon characters on their dress, most of the time in English; quite a few seem to be unaware of the messages they sport. Perhaps this is so because people are not in the habit of reading.

Books are rare. The so-called bookstores sell school needs, including mandatory texts, never-changing dull picture postcards, but normally little to read. Magazines and newspapers are sold at separate outlets in the streets, but there are not many; daily total of the national press sold that way is probably 300 to 400 hundred copies only.

Preferred reading is comics, and there are quite a few places where one can look at them against a fee. Equally popular are the video tapes many stores let to be screened at home. In response to the insatiable demand for sex and violence, a vast enterprise of clandestine copying has grown. Naturally, the resulting tapes need to be more discreetly distributed. Even so, spending time at movie houses remains attractive. On Sundays, action also draws the mainly male crowd to the cockpits, known as "Sports Plaza" or "Coliseum." The excitement is less in the bloody spectacle of two roosters hacking each other to death than in the betting on the outcome of the fight. As far as Lucena City is concerned, these cockpits are not very spectacular, although at other places, such as Tayabas, they may be rather conspicuous.

Behind the Kapitolyo, one finds another sort of public theater, the *ampiteatro*, normally referred to as the *ampi*, where minor events take place. On certain days, though, it becomes quite lively when traveling American preachers stage their Charismatic rallies, promising health to the believers whom they try to attract with posters inviting the populace to "be part of a miracle." More important events are staged in the vast grounds of the national high school which hold a big grandstand; there, incumbent national politicians arrange their rallies during election campaigns.

This high school is an important establishment. It offers 4-year standard curriculum to some 12,000 students who crowd the place from early morning to late afternoon. They are so many, because national schools are inexpensive in comparison to more prestigious private schools that cater to the other half of the student body concerned. With such quantities to take care of, it is clear that teaching must be organized in parallel classes.

At 50 to 60 pupils to a class, these may be spread over as many as 60 sections. These sections group students of comparable ability, the first few sections gathering the brightest and the best. In spite of the size of classes, the latter students, and their teachers, are sufficiently motivated to make the grade and to hopefully stream on to college.

Students in the lower sections are not very well taken care of. They are not as good, have little drive, do not achieve; they are a burden for teachers. In their case, big classes and noisy atmosphere kill curiosity and potential. They will never get through the hurdles of serious colleges and, if their parents can pay, will only make it to any of the abundant diploma mills. The latter bank on the race for certificates and the sacrifices Filipino parents make to get their children a formal education.

A Streetscape

Now we are at it, let us carefully inspect the road in front of Quezon National High School to gain some insight in the use of public space and the messages it contains. The school is located off the center of town, some 400 meters from town hall on the main road to Manila. In front of the vast compound, it has dual carriage ways, separated from each other by a fence to prevent people from crossing at will. We shall start at the northern street corner, immediately adjacent to a big Caltex petrol station, and move through the hundred meters along the school's fence in southerly direction to the next corner.

Before moving, we note that the side street to the right sports a long row of snack counters where pupils are hoped to spend some of their lunch money. It is also the appropriate place for jeepneys to wait for students on their way home. Yet, this is not strictly enforced by the policemen who sit, two or three of them, in the police box at the corner. At certain times of the day they tolerate that a long queue of jeeps lines up along the kerb of the main road to pick up students. At other hours, they may suddenly enforce the regulation that no passenger vehicle is to stop along that very same stretch. Jeepney drivers know this, although on a bad day they may unexpectedly find themselves fined.

The police box displays the following, somewhat enigmatic English text:

> "The PNP (Philippine National Police) is the administration flagship agency against crime. It must be the ship–shaped battle ready at all times in the war against crime."

Immediately next to the box, we find a waiting shed on which provincial politician P advertises his name. A sign there reads "No Smoking." The electricity pole carrying the ubiquitous overhead wiring has a small board reading:

> "Let us continue supporting a 'jueteng-free' Lucena."
> (Signed) City Mayor, Lucena Chief of Police, LCPS.

This message is, as ever so often, pure hypocrisy. A year earlier, in February 1997, Lucena was indeed free of "underground" lottery, which shows that the authorities have the power, if they have the will, to ban *jueteng*. To them, however, this bane of the poor is their boon: with three nontransparent draws a day, organized jueteng is capable of creaming off the little extra or the hopes of the poor. These days, it is back, and quite in the open.

Next to this message from the mayor, we come to the main gate with, again, somewhat conflicting announcements. On its arch it wishes us "Welcome," and mentions the school's name. At the doors we read, "All outsiders do not enter" and, addressing insiders, "No uniform, No ID, No entry." When the footway resumes, we see a board standing on it that advertises "SM Studios"; lifting our head, we see four further messages on a pole that entice us to buy things, to support a politico, and to advance our education at a certain school. On the surface of the road, we find two low, removable sign posts warning, "All students use overpass."

The pavement is then blocked by a row of three waiting sheds, "Project of Rotary Club of Lucena '82-'83"; "Project of Congressman M"; "Project of P," the politician we noted before. Above this all, we note a signboard spanning the width of the road, "Welcome to the City of Lucena." In between its supporting poles is a banner of the "Lucena Doctors' Hospital." In the middle of the road, at the beginning of the divider, we can still identify a meanwhile illegible commemorative plaque from 1972 about the "concrete paving" of the road.

The stretch of highway under consideration is dominated by a massive construction, the "First Pedestrian Overpass in Southern Tagalog." We have noted that all students are supposed to cross the road between Quezon High School and the state elementary school on the other side by means of this bridge. To compel them to do so, the sidewalk has been fenced-off. The bulkiness of this cheaply built structure leaves, like many of the waiting sheds, no room on the pavement, thus forcing all people who simply want to go straight ahead to walk on that part of the road reserved for traffic. This is particularly hazardous when jeeps are queuing there. Anyway, the purpose of the ill-conceived monstrosity, where indeed a few pupils pass, becomes clear when we look at the many messages it is expected to convey:

Iyam Pedestrian Overpass
Project of Governor Eddie T. Rodriguez
and Provincial Council
Ex-mayor Cesar F. Zaballero
and City Council
Initially funded from senatorial allocation of
Senator E. Angara Senator R. Saguisag
In Lucena: Discipline is Treasure, the Root of Unity, Progress and Peace
a project of the people of Lucena City

Still, a banner has been stretched just below the bridge's roofing:

'Healing Explosion'
with Fr. JF
St. Ferdinand Cathedral
'be delivered from all kinds of bondages'
18:00 hrs. February 26, 1998

On the southern face of the overpass these messages are repeated. Walking on, right along and among the cars, we come to a place where the fence leaves some space to rejoin the pavement. There, we are at waiting sheds again, "Priority Project of Congressman M," with the next one very visibly erected by Coca Cola. Then we reach the compound's other gate that is kept closed these days. Now it serves as a service hatch for six female vendors who install themselves with their snacks against it. In the evening they are apparently allowed to leave their tables on the footway.

The rest of the fenced-off sidewalk takes us past the school's canteen and burned-down DECS buildings. Sheets, mostly election-related, have been pasted on the few electricity poles. Then we reach the corner with another waiting shed under which we find an ice cream vendor. In the opposite branch street leading to the causeway, we see a tricycle and pedicab waiting station blocking one half of the narrow two-way street's road space.

On the opposite side of the highway, right in front of the Caltex petrol station, we find a huge outlet of the national brand Petron. In between it and the elementary school compound is the predictable row of vendors catering to pupils. On the sidewalk along the highway, we see the same common features, such as overpass and fence along the kerb. Part of the footway is roofed over, compliments of the Lions' Club. It was installed a few years before the pedestrian bridge was built, and served, apart from offering some respite from the rain, to advertise the Club's "civic-mindedness" and the names of all the members of the Lucena chapter.

Besides the usual small posters on electricity posts, we note the sign "No vendors allowed." On the school's fence we find, per segment, the names of its generous donors. Similarly, at the gate, the announcements of who paid for pavements and other things. Again we are forced to walk out on the road, where we find a removable short sign post, "Loading and unloading of students"; on it, the note, "A joint project of LC Engineer's Office and Jollibee."

In passing under the overpass, we see a banner, and a big billboard of Quaker Oats, "When you eat as much as you need, your weight will be neat," reminding us of the health-care weighing program of the very young. When looking into the school yard, we observe, like on the other side, a well-kept place with a national flag flying at its pole. Then we come to buildings that are so close to the road that their messages are clearly meant for the passersby:

> This 2 classroom school building is donated by Engr. and Mrs. Edwin G. Tantuco to the good people of Lucena City under "Operation Barrio Schools." This is another project of the Lucena Filipino-Chinese Chamber of Commerce and Federation of Filipino-Chinese Chambers of Commerce and Industry, Inc.

We find the names of the donors three times on the two classrooms, and the full message twice. Again we are assured that, "No vendors are allowed," on this stretch of sidewalk. Before coming to the corner of an unpaved sidestreet, we find a pile of garbage, left by vendors, and then come to a rickety row of shophouses, catering snacks and school needs, along a very narrow pavement, securely fenced off along the kerb.

Image

Near the high school, and at the entrance of town proper, it is natural to find a high density of messages. In the main, these were political, civic, and commercial. One banner excepted, we found no religious announcements. As far as the state goes, we found quite orderly school yards, with flags at the top of their poles. Respect for the rules of display of the national banner is shown by the grade school. At the high school, it flies day and night; at times, it is not well-kept either. Sometimes the flag is faded, torn and dirty. The other symbol of the nation, the burned-down DECS compound, presents a sorry sight.

Downtown, the density of religious messages is quite impressive, because of buildings, statues, and suchlike. Meeting places and schools of sects and congregations are certainly as numerous as those of financial institutions. Many commercial firms have holy names, such as "Sto. Niño Enterprises"; likewise, jeeps regularly sport references to biblical texts, such as "Matthew 6:9-13"; I especially like the signboard of a big supermarket, "Glory to God. $. Sioland." But for the rest, the impressions gained along Quezon High School correspond to those imposed by the inner townscape.

Messages are political, civic, and commercial. Politicos advertise their names and try to impress with their generosity and initiatives (paid for with taxpayers' money, their so-called pork-barrel funds). Civic clubs and associations remind us of their existence everywhere, through monuments they erect, anti-drug billboards they sponsor, and insignia their members display. Many commercial messages are merely to be expected in a lively urban environment. These range from billboards of private schools propagating the courses they offer to the ubiquitous fast-food outlets and the simple "50% off" and "Sale" signs at many a shop.

How conscious are people really of this cacophony of commercial and other communications? Probably not much more than they are of the general state of their urban environment. They are accustomed to it, and move around as a matter of course. When I told a teacher that I had difficulty in finding a certain text, she insisted I go to a particular store. They sold everything from writing pads to ballpoints, but did not have a single title in stock. Yet, in her life this teacher must have been to that store, and be subconsciously convinced that it sells books. So, what do people practically behold?

All the same, people are influenced by the surroundings they live in, and these may even reflect a mentality. When one regards the sorry state of the plaza in Sariaya, one notes disrespect for history and identity, traits in which Lucena apparently shares. Draping the town hall in straight banners of dark blue, white and red, or putting up a cluster of the 1896 *Katipunan* flags at official buildings, neither brings history to life nor does it inspire people to celebrate the 1998 Centennial (of the original proclamation of independence).

When one enters San Pablo. one rides along a rather well-kept avenue heading to the cathedral and its spacious front yard. This wide street is divided by always whitewashed center islands and lined by specially designed lampposts. The skyline along the avenue is controlled and kept at more or less even height. The first impression is that it breathes a civic spirit, that people take care of their town. In spite of all the civic messages one is surrounded with in Lucena City, there is no area or street that reflects the idea of pride in place.

What one sees little of, except for certain seasonal parades, are active manifestations of citizenship. It is rather the contrary one notes. Over the past ten years, lots of money have been invested in heavy concrete high-rise buildings, but the public infrastructure at which these are located has not improved. These days, public space where these buildings are situated is deteriorating, were it only as a result of traffic. When a councilman in Sariaya pushed for less noisy, less stinking tricycles, these became quieter and belched less exhaust. When Lucena's mayor was serious about jueteng, it completely disappeared. Then things get back to "normal," a mild state of anarchy.

Buses and jeeps stop wherever they like or where passengers want them to halt. Three quarters of them belch undiluted diesel fumes. With the traffic now clogging the streets, a lot of breeze is needed to have the idea one still breathes air. Sidewalks are in disrepair and uncomfortable to walk on. There is an abundance of obsolete traffic signs left on pavement or at kerbs. Other such signs, meanwhile, are illegible, or hidden behind trees that have since grown. Overhead wiring adorns every street.

Public services are of poor quality. People regularly enjoy "brownouts" when electricity fails; then bigger shops and establishments start their loud private generators. Water delivery is erratic, and many people resort to their own pumps and wells. There are no mailboxes. To send a letter, one must go to the town hall or Kapitolyo to queue in order to get it machine-stamped (most often postage stamps are not available). Telephone service is expensive, primitive, time-consuming, and lines regularly break down. Men are in the habit of pissing everywhere. There are no public facilities to take care of this urge of nature; irate residents have marked preferred spots, "Only dogs pee here." People usually drop their litter as they go; there are no public trash cans.

Does all this mean that Lucena City is dirty? Not really; it is drab. The streets are regularly swept, and these days garbage collection is rather effective. Many people burn their rubbish along the roadside. No, what the above two paragraphs mean is that there is an absence of politicians, and of a civil society, who take care, who identify with the place, who take pride in it. Organized civic action or protest hardly exists, if at all. People know about graft in public tenders, and are prepared for the poor quality they receive. "Such is life in the Philippines," they will explain. The many civic clubs seem to leave it at that, too. They are a purpose unto themselves, and do certainly something for their members. But as exponents of civil society, they appear to turn their back to public needs.

The latest telephone directory describes Lucena as "city of charm and beauty." It is a lively place of business, finance, commerce and industry, in brief, progress has taken hold of the town. This is obvious from new buildings, among which the eight-storey Ocean Palace Mall is singled out as most exemplary because of its "ultramodern ambiance." If, with this last observation, the author hints at the phenomenon "mall" itself, or at the four fast-food restaurants, Chow King, McDonald's, Buddy Pizza, Queen Square, that occupy its first floor (together with a public karaoke machine), then I have little to disagree with but the first statement.

Markets have their charm. They are busy, somewhat chaotic, somewhat like an ordered anarchy. They are loud and lively, get dirty and dusty, and are cleaned again; they are driven by the pursuit of money. Their agitated activity is like that of the Filipino Jack-of-all-trades, the jeepney driver who steers his vehicle while collecting his fares, changing the money, adjusting his radio, greeting his friends, discussing with passengers, and being all the time attentive to pick up potential customers while alert to any of the five or six signals indicating that somebody wants to get off. He is the genius mastering chaos. He exudes the atmosphere of the market. Lucena City is such a market.

2
Mirror of the Public World

THIS CHAPTER is about the images newspapers evoke of the public world. Traditionally, the written press is held to mirror life in wider society, and to make a crucial contribution to public opinion. While I hold that mirror to be a distorting one, I think that the messages newspapers contain have more impact than those sent through electronic media. The effort of reading presents more of a challenge to the mind.

Communication through the printed word is somewhat dialogical. It stimulates to think, it shapes opinion; because of this bias of mine, we shall give here three manners of newspaper analysis. The first concerns an exercise in intensive reading, with the question in mind what images it possibly evokes. Then issues of the press will be compared to find out about everyday preoccupations. This, again, will be followed by a topical presentation of certain dominant subjects. Lastly, we shall summarize the image newspapers probably call forth.

First Impressions

On the third day of December, I boarded a PAL plane in Bangkok and, during the long-delayed take-off, I had a good go at the *Philippine Daily Inquirer* of Monday, 1 December 1997. On its front page, there is little to draw acute attention. A water shortage is evidently threatening the capital, but with so many disturbances plaguing weather patterns all over the globe, it may be expected that the El Niño phenomenon plays havoc with the Philippine islands too. On page 20, though, immediate water rationing is announced: the city will be divided into sections where water is said to run by 12-hour shifts. This news is worrying, because it may affect my well-being upon arrival.

Besides water, the front page headlines other major concerns: crime, politics, economy, corruption, and environment. These do not sound very exciting; they constitute the normal fare of newspapers anywhere. These are but ordinary news filling the public world. Close reading, though, makes the issues at hand more specific, possibly even particular.

According to one headline, the anti-crime campaign is to be stepped up. The president ordered it himself. Why? Isn't crime fighting one of the normal tasks of good government? The Philippines even appears to have, next to the usual instrumentalities, such as Police, Army, National Bureau of Investigation (NBI), Department of Interior and Department of Defense, a Presidential Anti-Crime Commission (PACC). Now, however, all these are supposed to cooperate, and to ensure "prosecution regardless of personality or status of suspects."

Why then, does Cardinal Sin think that the government has performed poorly in stamping out crime? The same article gives a clue. A "highly placed and intricately organized crime group was found to be headed by a Cavite police officer." At other places in the issue, too, we find that highly placed involvement in crime is expected, and thus considered to be normal.

Elected and other officials are said to protect drug traffickers, and Manila Mayor Alfredo Lim says such individuals deserve double the death penalty. As far as he is concerned, law and order must come first. From this condition, political stability will ensue, leading, in its turn, to economic prosperity.

Nevertheless, crime seems to be irrepressible, or simply unrepressed. The first impression derives from the variety of reported items; the second from the protests of Filipino-Chinese against the apparently relentless wave of kidnappings for ransom. According to their spokesperson, in 1996 there were 147 kidnappings of 241 victims, and ₱109 million-ransom was paid. In the first ten months of 1997, 124 kidnappings involved 193 victims, which netted the criminals ₱292 million. The limits have been reached; Binondo (Chinese enclave located in Manila) schools and shops close for the day on which a victim is buried.

It is not only Chinese Filipinos who are kidnapped. A police chief and an army sergeant have been taken hostage by the NPA (New People's Army), the armed branch of the NDF (National Democratic Front). The details of the small news item reveal that the NPA/NDF is considered to be a serious negotiating partner of the Philippine government, but also that a civil war is being fought in the country. This impression is reinforced by the political cartoon on the opinion pages; there a de-feathered peace-process pigeon is seen fleeing from the violence unleashed by insurgency and internal military operations.

Whether or not corruption is a crime, I do not know, but from what we read we may conclude that crime is for criminals and corruption for politicians. The latter species come prominently to the fore. Elections are at the horizon, and all sorts of "presidentiables" surface in columns and news. Of special interest is the discussion about voting. Fraud seems to be intimately related to elections. There appear to be many ways of counting votes. To ensure cleaner and more honest elections, computerized voting is being proposed. Yet, not everybody is in favor. The counting machines have appeared to be as manipulatable as vote-counting human beings are frail. Besides, "the machine counts fake ballots faster than genuine ones." As a result, people pinning their hopes on machines have been thwarted by politicians, even "presidentiables," who are not inclined to put their fate into the "hands" of dubious machinery.

All this has to be argued, and with so many people in politics and law there is no end to reasons, suspicions and accusations. In addition to the front-page discussion of the demerits and vulnerabilities of machines, the Editorial and a columnist take contrary positions on the subject on opposite pages. The Editorial reviles those who go slow on computerization. The people concerned are quick to point out that the machines cost a great deal of money, and that certain parties involved in procuring them could enjoy a windfall profit, "commission," from the transaction. These opponents of rapid computerization require transparency rather than hurry, to which the Editorial retorts, "If every program that might possibly be tainted by corruption is to be junked, what could government possibly undertake?"

The columnist on the other page reverses the arguments, and opens on, "When high-strung, excitable JC of the Namfrel (National Movement for Free

Elections) meets fiery and fearless MD-S of the Philippine Senate, it is like an irresistible force crashing into an immovable object. Sparks fly and the din is deafening." Many well-written sentences later, the senator declares, "If he (JC) wants a fight, he'll have a fight. I have been extremely patient with this bungling fool. But now he has forced me to defend myself. He's dead meat."

There is fun in reading Philippine newspapers. Repeatedly, we are confronted with biting sarcasm and resounding rhetoric. Obviously, Filipinos take pleasure in linguistic circus. Commenting on the "presidentiables'" penchant to cultivate religious groups, a columnist proposes, "If their poses present the true picture, the 12 or so presidential hopefuls may be considered to be the most prayerful and God-fearing group of men and women ever to aspire for the highest post of the land . . . They don religious attire . . . pray the rosary . . . carry icons, sing prayers . . . shout 'Praise the Lord' or 'Hallelujah' . . . or perform any act that a religious group considers part of its rituals."

To this, a letter-to-the-editor writer opines that politics comes very close to prostitution:

> You won't see Budget Secretary SE prowling the lonely, dimly-lit Quezon Avenue stretch late in the night or the wee hours of the morning. He doesn't deal with pimps. Neither will you catch him all made up, a naughty Marks & Spencer teddy under his trousers, plying the Susie Wong trade at a five-star hotel. He isn't involved in the escort service business. [Yet,] E, minus the false eyelashes and the stiletto heels, admitted he and several other Cabinet members switched their support to RDV because of fears they would not be included in the senatorial lineup of JDV . . . 'That is important to me. That must have influenced our decision.'[1]

Politicians, aspiring for, or in power, stand in the spotlight. In this *PDI* issue, they occupy center stage. "Globe-trotting President Ramos needs to make tough economic decisions that could spell defeat for his party at the polls." Let us hope that the president is more of a statesman than a politician, and that electoral strategy will play second fiddle to economic rescue.

Well, one of the immediate issues confronting the president is tax reform. The Legislature seems to be deadlocked about the height of the level of income tax exemption, an issue that is exploited to the hilt by certain representatives whose posturing for a higher level, for instance ₱116,000 versus ₱92,000 is argued as being "pro-poor." Such an incoherent argument is bad reasoning and dangerous populism.

People earning that much are by no means poor, and the demagogues concerned are either mentally weak or irresponsibly profiting from downgrading the severity of the current financial crisis. The presidential aspirants, too, seem to shy away from addressing the unpopular measures needed to restore economic health. "With the elections less than six months away, brace yourself for more antics and activities that unwittingly expose the true nature of the people who want to lead this country for the next six years."

Well, some do expose themselves unashamedly, and seem to relish the sweet taste of power. The governor of the Autonomous Region in Muslim Mindanao appears to be one of them. He is extensively chastised by one of the columnists for his high-living, long absences from the Region, authoritarian handling of his critics, being ill-informed, and not paying the salaries of teachers and other officials. In short, he seems to be vaingloriously enjoying his power; arrogance and ignorance are perfect bedfellows to that syndrome.

Perhaps, therefore, Richard Gordon is right when he observes that in the present personality-centered political culture of the Philippines, the politics of goons, guns and gold, he does not want to run for office. He hopes to find the people, especially the young, prepared to accept new leaders with new ideas.

Among the other items, we still discover a few things of interest. Canadians are said to have pledged heavy investment in the country, and such is welcome news. Yet many people are questioning the administration's claim of six percent economic growth over the past nine months. Opposition politicians dismissed this as a "political mirage," and particularly poorer wage-earners disputed the assertion as meaningless. "If there is growth, why is it that we only get less?" they seemed to ask.

Consumer prices have been leaping since the peso plummeted. Wages cover less than half of the recognized daily needs. Clearly, these things are expressed in the labor unrest the paper also reports on. The people concerned want a legislated wage increase; they condemn the policy of reducing the number of regular workers in the country which, as a result, is also threatening to the existence of organized labor. With the government pursuing a "cheap and docile labor policy," six-percent growth claims merely seem to serve to cover up and distort the deteriorating plight of the workers. Not everything on the labor front is bad, however. At least two major firms have attested that friendly relations between management and unions prove to be beneficial to them. This demonstrates that collective bargaining negotiations are indeed productive, and can result in "social partnership accord."

The paper under review contains a fair amount of environmental observations. "Dirty ice" is held to be responsible for a good deal of diarrhea. Fishing in Laguna de Bay, the great lake to the south of Manila, is a dying industry; there remains little water, and whatever there is, is heavily polluted. In places as far apart as Negros and Pampanga, citizens are protesting economic expansion activities that threaten to destroy their living environments. AIDS takes many victims in the islands. Contributing factors are poverty and ignorance: many children roam the cities, and are very vulnerable to sexual abuse and exploitation. Yet, everybody can be infected and nobody can afford to ignore the risk.

The current drought, too, is having nasty consequences. Fires freely spread because of the water shortage, and we should fear the worst of the year-end's fireworks extravagance. The firefighters simply lack the water to douse conflagrations.

Miscellaneous items still deal with corruption in the awarding of contracts; crimes; a success in crime-busting; historical awareness among street children (Question: "Who is Bonifacio?" Answer: "That stone carving over there!"); suppression of academic freedom at the national university; a Bible reading; winning lottery numbers; some readers' observations about bills, traffic safety, con-men, drugs, and political culture; a little scattered foreign news; endemic red tape; accidents.

Finally, we may still be struck by a few more telling observations. The twenty-four pages of the main section of the paper carry almost fourteen pages of paid advertisements, and one full page on which the Philippine press objects against the bill banning political advertising. The press argues that said act violates the freedom of speech and is tantamount to censorship. In view of the approaching elections, the media have a point: they stand to forfeit considerable income if the more affluent politicians cannot fight it out by way of paid ads. Nevertheless, advertising does saturate the *PDI:* next to the 15 pages reviewed, the paper's 58 extra sheets feature some 30 full-pages of ads. Not bad, isn't it, for a Monday-morning newspaper: 82 pages in all, among which paid-for messages take the bulk.

I did not spell out every single page during the three-hour flight. The Sports and Entertainment section took up a full 14 pages; 18 were devoted to business, and next to the usual financial info, I noted two articles featuring the success of women as managers and real-estate brokers. Sixteen pages about lifestyles sported an amazing amount of facts about painting (especially

Amorsolo), architecture, and Christmas traditions among the very rich. Altogether, the copiousness of the issue, and largely commercial publicity-seeking left the impression to be headed for an Asian Tiger economy, and a society that, despite some not-so-extraordinary problems, is well on its way to affluence.

Apart from this, people unfamiliar with the Philippines could have noted that most Filipinos go by Spanish names, even though quite a few Chinese and a number of possibly native names do indeed pop up in the pages. Apparently Filipinos are not afraid of some highfalutin statements, and seem to be inclined to both rhetoric and sarcasm. These arts are freely exercised by the columnists who are allowed to fill two full pages that often make for amused reading. Play with language also seems to inform the naming of groups. In this issue alone, three interesting acronyms were proposed, to wit FREE (Federation of Reporters for Empowerment and Equality); AWARE (Alliance of Workers for Wage and Reform), and ACCESS (Agno Concerned Citizens for Ecologically Sound and Sustainable Development).

Everyday Fare

On Thursday, 11 December 1997, I bought three different English-language "quality" newspapers and three vernacular tabloids in order to compare their appearance, contents, and comments on the issues of the day. The first thing of interest I noted was the dissimilarity of the front pages of the *Manila Bulletin, The Philippine Star,* and the *Manila Standard.* The only things in common among their headlines were the topics of kidnapping and presidential elections, about which each paper had something different to say. Due to this variation, it may be best first to briefly review the papers one by one, and then to compare and conclude about the impressions they make.

Manila Bulletin, "since 1900," is the most continuous paper published in the country. It fits itself to times and circumstances, and therefore exudes a certain insipidity. It hardly ever gives any offense, and does not advance much original or courageous thinking. Being fit for all, with a considerable business section, it is probably the main newspaper in circulation. As a result, it is heavily freighted with paid advertisements (31 of 64 pages), while further carrying obligatory pages with the names of successful professional licensure examinees, media programming, and movie schedules.

On its front page, twenty topics are broached, and the reader needs to do a lot of flipping through the pages to find out what these substantially amount to. We notice that 50 percent of some 8,500 candidates passed their nursing licensure exams. In the business section, we find their names listed on two pages. An Agri-fisheries Act has been approved by Congress. Other reports vie for attention:

- The Philippines is determined to recapture its No. 1 position as "rice capital of Southeast Asia";
- Water must be conserved;
- El Niño is waning; and,
- The masterminds of the kidnap-for-ransom syndicates will be arrested.

Also in the news is the president's anointed successor, JDV, who engineers reconciliation in the party. Others, seeing how the cat has jumped, are quick to join the bandwagon. Yet, diehard backers of the chief competitor, RDV, urge the latter to run for president. Another presidential candidate boasts that her position is firm, in spite of vicious attacks. Landowners join hands to promote their interests. No funds available for computerization of the May 1998 elections. Soldiers must be housed decently. Education should be better supported. A vice presidential hopeful launches his campaign. A grassroots justice movement is surviving into its fourth year. The weather will be very much like yesterday's. There is a picture of somebody making Christmas decorations; another of a dirty and muddy river running dry.

On pages 2 and 3, we find a trifle of irrelevant foreign news (Iran blasting West; Korean election tactics; names of Nobel prize winners; a hijack). Page 4 continues with similar easy-to-digest tidbits. The ad on page 6 lists the three women and four men elected for "The Outstanding Young Filipinos" for 1997 Award. Page 7 offers miscellaneous items on OFWs (Overseas Filipino Workers), the water crisis, and several civic groups.

On page 8 we find the continuation of many of the items announced and initiated on the front page. About the presidential race, it is said that RDV is the only candidate who "can make politics honorable again." He is the corruption fighter, so, even if not anointed by the incumbent president, he will be anointed by God and the great mass of Filipinos.

If he still lacks a party, RDV could be the guest candidate of another political group. Let RDV bear in mind President Quezon's motto, "My loyalty to my party ends when the loyalty to my country begins." Other observations about the "presidentiables" predominate. One of them keeps chiding the shortage of educational facilities, and some people opine that said opposition candidate can easily best non-charismatic JDV. The League of Municipalities of the Philippines (LMP), though, let it be known that JDV is the best candidate to win and to see to economic growth. A female "presidentiable" foresees no role for JDV; she will be the one battling it out against the main opposition candidate, current Vice Pres. Joseph "Erap" Estrada; it will be woman against womanizer!

Among the comments on bills passed, we find that 29 million Filipinos are thought to be marginalized, and live below the poverty line. According to another article, election fraud must be deemed normal. It can also be expected that high-ranking police and army officers protect criminal syndicates.

This brings us to the two opinion pages. The Editorial is dedicated to the 120th anniversary of the Chinese Charitable Association in the Philippines. G's column consists of clippings from the news, mainly political tidbits. Another column presents us with the anti-Church and pro-President points of view of two letter writers. Two lady columnists comment on Rizal, the national hero, and the Iraq crisis, respectively. A priest reminds us of the value of a positive attitude in facing life's vicissitudes.

The president "breaks a lance" for alternative and native, or folk medicine. According to his speech, on page 11, Filipinos should be more conscious of the value of their own knowledge:

> Filipinos should be more conscious of the value of their own knowledge: We have looked to other nations for new technologies and cures, even for ordinary ailments. Indeed, many other nations have been exploiting the potentials of our resources, claiming them as their own discoveries without giving credit to us, and making tremendous profits at our expense.

We further find comments on Filipino civil war refugees in Malaysia (in Sabah and Labuan); they are said to number up to half-a-million. On the manipulability and ineffectiveness of the law. On the development of English, Tagalog and *Taglish*, all three of them apparently heading for sloppiness and confusion. On the flu pandemic. This then brings us back to miscellaneous national news items. Four thousand former members of military rebel groups have been granted amnesty; henceforward they will be free to travel abroad. Imelda Marcos is also free to do that, despite her conviction on corruption charges to up to 24 years in prison. The Chinese, even in the teeth of rampant kidnapping for ransom, should cultivate "sobriety and calmness." Civilians are commended for their role in the freeing of two police officers taken hostage by a Luzon-based command of the NPA.

The rest of the main section is made up of diverse items without particular interest. On page 24: "The University of Perpetual Help is encouraging medical health graduates to pursue a post-graduate course on sex education to help in the government's crusade in reviving the old Filipino traits and values in an effort to bring back the lost morality among the people."

We find three pieces on environmental issues, several on various seminars. Other reports are on: "poverty is the source of criminality"; Marikina City's renaissance; electoral fraud; peace talks with the NPA; awards; and, the inevitable, election-related political tidbits.

The Business and Sports sections, which incidentally also carry some regional, agricultural, and social news, do not contain anything but the expected routines, although the fact that, "the 32,000 Filipino seafarers on board Norwegian vessels outnumbered the Norwegians in those ships," as reported on page B-9 may interest some people. Abuses of power-holders, such as mayors and officials, surface several times, but are as common place as what a business columnist opined on page B-12: "We cannot go on being as morally corrupt as we are now if we are to hold faith with what they all (national heroes) died for."

The Life-and-Leisure and Entertainment section does not contain anything unusual. It is the run-of-the-mill sequence of glamour, fashion, movies, cult stars, and suchlike, that fills up the pages. The special Real Estate section holds news that may be of interest for insiders, and leaves the impression that the islands are hit by a building boom to which only the sky sets the limit.

The Philippine Star of 11 December 1997 is refreshing compared to the *Bulletin*'s tastelessness. What I like about *The Star* is its recalcitrance. In spite of this quality, the paper carries a hefty 17 out of 44 pages of ads. Expectedly, this is considerably less than the *Bulletin,* although it still is impressive. The front page offers different fare from the latter, too. Politics is less prominent, with one picture of the "reconciliation" presidential candidate JDV engineered, and a fun-poking column-like item about the "woman versus womanizer" race to come (Erap is depicted, saying, "You are cute when you say 'womanizer.'"); it is further said that the moralistic presidential hopeful, Francisco Tatad has called the incumbent vice president an "inveterate philanderer." In a lesser item the current president still lets his intention be known that he expects to play the role of "elder statesman" in the future.

The main headline and the lead picture draw attention to other aspects of Filipino life. "Military colonels and police senior superintendents are believed to be among the masterminds of twenty-one kidnap gangs operating in Metro Manila." The picture, made on World Human Rights Day, shows security guards beating up striking employees. The photographer himself was also hit.

Cardinal Sin made it to the front page, too, with his, "It is not a perfect Church"; to belong to it means to be part of a community of faith that is far from perfection and bliss. "It was the first time in recent memory that the Cardinal asked for apology and understanding for sins of the Church." We further find a headline about presidential hopeful RDV, and miscellaneous items about foreign assistance; the temporary release of 20 alleged political offenders (APOs). According to the Task Force Detainees of the Philippines (TFDP), there still are 169 "political prisoners" (in jail); urban Filipinos are eating more bread than rice; the amnesty of 4,000 members of military rebel groups; a university homecoming; a chopper crash. Further on, most of these stories are continued.

Page 2 offers a mixture of world news, which is followed by national items that are more routine than exciting: some environmental observations; a new jail; car theft; a drug ringleader killed; legal advice; a murder; an accident at school; road building; conserve water!; anti-smoking law; budget allocation; control of rents; tax revenue. The real fun of *The Star* is in its two daily opinion pages. The Jaywalker column takes the government to task about its economic optimism which, in the eyes of the suffering people, cannot be seen but as hogwash and lies: "The economy is suffering from a melt-down . . . there is no sector in the economy whatsoever that is thriving–except probably drugs and gambling and kidnapping for ransom." The cartoon and the Editorial are precisely about the last subject. "The citizenry wants the bad guys not just arrested but tried, convicted and locked up in jail." Trust in law enforcement, though, seems to be extremely battered.

Max Soliven, *The Star*'s publisher, takes Senator Tatad to task. The latter announced his running for president on a moralistic ticket, "I did not seek this burden. But God knows best; we must be docile to his will." No wonder that such being-the-elect pretensions draw flak from a former (Marcos) political prisoner who recalls, "It was Tatad who went on radio and television nightly to proclaim the glories of Marcos martial law and condemn those of us who were in jail because we were evil-doers belonging to the discredited 'Old Society.'" This diatribe flows over into the next, namely an exposure of Opus Dei, of which several ranking public figures–Tatad also?–are members. So, "Whither now, *quo vadis*, Bishop Tatad? To Malacañang (presidential palace)?

I doubt that the Filipino people, although Catholic for almost four centuries, are really ready for Octopus Dei."

The columns "My Viewpoint," and "Roses and Thorns" take opposite positions to the presidential wisdom of anointing JDV instead of RDV. There can be little doubt that JDV is a very clever *traditional* politician (*trapo*), at the same time that many people are tired of the non-transparent wheeling and dealing of traditional politicians. RDV is, by all means, a nontraditional politician, but does that mean that he can turn the wheels of politics to great effect? This leaves plenty to comment on for the writers concerned.

Aptly the column, "Sundry Strokes," opens with the line, "While a number of *trapos* and government officials are doing their best to wreck the country's economy, . . ." but then looses its way into various historical and philanthropic musings. "From the Stands" is, like the previous column, written by a woman, and tackles the problem of gender bias in a male-dominated world.

On the following pages, an article about the respectability of alternative, or folk medicine and healing practices attracts attention; so does the environmental observation about the relationship between wet-rice cultivation and the emission of greenhouse gas. Imelda Marcos (Leyte representative, and widow of the former dictator) "gives away rice to House (of Representatives) employees"; she knows how to keep herself in the news. Mental patients killing themselves seem to be a regular occurrence. Security officer robs bank. Protest on the government's human rights record. Prisoner escaping. Safety at construction sites is questionable. The water problem. Misplaced luggage. Rape of a minor. Moral values needed in the fight against crime. ("D underscored the need to instill upon the youth the fear of God, respect for authorities, obedience to laws, honesty in everybody dealings [*sic*], and hard work").

The Star always gives generous space to religious and moralistic subjects. Apart from the daily Bible fare on the editorial page, we still find the regular contribution "Straight from the Word" and half a page devoted to "Our Lord of Love and Redemption of the Mt. Pinatubo Shrine." The female columnist assures the readers that "our eternal life is constantly jeopardized." Happily, though, the Philippines enjoys the special attention of heaven, and Filipinos are well-advised to pray more regularly at their shrines. And these are auspicious!

"Last November 2, 1992, in response to our request for His own message to be put up at the shrine of Mt. Pinatubo, at Palan, San Marcelino, Zambales, Our Lord of Love and Redemption, Jesus the Christ spoke through our guide–Mrs. PKF–declaring Palan as a 'spiritual rehabilitation center.'"

We further find a highly personal, many-names-mentioning column, which is a rather common feature in all sorts of newspapers; a piece on health care, "The Republic's Next Debacle?"; the announcement of a civic club meet; letters to the Editor. The latter express political partisanship; worry about kidnapping and optimism about fighting the crime; indignation about unrewarded war-pension claims; praise of American schools. On that page we also find the last lines of Soliven's column:

> I don't appreciate the nonsense that the world owes the poor a living just because they are poor . . . Isn't this land-grabbing and squatting under another guise? What kind of people have we become, owing to juicy government promises which encouraged parasitism? A nation of squatters, swindlers and cheats? It's time we reminded our people that you don't get something for nothing.

Two pages about national and international sports bring the main issue to an end. The eight pages of the Business section are conventional: it is about stocks, exchange and interest rates, and some corporate news. The same goes for the Entertainment pages: they are about movies, TV stars, the horoscope, and two pages of names of new nurses. The Fashion & Beauty pages are just about these, and contain also three sides about the "beautiful people" who make "society news."

Compared with the other two papers, the *Manila Standard* offers a most disciplined front page. It attracts modest attention to some features elaborated on its interior pages, such as showbiz; sports; business; global warming; a bank robbery, then the lotto results and the weather. The leading article is about kidnapping, followed by the president declaring 1998 a "Human Rights Year."

Other items are about the computerization of the polls; the expectation that presidential hopeful RDV will not break ranks with the ruling party; the oil deregulation law; two small international items relating to the currency crisis. The most telling sentence, in my view, is, "The group said they will (form a new party for RDV or) find a way by which he can be a guest candidate of another party." It appears that political parties are not organized around ideological lines, but around personalities.

The following three pages either enlarge on the subjects headlined on the front page, or broach fresh topics. The president signs tax bills "that also grant 100 percent income tax exemption to close to four million overseas Filipino workers." Under "IMF letting Asia's tiger cub out of the woods," we learn that, "Philippine officials boast that their economy, once Asia's basket case, is in better shape than its neighbors . . . the Philippines can finally hold its head up among Asian economies."

Gas emissions from rice fields; pardon of political offenders; nursing examinations; foreign aid; amnesty for former rebels; crime and its masterminds; work-site safety; presidential hopefuls, are the items that correspond to the other papers reviewed. New are the: presidential assurance, "Nothing is secret about . . ."; intra-ASEAN negotiations (two reports); twelve killed in Mindanao; illegal labor recruiters; the Philippines is an "illiberal democracy"; political ads ban; environmental monitoring; commemorative stamp; urban transport.

Four business pages follow: investments; disinvestments; interest rates; take-over bidding; taxation; import tax, et cetera, plus stock exchange and currency crisis. Then local news is resumed: bank robbery; cop shoots down one of three men. . . ; two others slain in Quezon City; unsafe worksites; prosecute water-wasters; miscellaneous items. Three sports pages conclude the 12 sides of the main issue. Though apparently short, the volume of text is considerable since advertisement takes up only three quarters of a page.

The same goes for the second section of the paper: just one-tenth of a page for a movie ad, leaving the rest free for the Editorial and opinion columns (three sheets), and one page each for "Regions," "World," "Trends," "Entertainment," and more "Trends." The generous allotment of space to Editorial and opinion columns results in some interesting comments on global warming; (Internet) information addiction; the presidential race (mentioned five times!); peace talks with the NPA; police and kidnapping; a happy recovery:

> God works in inscrutable ways. He must be reminding you that there is more to life . . . there is a need to realize and appreciate your oneness with God . . . To The Almighty, to Mama Mary, and everybody who helped me make it through the long night, thank you." A letter still adds that, "Our present breed of politicians . . . are wanting in integrity and principles . . . We can only wonder why idiots are doing the sensitive task of legislation while we have the right men for the job.

The "Regions" page mentions environmentalist concerns; presidential polls; a political speech; road project; interest rate; outstanding leaders; some historically-wrong information about the Iglesia Filipina Independiente, and "Jesus Christ, who is Prophet Aisiah in Islam." The world news on the next page is routine and of little interest. "Trends" and "Entertainment" do not contribute much to the readers' enlightenment either.

Summary Image

The image of the public world that appears in the newspapers we scrutinized is rather messy and highly politicized. That is to say, a lot of attention is spent on individual politicos who seemingly preside over an untidy society, but who have little to offer in terms of clear guidance. Justice appears as faltering and ineffective. Violent crime and killings are everyday fare. All this seems to stimulate many negative remarks about "the Filipino" in the public world. At a more private plane, though, the latter may seek solace in religion and moralism. Individually, therefore, there is hope where society is disheartening.

Tabloid Press

Of the three tabloids bought on 11 December 1997, two were selected for their massive circulation, and the other because it is published by *The Philippine Star*. The last one is not really different from the others, but since we have to start somewhere, let us give it pride of place.

On the front page of *Pilipino Star Ngayon* (XII/267), we find a "biggish" picture of MM, a young and sexy movie star. We also encounter a political cartoon advising the president to dismiss certain high officials. Next to modest advertising, the remaining space contains headlines: "3 Kidnappers Will Be Executed by the MILF!" (Moro Islamic Liberation Front); "2 Traders Shot, 1 Dead"; "Grandmother Killed by Drug Addict." We have to move to the interior pages to read the stories. On page 2, the front page cartoon and the MILF story are elaborated. We find further news about kidnapping; the presidential race; the disappearance of a Filipino entertainer in Japan; the freeing of 20 political prisoners. On page 3, we are confronted with a picture of the badly-damaged grandmother, and further with the halting of construction at unsafe building sites; a picture of a killed robber; somebody knifed down by robber; somebody running amuck, knifing two people; a thirteen-year old raped by five men.

This brings us to the one-and-a-half opinion pages. We find some wise advice ("rein in your desires"); a comment on biblical text; legal counsel; an editorial on new weaponry for the police (in order to make them more effective against well-armed criminals); a fun-poking column on exploited credulity; a lengthy article about the situation of the people in Pinatubo resettlement areas; a denunciation of "bad eggs" in the police force who can continue in their devious ways because of high protection; incorrect behavior of jeepney drivers; a "Mystery File" on premonition. The next page announces, "Two Dueling Traders; 1 Dead, 1 Wounded"; "A (a rapist) is Worried About the System of Justice"; "Two Workmen Killed in a Landslide"; "Helicopter Crash Landing"; "Lifelong for Massacre Suspect"; "Land Affected by the Drought." Two pictures illustrate the manufacture and sale of big Christmas lanterns.

The next ten pages are about showbiz (mostly movies, the starlets, the juicy stories these generate, and lots of name-calling); puzzles; comics; letters to and from Dr. Love; horoscope and sports. Out of the 16 pages, 2 1/2 were taken up by ads (mostly movies to go to, and one page of classified ads, almost all of them official announcements).

Abante's 11 December issue contains only 12 pages. Its front page features a scantily dressed starlet and the pictures of people relating how their bank was robbed. The main headline announces that certain members of the legislature are suspected to be involved with the kidnap-for-ransom syndicates. According to the minor headlines, the film industry is about to clean itself of "bold actors" and "TF" (titillating films); the election expenses of all presidential aspirants will be carefully investigated; the government keeps pursuing its talks with the communists; 3 Air Force men injured in chopper crash.

On the following three pages, said headlines are substantiated. These news items are complemented by an item about the water crisis; the outbreak of diarrhea in Quezon City; a hoped-for across-the-board compensation for lowly paid labor; a jailbreak; Imelda Marcos; workplace safety; impending oil-price hike; environmental destruction; official budgetary problems; rapist challenging court; a murder case; a snake charmer; a missing girl, and a column about destruction caused by quarrying.

The opinion page offers an Editorial on the social problems, irritations, and even thievery caused by the drought when people have to queue for hours to fill a pail of water. One of the two other columns deals with the presidential anointing of JDV, the other with legal advice. Follows a full page of "hot-line" ads: "Direct to the Girl"; "Hidden Secrets"; "Meet your Match." Callers are supposed to be at least 18 years old, sometimes even 21! Then come the two showbiz pages, a column about the broken family, puzzles, two sports pages, and a last page with a bank robbery, a rape, a woman killed by robbers, a bad-checks ring, children playing with live ammunition and thus wounded, and a triple life sentence for a killer. Two and two thirds sides of ads fill about one fifth of the issue; apart from the erotic phone lines, two ads of VD (venereal disease) clinics stand out.

The twelve-paged *Taliba* headlines the three life sentences for one murderer; the granny killed by an addict; the expected sentencing, for child rape, of the MP RJ; the bank robbery; the presidential race. On pages 2 and 3, these items are elaborated. These two pages are clearly laid out, and thus the following words jump to the eye: "killer"; "rape"; "robbery"; "killed"; "throat cut"; "kidnap-for-ransom"; "death penalty"; "rapist"; "will be executed"; "drugs ring"; "JDV"; "FVR and JDV"; "bank robbery"; "hold-up"; "shoot-out"; "fight because of gossiping"; "lasciviousness and child abuse"; "political offenders"; "FVR"; "RDV"; and, "JDV." Some space is given to striking yet irrelevant foreign news ("hijack"; "beauty queen").

Pages 4 and 5 hold the columns. The Editorial discusses the new tax law: it is a boon for those who have to make do with little. The anointing of JDV, an old-style politician *par excellence*, is the subject of the first column proper: JDV's prayers at Mt. Banahaw (a source of mystical power) have been granted. The second one contains letters from, and advice to, women about their love life. Column number three is concerned with the presidential race; with cyanide fishing; with the public blaming officials, even the president, for the kidnappings. The last column is on legal advice. The sole news item on the opinion pages is about an officially intolerable relationship between a high-ranking female civil servant and one of her underlings. The usual three *showbiz* pages follow, and so do pages with classified ads (mostly pawnshop auction sales; legal notices; official announcements), and simple society news. The rest of the issue goes to sports. The bulk of the three to six sides of ads promote movies, although a two-thirds-page advertisement of men's briefs also stands out.

Image

There is little that is unexpected about the three tabloids reviewed. Perhaps the most interesting fact is that all three of them sport a legal advice column. The bulk consists of reading feed, plain entertainment, and the reporting about the big-big world consists of crime of all sorts, and (closely related?) politics. Columns and editorials are routinely written, but refrain from in-depth reporting and investigative journalism. They have been written in a hurry. This is characteristic of the tabloid culture: the reader flips through the pages, and in a short-short time really, he is through. The tabloids do not demand a prolonged attention span, and there is hardly an image of society that emerges. Tabloids are entertainment.

What Are The Issues?

From early December until the last day of February 1998, I have been reading and clipping from the Philippine press. It was a tedious task, more so than on other occasions. Perhaps this can partly be understood because of the political season it was. In the last half-year running up to national elections, the political circus, with all of its clowns and gimmicks, its jokers and jugglers, its trapeze artists and animal tamers, goes into a frenzy, drawing and directing attention, manipulating, hoodwinking, boasting, exaggerating, and the public seems to love it. Even if they don't, this is what they get, day in, day out. In my case, *ad nauseum*.

Every time one reads these newspapers, he is confronted with an overdose of political information, that is to say tidings about individual politicians and their moves. A few years ago, not during any particular political season, I remember the new year's wish of a columnist that she and her fellow writers may find other topics than the antics of popularity seekers and presidents to write about. Were they only commenting on the affairs of state and society, on issues and substance! No, the same columnist and her colleagues babble on, filing their obligatory pieces and filling obligatory space.

Under Suharto, Jakarta newspapers showed a stark contrast: a near-absence of politics, that is, of political discussion, and an apparent paucity of politicians. There, it took a lot of courage to incisively comment on the affairs of state, although there always was space to write about its culture, morality, and want of justice. As we shall see, these are also topics that regularly surface in the Philippine media. Another aspect attracting attention is that Indonesian newspapers have few regular columnists but give considerable space to lengthy topical articles discussing, for instance, education, religion, or history.

Such half-page features, written by specialists, have evolved to high-quality contributions in the Thai press. Political subjects are not taboo. Such matters gain perspective in the critical exchanges about the understanding and actual practice of human rights and national law in the country. The spread of relevant topics, from public health to the interpretation of history at school, is quite amazing, and the standards of investigation and commentary have grown to become quite respectable.

Detailed and well-researched information on matters affecting nation and country is generally missing in Philippine papers. In a way, the press is stagnant. Most broadsheets entertain a bevy of regular columnists who are supposed to fill, together, two pages, sometimes more, a day, and although there is a lot of interest in their commentary, it remains comments on the happenings of the present that normally lack a basis in investigation and research. Moreover, space available to them is severely limited. Since they are supposed to fill these two or more sides in an absolutely regular fashion, there remains almost no room for lengthy in-depth features. What remains are gratuitous opinions and political partisanship. Unfortunately, the present press has largely lost the fighting spirit and substance that characterized the opposition-to-Marcos-papers in the waning days of the dictatorship.

When democracy was restored, it resurrected the *status quo ante*. The old oligarchy came back to power and, within one year, the high-flung ideals of a just and equitable society were drowned in the blood of the Mendiola massacre. The real issues, such as maldistribution and abuse of economic and political power, vanished from the pages. The fight against the Communists became prominent. The related human rights abuses were censored out.

The Philippine press may be free, even licentious, but it is not independent. Ownership is largely with individual ruling families who use the media to fight their economic and political battles. It is only on the rarest occasions that reportage surfaces which tells us something relevant about what is happening to the great majority of underdogs. Systematic violations of human and constitutional rights, open democratic debate, the real state of the environment, all these and related issues do not make it to the pages. Informed political discussion, platforms and plans, do not try to find these in the daily press. At best it offers commentary in the margin; its contribution, contrary to the late Marcos days, to pluralistic and astute public-opinion making is slight.

Justice

While the subject of politics is unavoidable, it may be of interest to begin with some different matters that are, equally unavoidably, related to politics. In the Philippines, it seems, everything revolves around the exercise of power, and the administration of justice is no exception. A perennial issue, in this respect, is that many people hold themselves to be well above the law. On the occasion that such untouchables are brought before the court, news is being made.

People who enjoy privilege and power think that they can get away with anything they do, and if they stumble in their course, the public, and parts of the press, delight in the case; yea, they even get excited, and hope that justice will catch on with representatives who rape, congressmen who kill, mayors who murder, prosecutors who pervert, Imeldas who embezzle, cops who kidnap, and politicians who protect criminals. What everybody knows is that the powerful can do as they please; that a maid must expect to be molested; that a worker will be squeezed out of his wages; that witnesses live in fear and will not be forthcoming; that connections are more convincing than the canon of the law; that money has much weight on the scales of justice. Yet, news of this sort is scattered throughout the pages, every day.

It took about a year to get Congressman J convicted, and running up to elections, his case still draws attention. When a warrant of arrest was issued against him, he went on the run, hoping, perhaps, to leave the country. Anyway, he was brought before the court, having been challenged by his victim, an 11-year-old girl. Her pimping stepfather had let her out to J, who finally drew a double life sentence for raping and committing acts of lasciviousness on the child.

At the time, his being on the run, then being arrested, drew considerable attention. Then, J's antics were fun. He had his place of remand refurbished in grand style. There he was visited by fellow members of Congress who, in good democratic fashion, would not find such association disgraceful until the man was proven guilty, or had exhausted all his means of appeal (which still keeps him in the news). His company was also appreciated by the prison staff who allowed him in on their parties (cause enough for one superintendent to be sacked).

In the early days of his detention, J treated everything as a big joke, "Mind you, do you think I ask for the birth certificate of every woman I (go to) bed (with)?" Soon, there were claims by others of having been sired by J, such as an almost 30-year-old man who delightedly demanded to see his daddy. Predictably, he was the son of a servant girl abused in a distant past. So much became clear: J was a fecund and high-frequency philanderer, a trait that is often admired in the Filipino male. As *PDI* columnist RJ-D had it:

> And how are women and children to believe that the legal establishment, still largely under the control of men, understand rape and sexual exploitation, and take it seriously as both a crime and a social issue when a convicted rapist is given such a cushy treatment?
>
> This is why the case became so controversial, not just because the accused was a prominent and powerful individual, or the victim so young, but because it was so "common." Wealthy men think nothing of buying

sexual services from young women, and Filipino society considers this not only right but the men's due.

Everyone says exploiting the sexuality of children is repugnant and wrong. And yet the pillars of our society, specifically J's colleagues in the House of Representatives, cannot even bring themselves to concretely express their repugnance at this deed, if not at the congressman. What are they saying by their reluctance to expel him from their ranks? And what do we make of J's firm belief that his constituents not only believe in his innocence, but that they will translate this belief into votes come May? (*PDI,* 24/12/97)

Newspapers were quick to hail J's conviction:

The Makati Regional Trial Court yesterday delivered a powerful blow for an impartial and courageous administration of justice . . . The decision revives public confidence in the courts' ability to conduct trial without fear or favor . . .

The rise in the number of convictions of powerful officials reflects the effectiveness of the witness protection program of the government, without which witnesses and even victims of crimes are extremely vulnerable to threats and pressure. (*PDI,* 13/12/97).

The Editorial of *The Star* (18/1/98) also finds occasion to report about "An opportunity for truth and justice." This relates to the killing of labor leader Rolando Olalia in 1986. In the run-up to a coup to oust then President Aquino, the participants in the conspiracy wanted to rid the Aquino administration of leftist elements. The plotters were members of the RAM (Rebolusyong Alyansang Makabayan), originally an anti-Marcos faction within the military, who apparently took it upon themselves to kill and stage coup attempts. At the time of the Olalia murder, no conclusive evidence was forthcoming, but the affair rolled on in the sense that people in the know were rubbed out in regular succession, which suddenly brought out witnesses who feared for their own lives. While this case is under consideration of the Department of Justice, it must again be observed that the RAM boys are well-connected. Wasn't their leader rewarded for his coup attempts and consequent killings by being elected senator? Really notorious people get their deserves in style!

Take any Filipino without name, wealth or power, accused of a felony; chances are, in the next minute, the police would collar him, drag him down to indignity and shame, and to the usually dingy police station.

> But take a member of Congress with a name (no matter stained), wealth (whatever its source), or power (and its appearances), accused as a conspirator in the murder of two sons of his political rivals, on the testimony of a supposed witness. Have a court issue an arrest warrant for him. For days, the congressman promises in media interviews that he would surrender, but only to officials of his choice, and not to the police.
>
> Ten days after the murders were committed, he actually did show up, with wife and five children and a coterie of reporters and photographers in tow, at the house, in posh Dasmariñas Village, of the Speaker who is aspiring to be the next president of the Republic. Oblivious to the royal treatment that has been conferred on the congressman, the Speaker even lauded the former for turning himself in. 'Congressman JV is giving a very beautiful example, unlike others who are on the run for the law,' the Speaker said. You might think it was said tongue-in-cheek but the Speaker went on to hail the congressman as the paragon of a law-abiding citizen. (*TMT,* 8/1/98)

When the hearings took place, the honorable congressman had well prepared his case, to the point that his accusers walked out:

> We are sorry but seemingly, the honorable committees have lost all moral right and credibility to further undertake any impartial and objective inquiry. Ms. Q criticized the House for allowing Rep. JV 'to act as judge and prosecutor' during a hearing last week, wherein witness EH recanted his statement linking the congressman to the killings.
>
> What happened at the hearing was an unprecedented display of power and influence (and) an uninhibited disregard for *delicadeza* and an apparent mockery of the justice system, she said.
>
> The House committees are investigating allegations of torture, illegal arrests, and salvaging allegedly carried out by the National Bureau of Investigation in connection with the double murder. (*PDI,* 5/2/98).

Justice is not easy to come by, and it appears to be very biased in favor of the few who rule, who have means and power, and who can delay and appeal to higher courts. Justice seems to be swift in the case of the underdog who may languish in jail for long periods before ever seeing a judge. There also is the justice against the Left, or defenders of human rights. That the ghost of Rolando Olalia has been revived is felicitous; whether it will lead to anything is another matter. About the killing of journalist F, we could read:

> I am not expecting anything from the government or even the police,

> what with the slow-paced progress and a visible inaction from their end, (the widow) stressed . . . Invoking divine intervention, (she) said: God is really working among us. Look what happened to the Olalia case, for 11 years the case was unresolved but now at least there is something. I hope F's case will also be resolved with God's intervention. (*PDI,* 12/2/98).

Yes, ultimately justice must be hoped to descend from heaven, or may even be postponed until one's soul has arrived there. And then, isn't there such a thing like the forgiving of sins?

Perhaps Bongbong, the former dictator's son, was right when he observed, "My father must be laughing in heaven," about all that questing for ill-gotten wealth and Imelda's antics. After all, she is running for president, too, and if she indeed sits on the famous pile of pelf, she may have a point with her election promise to bring the miseries caused by the country's foreign debt to an end. One way or other, campaigning, dancing with schoolgirls, traveling abroad, distributing rice, or being judged in court, she has her ways to remain in the news. The *PDI,* especially, made a lot of her conviction; it was hardly mentioned in the *Bulletin,* but then, would such a trifle as a 12-year conviction land her in jail?

> Jailing Imelda, as everyone says, will send a stern warning against corruption and venality. Yes, it will. But it will do much more. It will help to restore the balance in our skewed moral universe.
>
> At the very least, jailing Imelda will help push back our malignant belief that politics is impervious to morality. That whatever a king, or a president, does may be judged only by God or their conscience. That they have the right to rob and torture and murder for the common good. No, it is not true at all that if you kill one person, it is murder, but that if you massacre thousands, it is war. It is not true at all that if you steal a loaf of bread, it is theft, but that if you embezzle millions, it is ingenuity.
>
> At the very most, it will help to push back that even more malignant practice of *areglo*, or compromise, that we constantly resort to. No, more than a practice, it is a culture. It is a culture premised on the idea that since we can never have justice, we might as well settle for the next best thing, which is a settlement.
>
> It has become frighteningly prevalent. How often have we seen it in daily life? A child is murdered and the parents, after sending their lamentations to heaven, accept a suspect's *abuloy*. They are the ones who, despairing of justice, find ways to reconcile themselves with the injustice of it. (*PDI,* 4/2/98)

Morality

In order to create national community, we need to instill the values of pride in nation and self-sacrifice; to give it substance, we need to celebrate centennials, Rizal years, and People Power at EDSA. In order to create conscious citizens, the Constitution must be studied at school. In order to revive the moral fiber of the land, people should be exposed to a Moral Recovery Program. The Preamble of the Constitution opens the perspective on the good life; school teaching, from elementary up to college, reserves special sessions devoted to morals and manners. In brief, values education sometimes even called "eugenics" or improvement of the race, is deemed to be an important means for achieving a desirable society.

This pattern of thinking is widespread in East Asia, and fuels the discussion on the so-called Asian values. Such values are thought to be effective in themselves. People who load up on them, will behave nicely, work hard, be docile, be good citizens and good family men. It is values that create the system; it is the absence of morality that makes it a mess. A sociologist may wonder at this reasoning, but it surfaces all the time in the evaluation of and prescriptions for life in the Philippines. And, as just mentioned, school, basic law, and recovery programs are thought to be important ingredients for national wholesomeness.

Predictably, the newspaper often comments on the mess, and thus, the putative paucity of morality, of values:

> What this country needs most is not economic recovery, what it needs most is moral recovery. The signs of economic recovery are there, however feeble and sporadic they are. The signs of moral recovery are nowhere to be found. The signs only point to a nation getting sicker. There is no justice in this world, but there is even less so in this land. That is what makes this country the Sick Man of Asia, notwithstanding the colorful sheets from Philippines 2000 that shrouds it in the dark recesses of a charity ward. That is the greatest impoverishment we have. That is the deadliest virus we have. (*PDI,* 4/2/98)
>
> However, there will not be a permanent solution unless a moral reformation takes place among the people in private business and in government service. Once and for all, society will have to confront the issue of bribery and corruption. If we do not change to restore honesty and integrity in our way of life, we will always be threatened with lawlessness. We have to restore our civil society as we start the new century. (*TPJ,* 6/12/97)

> This is supposed to be funny? In these times when dishonesty and graft and corruption are rampant, anarchy is everywhere, and morality appears to be non-existent, it is appalling to see a prime-time TV show add to the sorry situation, teaching the audience to cheat and inflict harm on innocent persons. (*PDI,* 27/1/98)

The last observation hits home. Television floods the audience with inane shows, basketball without end, lowly-rated American programs and, together with the movie and video industries, with huge quantities of unsavory violence. It strikes me every time I enter the country, and sit on my first bus to Lucena, that I am forced to watch sheer endless brutality, ferocity and destructiveness, thanks to the bus company's complimentary video entertainment. This jibes with what is shown in the downtown movie houses.

> But who cares about values? That's Greek to Tagalog movie fans. Filipino movies or showbiz entertainment in general are essentially and explicitly non-Filipino simply because they stress a different type of negative culture and values alien to the Filipino soul and society. They glorify the violent, not the heroic, the smutty and perverted not the romantic and the beautiful in sex, the stupid and the gross not the amusing and humorous in comedy.
>
> With these ideals being commonly exploited by local movies, how can the Filipino movie ever promote national unity? On the contrary it divides instead of unites, it confuses instead of enlightens, it insults more than it entertains the human mind. (Of course, there are still Filipinos who believe that to be insulted is humorous and entertaining). (*PDI,* 1/1/98).

According to Sen. Francisco S. Tatad, stupidity and violence are not the preserve of the electronic media alone. The press feeds it; politics provide it:

> While the national election is 'expected to help educate the electorate,' politicians have already succeeded in 'idiotizing the nation.' The spirit of the law is being 'flagrantly violated' and the Commission on Elections seems 'completely powerless to do anything about it.'
>
> The situation is getting more insane with every passing day, and the media may be unwittingly contributing to it. They are having a field day screaming headlines about the worthless antics of politicians at the expense of more important news affecting the continued stability, if not viability, of the social order. (*TMT,* 6/1/98)

The good senator did not leave it at this. He founded a new party to contest the presidential election. Under the name *Gabaybayan* ("moral guide of the nation"), a party of the family, of women, of the young, he wants to invest the nation's leadership with morality, and promote material cum spiritual progress. And he wants, no, rather he has been entrusted by God to seek the presidency: "I did not seek this burden. But God knows best; we must be docile to his will." Even so, should he be taken seriously?

> Poor Senator Kit Tatad. All he did was pronounce that dreaded word, 'morality,' and immediately everybody started making fun of him. In the case of Tatad, the question now going the rounds is: "*What* is he? Is he fish, or foul?"
>
> When he announced his bid for the highest post in the land, and launched his strange-sounding political party, Kit wrapped himself in the Philippine flag, as well as the revolutionary flag and the Katipunan flag. Whenever a would-be patriot wraps himself in the flag, the public immediately begins to suspect he is trying to hide something.
>
> Tatad claims that he is running so as to stop 'the most amoral presidential aspirant from becoming the next President of the Republic,' clearly referring to his enemy, Vice President Joseph "Erap" Estrada whom he accused of cohabiting with too many women. (*TPS,* 11/12/97)
>
> Tatad does not come with clean hands. The idiocy one finds in present-day newspapers cannot even come close to the sickening fare that the former information minister used to offer the Filipino people every single day of martial law. His was the face and the voice that Filipinos woke up to in their daily miseries. And when he finally parted ways with the dictator who mischievously referred to his young ward's accumulated wealth, the latter retorted that if he was smart enough to become press secretary at the age of 30, he should be smart enough to make that much money. (*TMT,* 7/1/98)

Naturally, politicians pontificating on morality must be mistrusted. Yet, there is a widespread perception that the absence of positive values in public life stands in the way of meaningful transformation. That is why Richard Gordon withdrew from the race: "I will not announce my candidacy unless the Filipino people, especially the young, are ready to reject the politics of personalities and the politics of goons, guns and gold, and unless the people are ready to accept the kind of new leaders with new ideas." (*PDI,* 1/12/97)

Sen. Raul S. Roco thinks differently, and is not about to withdraw. He:

> declared the dawning of a new politics of light; the style of governance he calls the sunshine principle. With this kind of politics, Roco called for an administration where truth and transparency will be the rule of government. No longer will the government act without a sense of accountability to the people. A kind of moral light will penetrate Malacañang in a Roco administration . . .
>
> Moral force should be the source of political power. A few good people doing good can change the world. Roco deepened this idea with the metaphor of sunlight's power to disinfect. Germs die in the sunlight. The force of a moral presidency which is transparent and honest will rid politics of its darkness and corruption so that our country can rise towards its true potential. (*PDI,* 23/2/98)

Roco is not the only alchemist among those who have set their eyes on the presidency. The most visionary among them is probably Andres Ugboc: "His government, he says, will be known as the Horoscopic Spiritual Form of Government, and his country the Horoscopic Republic of the Philippines." In his own (unexpurgated) words:

> In order to stop hunger, *Gobyerno Horoskopio* will cultivate uncultivated Land for farming so that rice and corn production will improve and there will be oversupply of production. And rice and corn could sell to P3 a KILO. If this is not enough, I will ask owner and developer of golf course and subdivisions to transfer their business to the mountain which land area is not considered as Agricultural. Or face the charges of Economic sabotage. (*PDI,* 13/12/97)

It cannot be denied that Ugboc has some very sound ideas, and his way of reaching decisions through horoscope is probably superior to the hanky-panky of traditional politicians who, according to the same issue of the *PDI:* ". . . are almost always unpredictable because they are almost always illogical in their ways. In a country where there are no rules, anything goes, including logic."

Traditional Politics

The two core institutions of Philippine society are politics and the family. The first takes care of the public world, the second constitutes the private domain. This clear-cut division is, certainly, too neat, but it may be analytically useful, especially when we consider the realm of politics. Anyway, both institutions operate in common ways: firstly, bonds between participants are personalized; secondly, such links reach up to a patron. Yet, whereas such relationships are expected to preserve and foster family solidarity, they are assumed to be opportunistic and self-serving in the case of politics.

The politics of patronage, of pork-barrel allocations, of perks and positions as personal rewards, of heavy investments in reaching elective posts, and of individual profit from such posts, is called traditional politics. As a system that politicizes nearly all public offices (and erodes bureaucratic integrity), it has been firmly established by the first strongman of the Philippine polity, Commonwealth Pres. Manuel L. Quezon.

It is a system which rests on favor and counter-favor, on being in the league or in the cold, on being elected or suffering losses, on receiving pork-barrel funds or having nothing to show. It turns the distribution of taxpayers' money into the personal largesse of politicians who provide their constituency with waiting sheds and roads, especially during campaign seasons. The waiting sheds are there to advertise the names of the politicians concerned, who also see to it that their names are well displayed at other projects they initiate. They can be generous because of pork-barrel funds made available to sitting politicians.

Apart from this money, the president holds a vast discretionary reserve which enables him or her to influence, and ingratiate, many, many people. In brief, politics means business. Altogether, this is the system referred to as traditional politics. It is run by traditional politicians, *tradpols* for short and, nowadays more popularly dubbed as trapos, literally, "cleaning rags," thus, expressing a sense of public contempt for the political profession.

But unless things radically reform, this is the system Filipinos are stuck with, and since politics is the national pastime par excellence, it draws lots of commentary. Because it is very hard for most to imagine programmatic politics, these comments are on individual politicians. It is they who draw the attention, and as a result the electoral season assumes the qualities of a popularity contest. In that way, actual or former movie stars can do well in politics; a charismatic coup-staging colonel could make it to the Senate; in the current race, we find actors and a national basketball hero:

> Of course, people vote for them not only because they look better, speak better and act better but also because the voters are tired of the *trapos*. Also, people mistake the characters they play in the movies with

> the real characters who ask for their votes. The characters in the movies are all heroes: brave, honest, clever, wise. Often, the real-life actors who play them are the opposite. It is only after they are already in public office that we discover that they are like *ampaw* (puffed rice), big outside but nothing inside. (*PDI,* 24/12/97)

Politics does not only bring stars to the fore. It sets whole families in the limelight. These are known as political dynasties. They see to it that, under whatever dispensation, they always have a finger in the pie:

> Right now, there are many wives, husbands, brothers, children and all manner of relatives who would run for the positions of incumbents who can no longer run for re-election. In many instances, members of the same family run for different positions under different parties. Thus, whichever party wins, the family has a member in a position of influence. In Pasay City, Mayor PC's wife E will run, again, for Congress while a number of C's sons from different women will run for different positions in Pasay under different political parties. In nearby Makati, Mayor JB's wife will run for his position. (*PDI,* 24/12/97)

This highly personalistic approach to politics is well-established in the way people are supposed to vote. They have to write down the names of all the individuals they vote for, such as one president, one vice president, twelve senators, one provincial governor, and so on, down to more local positions, all in all some thirty to thirty-six names. Voters must really know what they want if they aspire to see the "right" people in power. Most of them cannot be expected to be able to survey such a scope of candidates, and many will vote on the basis of popularity, of inducements (vote buying), or of being directed in a certain way by a superior. Can this personalistic approach result in visionary leadership?

> Not in a long, long time has the Philippines been so arid in its daily existence and so bereft of leadership as it is today. Our politics are in utter disarray, the men who presume to lead us are a crude, even disgusting, pack of mediocrity. There is carping everywhere, recrimination, intrigue, talk and double-talk, cross and double-cross, and we wonder. Leadership for many years in our country has been transactional. Its totem is the Countrywide Development Fund better known as pork barrel, even better known as the pigsty of patronage politics. (*TPS,* 19/1/97)

The absence of leadership is, as we noted, often thought to be rooted in a deficit of morality. There are people, though, who are not very impressed by moral measures. One bishop even pronounced:

> that infidelity is not a primary criterion in choosing a president. More important is the candidate's sincere regard for the poor, in sum, fidelity to the highest standards of public office . . .
>
> The pronouncement is favorable to Erap in that he's the only presidential candidate openly accused of philandering or adulterous behavior, a charge that he admits was associated with his youthful wild days. (*PDI,* 16./1/98)

There is more that may be favorable to Erap. Part of his "winnability" may even lie in an absence of grasp of national problems:

> A candidate unable to answer questions on national issues but able to blurt out the funniest ripostes does have the bigger chance of landing a space on the front page. So does a candidate whose handlers have learned to present their client's sliminess as something useful. (*TMT,* 7/1/98)
>
> I heard this over the last couple of weeks from some friends, all professionals and well-educated. Two of them even former activists. They are going to vote for Erap, they said, because they are tired of putting geniuses in Malacañang. All the geniuses have done is brilliantly retard the country . . .
>
> Indeed, the other presidents were not just lawyers, they either topped the bar or finished pretty close to it. But the fact that they were so, and did so, did not make them exceptionally law-abiding, it made them exceptionally law-avoiding. It did not make them unravel the rule of law, it made them unleash a tide of lawlessness. That's the part that invites cynicism. (*PDI,* 27/1/98)

All this is a grave indictment of traditional politics and there is no shortage of comments on the issue. For that matter, it is almost daily fare. The Church, too, adds insult to injury. The bishops published their opinion that "no one among the presidential aspirants 'passed our criteria.'" To which Cardinal Sin added: "The *trapo* is characterized as a politician who utilizes 'empty verbiage,' lying, vote-buying, backslapping, back-stabbing, political treachery, massive cheating, manipulation of people and the 'common good' for selfish, private or party ends."

The Cardinal ultimately blames the trapo for the major ills besetting the

Philippine political system. He writes, "The *trapo* is responsible for a political culture of corruption, disrespect, if not disdain, for the spirit and letter of the law, and ultimately for the total separation of politics from the fundamental Christian values of truth, honesty, respect for the human person, and dedication to the advancement of the common good." (*PDI,* 5/2/98)

Not everybody is as big-mouthed as the good Cardinal. Not everybody agrees with him, either. The bishops' guidelines were denounced in the *PDI* Editorial of 5 February 1998 as, "a forceful intervention by the Church . . . By preparing the document, the Church draws a portrait of a highly politicized institution, competing with other democratic institutions (like the media and the political parties) to influence public opinion." Besides, by proposing a list of ideal criteria, the voting populace was not given realistic standards to go by. Which brings us to the question whether or not traditional politics is all that negative and bad.

According to columnist CNP:

> Traditional politics has a wider meaning than the pejorative *tradpol* that some self-styled political pundits would have us believe. Traditional politics includes the whole gamut of activities in the practice of democratic politics as we know it in the Philippines . . . In this sense, every Filipino politician is a '*tradpol*' And that includes Cardinal Sin and Cory Aquino, I am afraid, even if they make claims to the contrary . . .
>
> Traditional politics in a democratic society, while not exempt from sin and folly (not Sin and Cory) like any other human activity, is not necessarily bad nor contemptible. On the contrary, it can be said, traditional politics embrace democratic impulses, from the need to negotiate, to bargain, to hassle, to persuade, to the more sordid wheeling and dealing that makes governance possible in a democratic society. The alternative is to dictate, to issue decrees, to threaten, to shame, to shoot, to clamp in jail which are the hallmarks of a (Marcos) dictatorial government . . .
>
> In my opinion, a successful *tradpol,* if he is able to weave his way through labyrinthine wheeling and dealing within democratic institutions to get things done, is superior to a tough cop [meant here is Alfredo Lim], a dogmatic cardinal or an ignorant housewife pronouncing grand schemes to set this country right. Political and economic problems have never been solved by ex-cathedra statements or shooting from the hip, literally or metaphorically. (*TPS,* 10/1/98)

National Community

In the chapter concerned, we shall see that national community is a perennially problematic subject. The failure of nationalism has been said to have resulted in a damaged culture. The same failure has been attributed to the tortuous colonial history of the country. Perhaps a viable national spirit had grown in protest against Spanish oppression. Subsequently, it was thoroughly subverted through American colonial education and the new master's co-optation of pliable elements from the Filipino elite.

This class, by itself an eminently colonial product, has no interest in the egalitarian spirit of nationalism. As the neocolonial rulers of the land, they are best served by quiet continuity. They will not rock the boat. Those who try to do so, striking laborers, protesting peasants, NPAs, do so for other reasons than to remedy the deficit of nationalism. They protest against the yawning gap between the privileged and those who struggle for survival. They protest against a nation divided against itself in which the existence of exclusive classes commands more logic than the ideals of national community.

It may be argued that it was Marcos who succeeded in kindling the spirit of nation. It was a nation in protest, though. Protest against the dictatorship united disenfranchised members of the elite, middle classes, and underdogs. When it was over, a spirit of self-congratulation prevailed: "We" did it. The whole world looked at "us." "I am a Proud Filipino" stickers surfaced everywhere. Then, the oligarchy was restored; an all-out war against the Left, and much of the rural population, was resumed; within one year, hopes were smothered in massacre. Even so, the memory of the successful uprising against Marcos at EDSA still inspired celebrations a few years hence. Meanwhile, though, the event does not stimulate much enthusiasm any longer. Why is that so?

> Even more than June 12th 1898, which quickly dissolved from revolutionary bravado to re-conquest by another foreign power, EDSA's Four Days in February 1986 constituted a genuine victory of the people. Cory Aquino correctly took pride in EDSA, but this turned, over time, into a personal fetish and a most cynical tool for dominating the moral high ground of Philippine politics. Instead of becoming a symbol of national unity for fostering a broad-based triumph of the people against tyranny, EDSA has been misrepresented as a Corysta victory, with patents and franchises reserved for the Aquinos. (*MS,* 23/2/98)

As EDSA was sacrificed to partisan politics, other key players in the events of February 1986 were alienated. They refused to participate in that "national" event. Even the date of the commemoration became a bone of contention. The revolt against Marcos began on 22 February, and that is the date to celebrate. Others hold the 25th to be the right day: then the revolt was over, Marcos was out, Aquino in. Anyway, it had to last until 1998 to bring Sens. Juan Ponce Enrile and Gregorio Honasan together with former Pres. Corazon Aquino and Cardinal Sin.

With all of them on the platform, President Ramos said the people cannot afford to be complacent, years after the "miracle" at EDSA:

> We need to constantly revisit these glorious days to draw strength and courage for ourselves to confront the challenges that face us as a people. Unity was our strength then, and unity must be our strength today. Every Filipino can become a hero, and it does not take much to become one. Abide by the law, pay your taxes honestly and diligently, be vigilant in maintaining peace and order, excel in whatever you do, have pride in your work, choose your elective officials wisely–these are some of the simple ways we can be heroes of today. (*MS,* 23/2/98)

Interesting, to my taste, are these last remarks by President Ramos. Inadvertently, he breaks up the nation he appeals to into individual people. Thus, at the same time that opposing factions show signs of Ramos-orchestrated "reconciliation," heroism is located in individualism, which is probably very correct and realistic in the context of Filipino society. Aside from this, not many people were spontaneously drawn to the event to demonstrate their pride, euphoria, or unity.

> Only about 4,000 to 5,000 people attended the affair yesterday (25 February). Gathered around the People Power Monument at around 7 a.m. to listen to the message of President Ramos, the motley crowd was made up mostly of government officials and employees, military personnel, policemen and media reporters . . .
>
> Two school-teachers from the Camp Crame High School said that the last portion of the Chief Executive's speech was 'not relevant' to the celebration of the revolution. They said he was 'politicking' when he reminded voters to pick the right presidential candidate. 'We were just hauled here to be his audience despite our disinterest. It's a Sunday, we should be resting,' the teachers said . . .
>
> EC, the girl scout coordinator of Quirino High School, said they received a memorandum from the Department of Education, Culture and

> Sports (DECS) division of city schools requiring their attendance at the affair. The memorandum had also been sent to six other schools asking for the participation of their boy and girl scout units. But she only saw school representatives from the Camp Aguinaldo High School and Camp Crame High School. (*MS,* 23/2/98)

Apparently, even schoolchildren had to be mobilized to provide the semblance of an audience. These officials, and others who can be pressured, will probably need to be bused in to get a crowd to attend Centennial celebrations. Officially organized nationalism simply does not work. It is boring, not inspiring. It is overdone, such as the flag-raising ceremonies and the obligatory singing of the national anthem, sometimes up to five times in a single day.

> Hardly anyone, it seems, is inclined to tackle a problem that accounts (I suspect) for the lukewarm reception the Centennial has received. The problem is this: how are we, citizens of a Republic that has spent its entire existence trying to crush revolutions, supposed to celebrate the Philippine Revolution?. Particularly when the Revolution itself was crushed by the Americans, on whose institutions we have based our government . . .
>
> Our Republic is, ideally, dedicated to the same ideals. We have a Bill of Rights dedicated to the preservation of life and human dignity. We officially subscribe to the concept of social justice, and the rights of property holders are, except in certain, special circumstances, inviolate. Which is why subdivisions can keep their gates closed even if this affects the traffic situation, and landowners can successfully resist land reform.
>
> Since we have not fully weaned ourselves–government-wise, anyway–from dependence on the privileged classes, we have developed the upper classes' dislike for governance . . . But without a corresponding, healthy feeling of confidence in ourselves. In the end, this leaves us with the worst of both worlds. And a sense of rootlessness, of a lack of purpose, that reveals itself in our attitudes towards the Centennial. (*Today,* 7/2/98)

Miscellany

The main topic in the news is and remains politics and politicking. Related issues that are regularly reported on are police and crime. In the period of observation, the military was not often in the news, although it was fun to note the students' partisanship when presidential candidates visited the PMA (Philippine Military Academy). This demonstration of undiscipline fits the image of society. Even so, we shall not review how these topics featured in the news, because it would add little to our understanding. It is enough to note that influential elements within the police are thought to be in cahoots with criminals; that senators accuse each other of protecting, even coddling druglords; that the vice president associates with notorious figures and gamblers; that corruption is comfortably ensconced in the highest circles of government, and suchlike. It is everyday fare, and so there is small cause for wonder that *The Star*'s yearender of 27 December was headlined, "Peace and Order Elusive in 1997."

Political pronouncements of Cardinal Sin and the bishops regularly make it to the pages, inviting most newspapers to negatively comment on the Church's transgressions against its separation from the state. Apart from the daily bible readings most papers carry, we also find regular columns by priests, such as "Straight from the Word," giving spiritual advice: "Don't let negative thoughts put you down."

In the *Bulletin,* such pieces of advice come on a daily basis. Amusing are the animosities between the leaders of the charismatic sects, El Shaddai and Jesus Is Lord. Religion is prominent in the Philippines, and headlines such as, "Church turns to prayers *vs.* El Niño"; "New revelations from Angel Gabriel"; "Our Lord of Love and Redemption of the Mt. Pinatubo Shrine"; "Sto. Niño de Providencia draws Mindanao devotees," are normal.

Under the last heading we could read:

> The devotion to the miraculous image is phenomenal. Since He began to shed oil, he has been healing a lot of sick people. But not all those who came were sick. Some came as a way of saying 'Thank you.' Among them was an 88-year-old man. When Lorna G found him hovering near the chapel, she was afraid he might fall as he looked very tired. After he had prayed to the Sto. Niño, Lorna gave him breakfast and money for fare. She had a feeling he was an angel testing her. Or he could have been St. Joseph in disguise. He was tall and gaunt and his hair was all white. (*PDI,* 4/2/98)

In the Lifestyle pages of most papers, we may find interesting advice about how to live with philandering husbands; whether to marry or not when pregnant; how to live with wife battering, and the like. Granted, these are responses to letters written to the columnist-advisors concerned, but they do, I think, reveal the tip of an iceberg of common family problems.

Advice may be conservative, such as, "Your husband seeks his pleasures outside, because you do not make him feel comfortable at home," or progressive: "Separate!" Of particular interest is the absolutely regular discussion of the situation of certain marriageable girls. In their childhood, they have been raped by relatives. The problem was, of course, never in the open. They have been traumatized, and then they seek advice on the terrible fix they are in. Must they tell their boy friend? And worse, what if the latter finds out he married a girl who is not a virgin?

The OFWs (Overseas Filipino Workers) receive occasional attention. According to the reports, their numbers vary widely, from 660,122 in 1996 to "six million." So much is certain, there are many of them, and the main question addressed in the early months of 1998 was: What will happen if the (East) Asian economic crisis forces them to come home? Unemployment is already bad enough, and rising.

Other worries are steadily expressed in articles and commentary on the environment, the state of neglect and decay of which is indeed appalling. Yet, other problems appear to be more pressing. Before a protection law can be passed, a huge garbage incinerator must be approved. The water problem now appears as chronic. The traffic is a daily nightmare, to which a Cebuano observed: "I learned why many residents of Manila are hot-tempered. Drivers tend to take as much as they can without giving others an inch. If they can help it, they don't let other drivers turn or change lane. Maybe this has something to do with the terrible traffic situation and the hurry to get to one's destination." (*PDI,* 8/2/97)

According to a Manileña, the real picture is this:

> 'If you can drive in Manila, you can drive anywhere . . .' But whether or not this is a tribute to the Filipino's driving skills is open to question . . . (It) is more a recognition of the metropolis' poorly designed, shabbily maintained and often dangerous streets than a tribute to Pinoy driving . . . The average Metro Manila driver, by world-class standards, is a substandard driver because he generally ignores traffic signs, that is, if he can understand, much less read, traffic signs, and his knowledge of basic traffic regulations is usually nil . . . Worst of all, Metro Manila drivers have the habit of unilaterally forming a counter-flow whenever they are delayed by slow-moving, bumper-to-bumper traffic, especially

when there is no traffic officer in sight. Pretty soon, the two-way street is occupied entirely by motor vehicles going only one way, blocking vehicles going the other way and thereby creating gridlock. Summing up, our undisciplined driving habits or Pinoy driving, spotty traffic law enforcement and dangerous roads are why traffic in Metro Manila is a gigantic mess. (*PDI,* 5/2/98)

So much for the traffic situation in the capital city of "unrelieved ugliness." (*PDI,* 8/2/97)

Image

In the near-absence of reporting positive things, the papers offer a steady lamentation of doleful complaints about the mess the public world is in. A serious treatment of problems, an investigation of their roots, and solutions, or simple reportage on successful developments, apart from the occasional conviction of a high-ranking criminal, hardly ever occurs. Newspapers are obsessed by politics; these substitute for the public world, all other things being secondary.

Politics is predatory; politicians prey on each other. Society stumbles on the brink of anarchy. The intention of the image is clear; it is, however, difficult to imagine. After all, people go to work, arrive, and come home again; children go to school, and so do their teachers. Traffic may be slow, but in the end people come to their destination and, tellingly, the newspapers are at their stands every day and at predictable hours. In other words, the very negative pictures the papers paint are biased. They give full exposure to irregularity and legerdemain, and do as if indeed, the latter are normal.

3
National Community

IF WE go by the titles of some of the textbook series serving social studies pupils at elementary school, such as *Ang Bansa Natin* ("Our Nation/Country/People") or the programmatic *Isang Bansa, Isang Lahi* ("One Nation, One Ancestry"), there seems to be little problem. It is clearly suggested that there exists a national community. Besides, special reading exercises are offered under *Diwang Makabansa* ("The Spirit of Nationalism"), all the time intimating that there is substance to it. And the title of the official text for the fifth grade, *Ang Pilipinas sa Iba't Ibang Panahon* ("The Philippines in Various Periods"), even proposes continuity through time, over hundreds of thousands of years.

Maybe these titles are mere promises. Maybe it is the school's very purpose to create national community. After all, school texts constitute a very important part of national culture, promoting the "symbolic violence" that molds a people into a single image by spreading shared myths, history, and common wisdom, thus making a national community out of the diversity of "7,107" islands and "111" languages and ways of life.

Perhaps school is nothing more than propaganda machinery, although it cannot be denied that, if anything, it is the most powerful instrument for giving rise to a shared culture of what is supposed to be the national community. The fascinating thing about Filipino school texts is that they ooze with uncertainty about what the national community actually is.

These texts do not stand alone. They reflect and strengthen a sort of ambiguity of culture, of identity. The question, "Who are we?" is bedeviling, indeed. According to one of my Filipino friends, "A Filipino is an English-speaking, Roman Catholic Malay with a Spanish name who eats Chinese food."

The Educational Development Decree of 1972 was, among others, intended to solve "the problem of nationhood." In March 1987, President Aquino still expressed her satisfaction with Fr. Leo James English's *Tagalog-English Dictionary* as, "This (dictionary) will be extremely helpful in our drive for national recovery since Pilipino is our national language and therefore, a vital element in achieving national unity even as we are the largest English-speaking nation in Asia."[1]

Is a national community defined by a shared language? And which is that language, English, Tagalog, or Filipino? Or is Filipino just another word for Tagalog? And who are the speakers of that language? Even so, probably, a national community can be founded on other commonalities than linguistic ones. Shared history, or territory, may be more compelling and, although the line between history and myth is thin indeed, the modern idea of a bounded territory seems unambiguous. We noted, however, the "111 nations" inhabiting that space.

In modern times, the state delineates the nation. Heir to a colonial predecessor state that marked out its borders, the republic legitimizes its sway by a particular interpretation of history that is spread by way of the school system. Possibly it is the state as shared government, and the propagation of common knowledge, that define "national community" best of all.

Nevertheless, that very republican state does not appear to be too self-assured when it presents its views. Let us see what happens in the fifth grade when social studies in public school are presented as *Ang Pilipinas sa Iba't Ibang Panahon* (DECS, 1986-1995).

This book is divided into five units; the introductions to these are, in my opinion, sufficiently revealing. Paraphrasing them, they state:

Unit 1. The Way of Life of the Early Filipinos. There are important events in the lives of people and the nation that need to be recorded. This is history, the written record of the important occurrences in diverse periods. It is important to know the past and its relationship to the present as a secure basis to face the future. That is the purpose of the study of history.

Not all that happened in the past could be written down, such as the way of life of the original Filipinos. In order to know about them, scientists are engaging in research. According to them, people have been living in the Philippines for the past hundreds of thousands of years. They consisted of Aetas, Indonesians and Malays. Strangers came too, such as Arabs, Chinese and Japanese. They stayed and traded here. The mixing of these groups stands at the beginning of the first Filipinos.

These earliest Filipinos had their own culture. This can be proven by the remains and implements they left behind. It is also proven by research results of experts studying the culture of the ancient Filipinos. There are many indications that the culture of the early Filipinos was rich and had reached a high level. This can be demonstrated by the social classes to which they belonged, the method of government, and their types of livelihood. All this illustrates the way of life of the old Filipinos.

The society of primeval Filipinos was composed of different groups of people who came from different parts of Asia. Together, they established the settlements of our ancestors. Next to setting up their dwellings, they also molded a system of education. They had ways of worshipping and believing, too, although there were differences in practice among them.

When Islam, the religion brought by the Arabs, arrived in these islands, groups of people in Mindanao changed their religious practices. They embraced Islam. This had its influence on their way of life. Whatever the differences of beliefs among the original Filipinos, their culture remained one and the same. This is the culture that we, up to this day, develop, cherish and take pride in.

Unit 2. The Filipino Way of Life under the Spaniards. For 333 years (1565-1898), the Philippines was under Spanish domination. This brought changes in the Filipino way of life. This, however, did not obliterate native culture. There were changes in the system of government and in material culture. Most importantly, our country got a name. From then on, it has been known everywhere in the world as the Philippines and the natives living there as Filipinos. When Spain was defeated by the United States in the battle of Manila Bay in 1898, its government came to an end . . . It was the duty of the missionaries to teach the Catholic religion and spread Christianity.

Unit 3. The Incessant Endeavor to Reach Freedom. (The first part of the introduction to this unit states that the establishment of the various colonial governments caused important changes in the system of administration, in society and livelihood. Repeatedly, Filipino efforts to realize their freedom and establish their own government were frustrated, such as when the Americans and the Japanese enforced their dominion.)

The system of government the Americans introduced the Filipinos to was a novelty. They spread the principle of democracy that until this day prevails in our land. They reformed the educational system. Many children could study at public schools. They introduced the values of cleanliness and health. Transportation and communication were improved, which resulted in many changes in the livelihood of Filipinos . . . There is a strong relationship between these innovations and the present Filipino way of life.

Unit 4. The Way of Life at the Time of the Third Republic (1946-1972). The 4th of July 1946 is a great day for Filipinos. It cannot be forgotten in the history of our nation. That day the Republic of the Philippines was inaugurated. Be that as it may, it could not hide the poverty of the environment. The war had caused tremendous devastation. That destruction must be confronted with resolution. Hence, the period of the Third Republic was a veritable time of struggle, too. On that occasion, we had to fight against poverty of livelihood. Most of all, that time was a period to reestablish ourselves.

Unit 5. The Incessant Endeavor to Establish the Nation. Every period in the history of the Philippines illustrates some sort of serious endeavor of the Filipino people. Many decades have passed since they resisted the Spaniards, Americans and Japanese in order to become free. A variety of problems confronted the Filipinos upon their liberation and at the time they obtained their freedom. Among these problems were the slow development of livelihood and peace in the country. Another obstacle is the absence of identity as a free people.

A common quality of Filipinos is their capability to adapt themselves to any problem or crisis. Their reaction gives them the flexible power for overcoming any difficulty or challenge. How did the Filipinos face up to the problems and challenges of the 1970s and up to the present?

Comments

In the Introduction to Unit 1, several contrasting statements have been brought together, notably: (1) Filipinos are a highly mixed racial group; (2) In spite of differences in origin, they apparently mixed so well that they had one culture that was well-developed; (3) Even religious differences that resulted in different practices did not influence the basic way of life; (4) Their culture, therefore, remained one and the same from the olden days into the present; and, (5) This demonstrates the importance of knowing the past to understanding the present way of life.

Yet, there was a snag on that long way. The earliest Filipinos, from deep down in history up to Magellan's arrival, apparently did not recognize themselves as such until the Spaniards gave their country a name. Anyway, in spite of the myriad changes in the (unspecified) Philippine way of life brought about by colonial contact, native culture is said to have persisted.

The Americans bring development and progress of all sorts; they brought a superior system of government and policies. When the Filipinos become their own master, they face problems, poverty, unrest. They even lack identity as a free people.

So, on the way from prehistory to the present, something seems to have gone missing. Although it has been suggested that the population was united in culture, rich and at a high level, and that colonial contact, especially with the Americans, brought progress, the present seems unclear, riddled with problems, and stimulates absence of identification with community, or perhaps even absence of community.

This weird evolution is difficult to explain. The textbook's authors probably had an idea in mind such as: "When politics, or the state were not interfering, cultural community prevailed. Then, in spite of being named and despite progress, or perhaps the changes leading up to modernity, culture fails to provide cohesion. What remains are a weak state and a fractious society that both miss the integrity to provide identity."

As a result, history appears as the undoing of culture, and with it, of community. Of course, the book devotes its last pages to the protest against the degeneration of almost everything valuable in public life. Marcos out. Aquino in. People Power–rebirth . . .

Does this hope for renaissance mean that the "anarchy of families" will be replaced by a strong civil society anytime soon? Will such a civil society bring order to the public world? Will it restore dignity and responsibility to public office? Or is it that identity as a free people has meanwhile become illusory because the country is more like a market than a nation? Why identify with a market other than as a means of serving personal and particular ends? Besides, people do identify with what really matters, that is, with their families and sometimes, with their community.

Societal identification, as in the past, remains weak, and only the impositions of the state define national community and nationhood. The role of the school in this–generating officially sanctioned confusion, mythology, national symbols, self-doubt and cultural insecurity–cannot be overestimated.

Some Concrete Teachings

In an ingenuous, almost artless way the first chapter of the official series *Sibika at Kultura* ("Civics and Culture"; DECS, 1991-1992) begins to explain that all people living in the islands are Filipinos, whether or not their complexion is dark, brown, or white; whether or not their hair is kinky or straight; whether or not their eyes are slanted or round; whether or not they are Christians or Muslims. However that may be, "We can be proud of the Philippines," because the country is beautiful, which is illustrated by a standard listing of famous sights, such as the Mayon Volcano, Bohol's Chocolate Hills, the Island of Boracay, waterfalls, the colorful southern *vinta* outrigger sailing boat, the Nayong Pilipino, and animals, forests, mountains, water, and fish. From this follows an exhortation to take good care of these, to keep it all in fine order, and not to destroy but to plant trees while keeping the water clean.

The next section introduces some of the national symbols, such as the flag that should be honored; the name of the national anthem, *Lupang Hinirang*; the names of national heroes who made sacrifices for the sake of freedom, such as Rizal, Bonifacio, Sultan Kudarat, and Melchora Aquino; then, the national flower, Sampaguita, that stands for nice manners, and the national tree, Narra, that symbolizes sturdiness.

Under the inviting title, *Be Proud: We Are Filipinos,* the book for the second grade opens on a listing of positive qualities. Filipinos are courteous, polite, and considerate, especially in relation to elders and authorities; they have a loving disposition which is demonstrated by the bond between parents and children, respect for elders and the dead (*Todos los Santos*), gift-giving and sharing; they are diligent workers and quick to extend help; are resourceful and systematic, self-dependent (buying native products), and sincere. They are valiant, too, as illustrated by their fight against the colonizers.

Follows a list of national symbols: the flag that should be honored; the lyrics of the national anthem; the national language; Rizal, who became an emblem because of his peaceful method of resistance; the national costume (*barong tagalog* and *baro 't saya*); the national animal, leaf, flower, tree, dance [*cariñosa* (*sic*)], and game. Then comes an illustrated listing of eight historic places, from Magellan's Cross to the Rizal Shrine in Dapitan, while beauty and resources are indicated by geographical formations, tourist spots, and animal life.

Under the heading, "We Filipinos are United," mutual assistance and solidarity, along with the provision of basic necessities, are said to be essential elements for a quiet, orderly, and safe life in a clean environment where people functionally depend on each other, as illustrated by dentist, nurse, police officer, firefighter and street sweeper. As an ideal community, they cooperate, help each other when disasters strike, share tasks in agriculture, and deliberate in a democratic manner to solve problems. These people also rallied to recover freedom from the dictatorship, which was a period in which leaders were separated from ordinary people. Now, however, people enjoy freedoms again: they are free to vote and select their leaders; enjoy freedom of worship; may express their opinion, associate and deliberate; have the right to confidentiality. Then 15 national and local celebrations and traditions are listed; these include 3 Muslim feasts, and 1 for the Cordillera. Of interest is the observation about the 25th of February, the Day of Thanksgiving and Solidarity, "We are admired by the whole world because of it."

The third grade still uses an edition from the Marcos days. Its emphasis is on development and progress; the preface, however, formulates the book's purpose somewhat differently. The course should cultivate the spirit of nationalism and love of country; foster right attitudes and good character in order to become good members of family and community, imbued with national identity and feelings of unity and loyalty. So, after a repetition of some geographical knowledge, the text switches to, "Being proud of being Filipino," through taking the example of model Filipinos.

Then information is given about the legendary ancestors: Aetas, Indonesians, Malays, arriving in succession, each new arrival driving the earlier groups deeper into the interior, each succeeding group smarter than the preceding ones. Whatever their accomplishments, they were hierarchically organized under a *Datu* (chieftain); they were courageous, courteous, and naturally given to music.

These ancestors came into contact with the Chinese, Arabs, Japanese, Indians (*Bumbay*), Spaniards, Englishmen, and Americans. The Chinese were rather white, had slanted eyes, came for trade, and were diligent; they mixed with the Filipinos. Filipinos and Spaniards mixed too; the latter brought Catholicism, prayer, baptism, and formal education.

The Americans came with human rights, democracy, and the equality of all–whether rich or poor, in education and public life. From all this sprouts the new Filipino; he is the result of the mixing of the blood and cultures of ancestors and foreigners. Then follows his qualities: he is gentle, dignified, hospitable, religious, trusting in God, and respectful towards other religions; he is obedient and honors his parents, likes to help, and respects women: he is polite to them and defends them always. He is able to endure hardship and is diligent; he does not surrender to adversity. Moreover, he is courageous and filled with love for country, such as Gabriela Silang. We can be proud, we are enduring and steadfast.

Then, in the section on "Duties and Rights," the pupil is assured that a state needs loyal citizens and that, in order to progress and make it a better place, the latter have obligations and responsibilities to their country and people. The country asks us to give our direct and wholehearted support to all its ambitions and ideals. In exchange we have the right to a secure, quiet and prosperous life, which will inspire our loyalty. The services of the government are many; there is free elementary and vocational education for all, and books need not be bought as they can be borrowed. The center provides health services, and its police officers and firefighters are always prepared to help. There are orphanages, free legal assistance, a Government Service Insurance System (GSIS) and a Social Security System (SSS).

Image

The message of the textbooks for the first three grades can be summarized as follows: the nation is a functionally integrated whole in which the various occupations complement each other. Especially government appears to be extremely important to see to good order; its benevolent care obliges the citizen. The resulting image is familiar to the child: it is familial. The government becomes a super-parent, the world outside the home an extension of the family. If all people fulfill the obligations of their respective places, harmony, peace and order will prevail. This moralistic picture of social life does not differentiate between private-familial existence and life in the public world: national community becomes indeed village-like.

All social life appears to be hierarchically structured (parents and the child's obligations; government and the child's duties). The ensuing moralism is anchored in personal behavior, and children are urged to inspire themselves by following the examples of individual national heroes and successful citizens. Social causation is not considered, and problems do not really surface; inspired by the ideals of family life, the world will be in good order.

The Official Texts for the Upper Grades

The fourth-year textbook series of the DECS for the upper grades (DECS, 1986-1995) promises to stimulate understanding of self, fellows, and nation; its stress is on culture. Half the book is about geography; then Filipino culture is introduced in a historical perspective. It runs the usual sequence of Aetas, Indonesians, Malays, *barangay, datu*, and Bathala/Maykapal (the Creator God) to arrive at the connections with foreigners. The picture is familiar: the latter come and bring, the Filipinos learn. Orang Dampuan came from Champa, Orang Badjar from South Borneo. Indian influences came indirectly, by way of Sri Vijaya and Madjapahit kingdoms; they can be traced in literature, vocabulary, the *bahala na* (fatalism) attitude and, possibly, in the use of the sarong. Arabs came, too, but particularly relevant was Chinese cultural influence. They brought the *payong* (folding umbrella), porcelain, gunpowder, metalworking, and so forth; many customs, such as respect for elders and close family ties derive also from the Chinese. From the Japanese, the Filipinos learned duck- and fish-breeding. On the other hand, the Philippines exerted cultural influence on Micronesia.

Then, the Spaniards arrive. They bring Catholicism, roads, modern ways of doing things, hospitals, plants from Mexico, gambling and cockfighting (*sic*). Spanish rule provokes many rebellions, and Muslims keep the resistance going. After the revolution against Spain, Americans subdued the country. Subsequently, they began preparing for self-government. American influence can be found in education, the English language, democracy, and the "colonial mentality" that prefers to buy things stateside. "Nowadays, the Filipinos are little by little changing towards appreciation of our own things. Gradually we are becoming aware of the beauty of the things made in our own country." The Japanese occupation brought about the progressive lowering of moral standards.

This fast run-through-history is summarized in a realistic assessment of the country's cultural evolution. Before the advent of the Spaniards, there were: the barangay government, the own religion, simple housing, the high status of women, a writing system, a system of measurements and weights, agriculture, fishery, trade, and logging. Then came the Catholic religion, European crafts and sciences, literature, new plants, grammar, and linguistics, and European music: "Upon receiving the new culture, the natives renounced a good deal of their old culture." They also took to many of the vices of the Castilians, such as cockfighting.

By the end of the Spanish period, Philippine culture had been expanded and enriched; when the Americans came, the existing culture was an amalgam of Malay, Indian, Chinese, and Spanish elements. The Americans added education, democratic government, citizenship and rights, the English language and many American customs. However, this also resulted in the preference for imported, stateside goods. The Philippines is open to the West, yet also rebellious against western domination.

Similar to the books for the fourth and fifth grades, *Ang Pilipino sa Pagbuo ng Bansa* ("The Filipino in the Formation of the Nation"; DECS, 1986-1995) aspires to be complete, from the earliest times up to the present; it highlights government, development, the relationship between state and citizen, and values. According to the preface, emphasis is on civics and responsible citizenship, in the expectation of contributing to shaping a nation every Filipino can be proud of. To this purpose, appropriate values and attitudes will be given prominence, together with rights and duties, in relation to economy, government, environment, history, present, and future. All this will be conducive to forming a stable government and nation. "However much separated the islands where they live, the Filipinos had a culture and a history that tied them together and that united them."

Yet, it was only in the nineteenth century that the feeling of nationality developed as a reaction against oppression. A free country has a territory, sovereignty, a government to care for peace and progress, and citizens. The latter can make a country strong, and so their quality is important. When they are healthy, they can be productive, and thus the government sees to health care. General and vocational education is provided, too, and the country, thus, has excellent human resources. They have the right attitudes, they study, have ambition; the overseas contract workers (OCWs) are given as an example.

The section on "Values and Beliefs" states that, "good values create a good society and progress." People enjoy freedom and democracy; they are equal by nature and before the law, having the same rights and freedoms; all have equal opportunity and there are no privileges. Officials serve the government loyally; the type of people we need are those who do not abuse their positions and who realize that the welfare of the majority is more important than personal profit; if that is not the case, the people will have no trust in their government. So, be heedful of your obligations, and pay tax. People have trust in God, pray, and are concerned to help each other; they believe in the hereafter, and love their fellowmen.

Be these values and beliefs as they may, under "Values and Progress" we learn that, in order to progress, Filipinos must change. What are the obstacles? They have close family ties, and it is good to go to faraway places in order to earn more money for the family as an OCW. Filipinos also have a high regard for those in authority, such as parents, leaders, heads, and barangay captains.

Since power can also be abused, it should be used like a father would do, seeing to the success of his children and stimulating trust. Property, such as land, a house, a thing, is an important value which is also served by land reform. Filipinos highly value education and are willing to sacrifice for it. After all, the more education, the higher the esteem people enjoy; this is demonstrated by the diplomas on the wall. Education means progress. Filipinos also value gratefulness: when people help us, saving our life, or giving work, they create an *utang-na-loob* (debt of gratitude) that puts us under obligation.

The section on "The Philippine Citizen and the Government" has this statement, "Be a true Filipino, in thought, words, and deeds" as its motto. According to Rizal, the government is there to improve the life of the people and, in order to do so, it has to follow their wishes and suggestions. In earlier times all power was concentrated in the datu, but nowadays society has grown complex and government has become necessary. Still, it is an institution that expresses the feelings and thoughts of the people; it executes their decisions. It is composed of elected citizens who carry on the political process.

This is followed by a lengthy enumeration of the tasks of government, the most outstanding being the care for good order. Filipino government is democratic and republican; its power ultimately derives from the people. Some of the activities of administration are explained, then the laws of Philippine citizenship. Follow predictably, the rights and freedoms of the Filipino that are juxtaposed with responsibilities–"If the people do not fulfill their obligations, the republic will break down"–and so the government needs the support of the citizens. This can be done by respecting the flag, being critical of officials, serving the nation, being an honest civil servant, and suchlike. The relationship between government and citizen is one of mutuality and subject to law, rights, and respect. It is thus important to know and follow the laws.

The line to structure the section, "Government Support for Development," is taken from history, from Spanish times (concentration of landownership;

bad economy) via American and Japanese regimes (economic dependence) to Aquino. During the Third Republic all presidents do something, but the problems (opposition, corruption, inflation) remain until the economy collapses and the people have lost all confidence in government. It is up to President Aquino to regain the trust of foreigners. Just the same, we should realize ourselves that the success of the government depends on a solid foundation, consisting of human and natural resources, science and technology, and the promotion of the national heritage.

While government and citizen need each other, citizens should also be self-reliant and not depend on the government. Thus, take good care of yourself, be healthy, intelligent, and productive, that is, be gainfully employed. Exercise (sports), eat the right food and do not cultivate harmful habits; be clean, and keep the environment clean. Use scarce resources judiciously; buy goods made in the Philippines; choose your products carefully; pay taxes; save; trust in your own ability; support culture; be productive; be punctual; have the right productive attitude; be employed; all work is honorable; keep the environment clean and help each other; be good in your behavior to your fellowman; recycle materials; save energy.

Then the book concludes:

> The progress of the country depends on the development and health of its citizens, and so the Philippine citizen has a role in shaping a stable and strong country that can be admired by anybody. Also the government has its part to play; it should realize its obligations and responsibilities in caring for the welfare of the citizens, such as you. This book explained the basic and simple rules governing your personality, and the mutual obligations and rights of the government and of you as a citizen. Throughout history the government has been active to organize the economy and to direct the activities and obligations of every citizen to the strongly desired progress.

Image of the National Community

The image of the nation that the DECS course materials for the higher grades evoke is different from that projected in the lower grades. In the latter, wider society was imagined along the lines of a family, the government becoming a super-parent showering beneficence on its nationals. The general view was hierarchical and ethically obliging. The former picture is less orderly. While the little that is given about the family conforms to the earlier teachings, citizens and government are projected as mutually dependent partners who together shape the nation state.

A structural approach is avoided; while moving into the present, from the Commonwealth period onwards, perennial problems crop up yet, how they are rooted, where they originate, remain vague, and the few reasons given are unclear, such as "slow development," "absence of peaceful conditions," "lack of identity as a free nation," and "foreign dominance of the economy"; the last condition also "weakens freedom."

The government seems to be incapable and impotent. People lose confidence. The government does not apparently express the aspirations of the people, and the slogans about democracy and being a republic do not result in development, which is the self-proclaimed first task of the government. Perhaps that is why ideas like state, citizenship, constitution, and laws can be explained in a technical-legal sense only, but remain inoperative at the level of social life.

The picture that is projected of the American period is one of order, progress, and modernization. From 1935 onwards that order is gradually breaking down, and especially Japanese times subvert morality. Presidents and republic are confronted with corruption, rebellion, irregularities, and failure. In spite of good intentions, and knowledge of correct values, the outer, public world appears untamable, inconstructible and, in moving towards the present, the picture gets increasingly confused. Continuity is lost sight of; disorder and frustration become normal; the nation state appears to be rickety.

This noninstitutional approach that fails to reason in systematic relationships, naturally results in an excessive emphasis on individual morality; if individuals are good, so shall the nation be. For that reason people should be taught values. At school, they learn that Filipinos have good values, but also that they should have more of them to progress, develop, and achieve a peaceful national community.

Presenting Nation or State, Community or Society?

The weird thing that happens to the elementary school presentation of national community is that it disappears. What is built up during the first three years is thoroughly broken up. Community and nation are substituted by state and society, by government and citizen. What was originally projected as a wholesome belonging together within the parental embrace of government is replaced by a weak state unable to minister to the needs of its citizens. Wholesomeness gave way to the chilly language of rights and duties; trust was betrayed; people were exhorted to stand on their own feet, to help themselves, and not to depend. Where community was supposed to prevail, society, with its anonymous, businesslike and legal relationships, came into existence.

One keeps wondering why this is so. After all, one of the problems social studies supposedly address is the one of nationhood. The latter idea itself is bedeviling enough. A national doctrine seems to be missing. President Ramos' peptalk: *Kaya natin ito!* (We can do it!) notwithstanding, a spirit of common purpose does not seem to come to life.

His evocations stress the idea, "If everybody does/works/exerts himself," problems will vanish, pride in nation will arise. But is there such a thing as a joint project that depends on the individual efforts of individual persons? Where has the common effort gone? Is there a nation-building program which makes people "feel" that they belong together? As classes, groups and platforms, they are not even represented in the legislature.

There is little that brings them together as members of a national community and Rizal years, or centennials, EDSA celebrations, and suchlike, do not galvanize the people into action or invigorate their spirit of togetherness. The only real national celebration is the running up to presidential elections, an exercise that, at the same time, marks the fractiousness of and dissension within Philippine politics. This, indeed, is a blatant demonstration of the absence of common purpose. There is no national community, striving after equality, equity, justice or welfare, to identify with.

Interestingly, the emphasis on individual values, on rights and duties, individualizes and shreds the idea of nation. It places the responsibility for national community and good society on individual shoulders. In doing so, the collective is lost sight of: "If I've done my duty, I've done my thing," and people can continue to pursue their own purposes in good conscience. Social studies do not tie them together in a national doctrine, such as happens in Thailand, or Indonesia, or Japan. The approach is technocratic (valuable human resources) and legalistic (citizenship; rights and duties). This approach is not informed by an ideology of nationalism.

The slide from community to society, from nation to state is probably inadvertent. It does expose the absence of a nationalist perspective, though. It also reveals theoretical naiveté: community and society do not match, are qualitatively different, and no amount of individual values can bridge the gap between belongingness and anonymity. It does betray, perhaps, a deep sense of realism. The ensuing realistic portrayal of Philippine society, and its twentieth century history, brings many of its facets, many of its facts in view. Yet, because of the absence of vision, whether ideological or theoretical, relationships remain unclear, and no image of the whole arises. Such disjointedness is definitely experience–near to most members of the "national community."

Excursion One

The Living Environment

Agap at Sikap (expedience and diligence) is the home economics textbook for the sixth grade (DECS, 1988). If, in the main social studies course, the tendency is towards an increasingly formal, legal and distantiated manner of explication, then this tendency is somehow counterbalanced by the lessons on home economics.

These lessons are informed by economics and morality. In each of the nine subjects treated, it is observed that caring for your body, raising pigs, or civic activities are profitable, at least, do bring benefits. These benefits, though, are not thought to be material only. They are exemplary, boost self-confidence, and lead to proper living, too.

Attractive is the child whose physical appearance and clothing look orderly and clean. Its appearance demonstrates that it takes care of itself. The child whose body and clothing are orderly and clean will have more friends. It will feel at ease while boosting its self-confidence.

Stand in front of the mirror, and inspect yourself. Is your appearance attractive? Do you take pleasure in your appearance, or is it necessary to devote more minute attention to yourself? At your present age, many changes take place in your body and mind; because of this, you must give more attention to caring for yourself. A good deal of the development of your personality depends on the care you spend on your body.[1]

Among the 14 pieces of advice given to obtain the desired condition, I like the imperative, "Drink 6 to 8 glasses of water a day. The body needs water to flush out the dirty things within the body." The chapter then proposes a plan to follow in taking care of the body. Next, it dwells extensively on how to dress; to stand; to exercise; to behave and be polite; to take care of clothing–again proposing a scheme for doing so.

The second chapter is about the family: to always help, love, and be concerned about each other will lead to a happy family life. This happiness will further be promoted if everybody partakes in household chores. Many benefits flow from everybody's fulfillment of their tasks and responsibilities. Because of it, they will be appreciated by the other family members which, in its turn, will promote the formation of their own personality. This is also a fine preparation for adulthood, when people will have to shoulder the responsibility for their own families. Besides, helping each other is economical in that it wards off the need for hired help, such as a laundrywoman, a cook, or a gardener, that is to say, if any or some of the family members are skilled in said activities.

Then the various duties and tasks in the family are explained. The following qualities are stressed: voluntarism; concern; consideration; diligence; trust; harmony; acceptance; doing things together. Care for the baby is next, and we learn about changing diapers and why a baby cries. Since the fulfillment of duties around the house cannot be taken for granted, planning is proposed to solve the problem. Who will cook, and when? Who takes care of the yard? When do things need cleaning? All this requires time consciousness, and will lead to efficiency, to saving money and energy, and so we arrive at an apposite point to introducing budget making.

The next chapter is about the ethos of work and civic activities. It addresses the fact that people are part of communities and even society, and this entails individual obligations to foster the common welfare. While this is, in itself, not so interesting, it becomes so when civic initiatives and organizations are discussed. In this section, the word, "government" is not even mentioned; local life benefits through civic action. Examples are given, ranging from Girl Scouts and Community Chest to Rotary Club and Catholic Youth Organization. Then, the chapter abruptly changes to a discussion of economic activities; their classification into primary, secondary and tertiary industries; ethic of work. To be careless and wasteful leads to inevitable ruin.

Chapters about agricultural activities, animal husbandry, handicrafts, food preparation, sewing, and the cooperative store follow. Whatever the activity, the text maintains that they are greatly profitable, such as the cultivation of vegetables around the house. In Marcos' time, this was a national policy indeed, and still the book affirms:

> A family will give a good example to its neighbors when they cultivate vegetables in their yard. It is attractive and will be imitated by the neighbors. If all would cultivate their yards, our community would have a sufficient supply of food, which would be supportive to the health of every citizen and to the prosperity of the nation.[2]

Similar peptalk introduces the other chapters. The text goes into great detail about grafting and pruning, mixing of hogwash, raising of carps, repairing mosquito screens, butchering, cooking, and tailoring. All such activities need meticulous planning and budgeting, and so does the cooperative store.

The students may wonder why their parental generation has been so reluctant in initiating any of the activities proposed because, isn't it:

> The problems inherent in poor livelihood will be solved when the families of a community help each other and unite. One of the most profitable methods in which families can save and earn some income is to establish a cooperative store. If the members of such a store are familiar with its correct management, it can be greatly helpful.
>
> The assets of a community will be activated and developed through a cooperative store. A cooperative is an association owned by the members of the store. The members have a share in its management, and profits are divided according to the extent they make use of its services. This is different from an (ordinary) retail store, because many are managing the cooperative, and many profit from it, too."[3]

Let's leave it with this note of optimism.

4
History and Society

THIS CHAPTER presents an analysis of two books currently in use for social studies in the first year of high school. The aim of that course is to discuss Philippine history and government in such a way that the students will become good citizens, inspired by love of country and people, and instrumental in the development of the nation-state. It is not our purpose to evaluate whether these aims can be attained (that basically depends on teachers and their methods), but to investigate how the social world is presented in these two textbooks, and how students learn to think about it.

In presenting the school texts in this chapter, I have been quoting and paraphrasing the contents in a way that conveys the flavor of the texts. I have maintained inconsistencies and absurdities, yet only very seldom taken recourse to (*sic*) or (!). I did intersperse some commentary and hope that this is clear in the presentation.

Social studies schoolbooks are an important part of culture, molding how people are to perceive themselves. Based on the colonial American tradition of education, early Philippine textbooks were low on nationalism and United

States-centric, in which the Filipinos forever appeared as the passive receivers of blessings foreigners brought. This, of course, was noted and commented upon by many scholars, Filipinos and non-Filipinos alike. The still reverberating denunciation of the state of history and social studies teaching was Renato Constantino's essay, "The Miseducation of the Filipino" (1966). In his subsequent rewriting of Philippine history, Filipinos become the active agents of their own past.

W. H. Scott wondered at the ways in which pre-Spanish history was presented in the schoolbooks. In his dissertation (1968), he sifted myth from fact, exposing the migration theory that held that the various ethnic groups that peopled the islands came in successive waves, each in their own boat, speaking their particular language, while bringing along their characteristic culture. He also criticized the fantastic stories about early visitors, the Spanish way of viewing the people they came into contact with, and a few spectacular cases of deliberate fraud, such as the Kalantiyaw code of law, presumably written in the early fifteenth century, yet actually faked in the early years of this one. Such distortions of history can never substitute for critical explanation of the present, suggesting a false identity where authenticity is needed.

Doronila had other questions to ask. She investigated whether or not the stated purposes of Marcos' martial law educational development decree (1972) were attained, namely, "reform directed at problems of national identity in order to ensure "that every Filipino shall become conscious and aware of his roots and feel proud of it."[1] Her 1986 findings were depressing. In her attempts to measure national identity formation, she found that, "if these young students had their way, they would rather be citizens of another country."

Also Mulder (1990) was amazed at the curriculum content, and the depiction of the Filipino as perennially on the receiving end drew his ire. According to the texts he consulted, Filipino civilization derives from Hindus, Arabs, Chinese, Japanese, Spaniards and Americans, all of them bringing their beneficence to the islands. For instance, because of Chinese ancestry, Filipinos are devoted to their family; because of the Hindu connection, they could read and write while becoming superstitious; because of the Japanese, they learned to breed ducks. Spain brought Christianity; America democracy. With everybody bringing and teaching the Filipinos something, the recipients were gradually being dressed up to "become the most socially advanced of the Asiatic peoples who have shaken off western rule" and "the outpost of democracy in the Orient."[2]

Thank goodness! The contents of books change over time and, for a while at least, the EDSA "revolution" gave rise to the Proud Filipino, a self-confidence that was further boosted by the hailing of the Constitution of 1987 as the savior of the country's woes. The two textbooks to be discussed here were clearly written in that spirit, one under the auspices of the Department of Education, Culture, and Sports (DECS), and thus official, while the other book was written by a team of authors from the De La Salle University. The latter book also follows the DECS format yet, like all privately-issued texts, takes considerable latitude in emphasis and interpretation. The main task of the books is to explain the world beyond family and community. They concentrate on government, administration, and politics, thus, bringing the political economy and the use of power into focus, at the same time developing an interpretation of history.

The Establishment of the Filipino Nation

The perspective of this book (DECS, 1989) is immediately clear from the table of contents. In the first unit, *The Origins of the Filipino People,* are explained. This is followed by chapters on the oppression of Filipino freedom, and the sprouting and development of nationalism. The second unit, *Towards Independence*, covers the repression of Filipino nationalism and the delay of liberty. The third, *In the Period of Being on Our Own*, presents challenges to independence, and the authoritarian regime. The final unit is about *The New Filipino*, and discusses the reestablishment of democracy and the Filipino citizen/national.

The picture this evokes is that of the eternal Filipino, from primitive to present, whose freedom has occasionally been frustrated and who, so immediately after weaning, and thus on his own, had to surmount challenges and authoritarianism, while now facing the future with constitutionally-inspired confidence. This view, of seeing early history in the light of the present, raises its own problems and, as we shall see, presents an obstacle to the understanding of Filipino becoming.

The Chosen Land

Let us start, however, with the first, geographical chapter, "The Chosen Land." It begins with a fascinating set of questions: "Why were foreigners attracted to the Philippines? What special qualities did the land have to persuade them to occupy it? Has this perhaps something to do with the geography of the country?" In the last paragraph of the chapter an answer is given. It was the wealth of natural resources that drew foreigners to the country and made them conquer it; in that way they grabbed the opportunity to grow rich and to expand their Asian colonies.

Whether this is a valid answer, is not in question here. It is more to the point to note that the opening sentences demonstrate a remarkable preoccupation with foreigners who, from the third chapter onwards, seem to play an important role in the islands, but whose most crucial contribution, namely the creation of the Filipinos as a nation, and their country as a state, is not acknowledged. Yet, that there is something strange about Philippine unity is immediately apparent from the interesting statement that the country consists of 7,107 islands. This far-flung archipelagic diversity is recognized as a barrier to transportation and communication, and thus to uniting the citizens and developing a flourishing national consciousness.

The many different tongues, customs and traditions among Filipinos form the second obstacle to their unity and mutual understanding. This cultural diversity gives rise to strong feelings of local and regional chauvinism that are more powerful than the national sentiment. To overcome this barrier, the national language, Filipino, should be enriched and developed in accordance with the Constitution of 1987, in the hope that it may intensify the bond of union among the population. Just the same, there is something good about being an archipelago, too. With so much water surrounding the land, there is plenty of fish to be caught, and the islands offer many prized tourist attractions.

Basically, these observations present a continental view of the country, which raises an interesting question. According to most texts, the early inhabitants of the islands came by boat, and there is good evidence that, like all Malayo-Polynesians, Filipinos sailed the seas. Yet, in the school representation, after having arrived, the ancestors immediately unlearned their navigational skills, and so, for Filipinos, the sea became a barrier rather than a connecting element. It was the foreigners, Arabs, Hindus, Chinese, Spaniards and Americans who sailed the seas; Filipinos were fishermen, or tourists, at best.

The chapter about the origins of the population is definitely an improvement over earlier accounts. While the imaginative theory of H. Otley Beyer about the various groups of people who sailed to the islands, each bringing its own language and culture, is still presented, it is juxtaposed with other ideas, and no final mythology is forced upon the student. What remains, therefore, to be explained is the presence of so many ethnic groups who are all

Filipino, in spite of their marked differences, some of them even building their houses in trees!

This type of presentation, "We Are All Filipinos," and the diversity they display, forces the authors to write highly ambiguous and inconsistent paragraphs. By introducing the old-fashioned, or archaic, Filipino, they create a unity about which general statements can be made and a precolonial past that should either be idyllic or, contrarily, anticipate the present. Often these two points of view are at odds. Let us consider the following as an illustration:

> It may be noted that the production of the archaic Filipinos precisely fitted their needs. Presumably this can be explained by the lack of knowledge about methods of storage and preservation. They made sure that their production was just enough in order not to be wasteful.
>
> Presumably there is another reason still why the economic system of the archaic Filipinos was such, namely the absence of groups of people taking advantage of other groups. In those days the concept of private property of land did not yet prosper and Filipinos were free to farm or plant wherever they liked. In that way, all were equal, nobody taking advantage of the other's harvest.[3]

This paradisaical situation makes one wonder about the importance of enmity, killing, and weapons that was discussed in the three previous pages. It does not seem to fit with the Spanish interpretation of early society that is repeated in all textbooks. This society is stratified, consisting of the *datu*, or chieftain, and his clan; the privileged *maharlika,* or nobility, owing fealty to their leader; the ordinary freemen and freed slaves owing tax and services, and the slaves, or serfs, who were the property of the others. Moreover, in the following section in which it is pointed out that, "the family is the basic unit of archaic Filipino society," attention is drawn to the importance of inheritance, while further property considerations are introduced under "Courtship and Marriage":

> In those days the adult men and women were not so free in their courtship because normally parents arranged the marriage of their children. With courtship came a period of servitude of the man and his family at the request of the woman's family . . . Another marriage custom was the transfer of a dowry by the man to the family of the woman. This is called *bigay-kaya*. Normally these were land holdings, gold, slaves, or valuables in accordance with the resources of the man's family.[4]

On page 32, the theory of Otley Beyer is smuggled back in when the idea of *barangay* is explained. Indeed, it was the boats that brought the various Malay family groups to the country which explains the existence of separate, kin-based settlements of the archaic Filipinos. Apparently, they were well organized:

> Historians say that Filipinos already had political organization. This is known as the *barangay-state*. As a state, the *barangay* had a territory, a group of people, government, and authority (sovereignty). It also had a chief, laws, a juridical system. The head of the *barangay* is normally called '*Datu.*' The *Datu* holds authority and is the head to discharge the tasks of government. He is the chief law-maker, executive, justice, and military leader. The chosen chief has prowess, strength, and determination in order to defend the *barangay* against enemies. It is also necessary that he is a respected person in order that people will immediately submit to his orders. The *Datu* can be changed when he is not obeyed by his subjects. From time to time the *Datu* was chosen on the basis of his suavity and intelligence.[5]

Normally, however, the datu was succeeded by his (male) child, and he was assisted by a Council of Elders to formulate the laws. Most of these regulations were never written down, although the Muslims sometimes did. The text then goes on to explain judiciary hearings and trials, without any mention of the infamous Kalantiyaw Code, which is a definite improvement.

Another element elaborated in earlier texts has also been omitted here, namely the presumed contacts with other Asian people by way of trade, and the influence they exercised on the evolution of culture. So, there were no Hindus to teach literacy and superstitions, previously a sort of claim to Southeast Asian respectability. There were no Chinese traders bringing jars and exotic goodies while exemplifying commercial practices, frugality, and love of parents. Absent are the Japanese duck-breeders.

Only the Arabs figure in the account, as they must, to explain the presence of Islam in the South. While the role of Arab traders is subject to historical speculation, according to the text they arrived already in the islands in the ninth century, the presence of Islam itself can only be retraced to 1280 A.D. Yet, this type of inconsistency is so common in all Filipino school texts I have seen, that it is not worthwhile to comment on these aspects of the books. It is more positive to report that a little over three pages are devoted to Islam, the Muslim creed, its political organization, and resistance to Castilian rule.[6]

The Coming of the Spaniards

The coming of the Spaniards is the beginning of the oppression of Filipino freedom. The widely scattered, independent *barangay-states* and the Muslim sultanates did not have the opportunity to unite. The independence of the Filipinos as a nation did not prosper. When the Spaniards came, the freedom of the Filipinos was destroyed before it had the opportunity to sprout.[7] In the following 45 pages of the text this line is then explained, devoting almost half of them to Spanish rule and cultural contributions, the other half to the opposition to said rule and the evolution of nationalism.

The data selected about Spanish history in the islands are standard but rather unbalanced, and their relevance for the understanding of the present is dubious. By cramming the information about three centuries of Christianization in less than half a page, the missionaries have to appear as both benefactors and oppressors without much respect for historical process. Besides, and more serious, is the inclination to present the Filipino and the country as original and enduring, which prevents the authors from explaining the revolutionary nature of the changes that took place in society and political economy. By merely stating that the people were taught more efficient ways of agriculture and animal husbandry, the point is missed that sedentarization, irrigation, the introduction of the plow, and all kinds of new crops basically changed the way of life and are at the root of Philippine culture today.

The observations in the text about a new social structure deserve attention. Next to the Spanish officials, one finds the *principalia* and the mass of the people. The first group consists of teachers, local officials, and rich landlords. They are the aristocrats of society and enjoy rights and privileges, such as participation in elections, and freedom from taxation and servitude. There is also the *cacique* who administers the estates of the rich, among whom we find the Spanish priests and officials. He collects the land rent. (Five pages earlier he has, more correctly, been called *inquilino*).

Those who get rich in trade enjoy a high standard of living that they show off in expensive status symbols, such as big houses, fine appliances, expensive clothing and jewelry. They study and become professionals. They form the group of *ilustrados*. To the mass of the people belong the ordinary residents of the country, most of whom are farmers. They live in poverty and experience the burdens and abuses of the Spaniards and the nation's ilustrados.[8]

It is a pity that the presentation of a changing social structure is done in such a slipshod manner and that the arising of the various groups and strata is not linked to the changes in the political economy. Of interest is the influence of Agoncillo and Constantino. Ilustrados are a perfidious type of people, oppressors of the masses. The chapter then continues with a listing of other changes, such as the conversion to Catholicism, resulting in a new morality based on the Ten Commandments, thus changing the customs of excessive usury, polygamy, divorce, and enslavement; the establishment of hospitals and orphanages; the introduction of new entertainment and games, such as the fiesta, the horse race, the lottery, serenading, and kite-flying. This is followed by a further listing of developments in literature, education, arts and sciences. The observations about the Spanish language foreshadow the present language policy and the awakening of Filipino nationalism:

> Some historians said that the Spaniards did not voluntarily spread their language; it may be said that it was rather withheld from the Filipinos. This is related to the belief that if the Filipinos would learn Castilian, they could know and understand their rights and achieve unity. In those days, the Spaniards noted the absence of a single language that tied the Filipinos together and they thought such a situation excellent to their pursuit of colonizing the archipelago. The priests and government officials also held the level of Philippine culture low and not befitting of the Spanish language. Nevertheless, there were also many Filipinos who learned to speak and write in Spanish.[9]

The chapter concludes with the statement that, "The Filipinos who were subdued by the Spaniards, received, were changed and enriched by colonial culture that became a part of their own civilization," which is a sound assessment. It is, therefore, sad that it is not traced to its deepest consequences: without Spain, no Philippines; without Catholicism, no common culture. The relationship of colonization and the sprouting and development of nationalism is, however, taken up in the following chapter that begins by restating that the changes in the way of life ranged from the system of government to religious belief and conceptualization, and are expressed in literature, architecture, clothing, and food.[10]

The text's preconceived opinion about the perennial Filipino does not detract from a realistic and excellent discussion of the origin and growth of nationalism:

> While the Filipino Muslims were successful, most of the uprisings in the other parts of the nation failed. The unity of the Muslims is not something one could ordinarily find in other areas of the Philippines. Many uprisings happened because of the personal interests of the leaders.

> The Filipino custom of merely caring for oneself (to the detriment of others) helped the colonizer in separating and dividing the Filipinos. In those days, the Filipinos were not yet forged together as a nation. With each having his own interests in mind, Ilocanos, Tagalogs, Visayans, Bicolanos, and other groups fought each other; because of this, it was easy for the Spaniards to use Filipinos to suppress the rebellions of fellow Filipinos.
>
> However much the uprisings were frustrated, the consciousness was also growing that all Filipinos alike were experiencing oppression and maltreatment. They felt the absence of freedom and the low esteem the foreigners held them in. The quelling of the many uprisings cultivated a hatred that slowly awakened the Filipinos to the real necessity of uniting in order to obtain freedom. Is this the beginning of nationalism?
>
> Nationalism is a feeling for the nation of those people who show loyalty to their own country, and not merely to a single leader or chief. The root of this word is 'nation,' which is how an association or group of people is called who have a single desire and purpose in life and who are tied together by a single race, language, religion, and customs and traditions. It is not enough for people to have a place to live in, a recognized government, and (their own) officials in order to have the feeling of nationalism. These are important elements, but the most important is the unity of the people who acknowledge that they are members of a single nation and prepared to defend their freedom. This feeling is not natural to people, but sprouts gradually and can quickly or slowly emerge because it will be in accordance with the historical experience of the people. In the course of time, the forms in which nationalism is expressed will also be different.[11]

With so much honesty, and attention to the present problems of a pervasive "individualism," plus the weaknesses of common purpose and nationalism, the origin of the word, "Filipino" can then be explained. That the name of the country was given in 1542 in honor of the then crown prince Felipe, was already mentioned in the text which here continues with the conventional historical themes, such as secularization, Cavite Mutiny and Gomburza, the reformists and the Propaganda Movement, pro-Spanish nationalism, its radical variety, and the Katipunan. As we were prepared to expect, the role of Rizal remains underexposed and his true significance is not grasped by the authors who repeat the elementary-school wisdom that he "became an excellent physician. He learned several languages and had many alien friends. His foreign friends assisted his endeavor to improve the welfare of the Philippines."[12] So, this only omits the grade-school information that he "loved his mother and was obedient to her."

While the reformists are recognized to have first formulated the separateness of the Philippine nation from Spain, and even threatened that the country could dismiss the Spanish empire,[13] they remain ilustrados, too. "The *ilustrados* did not have the determination to use violence in order to obtain reforms. Also the groups constituting the middle stratum of society reacted like that. They avoided the use of arms and turmoil because that could harm their properties and businesses. While these two groups continued with their reform movement, the masses, under the leadership of Andres Bonifacio, grew restless and also lost the hope that there would be change."[14] Consequently, Bonifacio gets the spotlight[15] until he was to give way to Aguinaldo. By the usual itinerary, Biak-na-Bato, American-Spanish War, second phase of the revolution, declaration of independence, Malolos, the surrender of Manila, and the Paris Treaty, we reach the end of the Spanish period.

Towards Independence

The second unit of the text, *Towards Independence,* begins with "The Suppression of Filipino Nationalism," and an eight-page account of the Philippine-American War, complete with the American atrocities and the prolonged resistance of Macario Sakay. This is followed by a very boring, legalistic description of the evolution of political life,[16] the interest of which is that the American idea of "preparation" or "training for" self-government is not taken seriously; Filipinos are capable enough. The section also highlights the power struggle between Sergio Osmeña and Manuel Quezon,[17] and eulogizes the latter because of his impressive rhetoric,[18] his Code of Ethics, and as the Father of the National Language.[19]

In contrast with the political discussion, the evolution of culture is scantily treated and, while it begins with the acknowledgment that even up to the present the strength of American cultural influence remains a problem, the presentation is sloppy and inaccurate. The idea of the separation of church and state is not an American innovation; it was already in the Malolos Constitution. Town-planning was not introduced by the Yankees. We only need to consider the "plaza complex" to see the pervasive influence of Spain. Also municipal elections were first introduced by the latter. It is undisputed, of course, that the spread of Protestantism was a result of the American occupation, but the connection between the Iglesia Filipina Independiente (IFI) and the invaders is missed. Because the Americans sided with the Roman Catholic Church and with the friars, they disappointed their new subjects who desired secularization and Filipinization.

The way the book presents the origins of the IFI has nothing to do with the Americans, and one wonders why it is treated under the heading, "Assimilation of American Culture." If the thesis is plausible that the introduction of all those zealous Protestant sects was directly causing the rise of an Iglesia ni Cristo, then one wonders why here, as in virtually all textbooks, this Philippine contribution to Christian expression is not mentioned at all. Especially in view of its present visibility and huge membership, certainly well beyond the languishing IFI, such omissions are grave distortions of history while failing to clarify the present.

In the discussion of American influence on production, it is pointed out that they did everything to keep the Philippines an agricultural economy while flooding its market with stateside products, "in the hope that the Filipinos would grow excessively attached" to them.[20] This, of course, serves to explain what is currently known as "colonial mentality," the preference for things American over the homegrown. The colonizers' influence on schooling was impressive; the education aimed at "preparing the Filipinos to become citizens of a democratic state" and "to teach them the American system." With the benefit of hindsight, we can safely conclude that this project largely miscarried while, despite American plans, other Filipino cultural traits persisted.

In the schools the nobility of labor was taught. The course of industrial arts became part of the curriculum, but there was no interest for it. The Filipinos gave more importance to academic than to vocational courses. They held manual labor in low esteem. This is the reason why it is easier to find work after completing an academic than a vocational course. It became a status symbol in life to have learning, and to obtain a diploma.[21]

After noting literature in English, and influences on arts, music, sciences, transportation, communication, and sports, we are again presented with an American contribution that failed to take roots, at least in political life and in relation to self-esteem, "Apart from the new sports, the Filipinos learned another thing from the Americans, namely, to accept losing wholeheartedly."

With 25 pages devoted to the subject, the chapter about the Japanese occupation is very elaborate, and one wonders why. It is, of course, relevant to know that a Second Republic existed, and the Hukbalahap need to be explained, together with the collaboration issue and the precarious position of Commonwealth Pres. Sergio Osmeña. The chapter closes on an interesting question, "MacArthur abandoned the Philippines and left the management of their own government to the Filipinos. Having been subjected to foreigners for many centuries, would the Filipinos already be prepared to take care of their own affairs?"[22]

The Period of Independence

For obvious reasons this question is never directly answered, but paves the way for a rather critical description of the early independence period up to 1986. In the scheme of the book, the preparedness for self-rule should mature with the Constitution of 1987, but it takes another 56 pages to arrive there, and the unit, "In the Period of Independence," begins with the challenges to it, such as the destruction wrought by the war and the problem of collaboration.

Much of the unit's chapters are written in a style reminiscent of political analysis by better columnists and commentators. The parting of the ways of Roxas and Osmeña is clearly painted against the background of collaboration and American anti-communism. The text leaves no doubt that Roxas was considered to be a collaborator, but the interference of MacArthur, and the support he enjoyed among landowners, brought him comfortably to the presidency against an Osmeña who had to rely on the support of former anti-Japanese guerrillas, among them the Huks.

Roxas' presidency is frankly treated to highlight the major problems of the day.[23] According to many Filipinos, the inauguration of the Third Republic did not mean that the Philippines was truly free. With Roxas strongly relying on the American connection, their friendship and anti-communism, the collaboration question is dissolved while the economy becomes hostage to United States' "beneficence" that is expressed in trade acts, parity rights, and war damage compensation, all leading to the necessity of amending the constitution.

Roxas serves the Americans hand and foot. In his thinking, the stability of the Philippines is contingent on the friendship of the United States, thus leading to agreements about military assistance and a 99-year lease of military bases. Meanwhile, the "problem of communism" needs explanation; it is traced back to Spanish times and rooted in the unjust ownership of land. A few, the aristocracy, lord it over the majority who wallow in poverty and who receive less for their labor than they need for their livelihood. Being forced into debt, even their children have to serve in the homes of the rich in compensation. Neither the Revolution of 1896, nor the coming of the Americans changed the situation of the farmers.

This information serves to introduce the discovery of socialism, with which Lope K. Santos, because of his novel, *Banaag at Sikat* ("First Rays and Full Brilliance," 1906), is credited. Subsequently laborers and farmers begin to unionize, and socialist and communist political parties arise that are not well received by the American colonial government. They receive more positive recognition from Quezon. The war leads to the formation of the Hukbalahap (Huks), its aftermath to the Democratic Alliance, whose six victorious candidates are prevented from taking their seats in Congress. Soon this leads to rural unrest in Central Luzon that, after the kidnapping and murder of prominent peasant leaders on visit in Manila, escalates to the armed struggle between Huks and government.

It takes little imagination to expose Roxas' high-handedness, his non-democratic attitude, and his reliance on the Americans to safeguard his position, even at the expense of the 1935 Constitution. The only salient point that is not mentioned is his revenge against the people of Central Luzon who had challenged him by electing six representatives not sympathetic to the big landowners. His unleashing of a reign of terror contributed most to the decision to revive the Hukbalahap. The idea of state violence and military abuses has to wait until the Marcos presidency to be explained.

The account of the ensuing presidencies highlights the perennial problems of American interference, frustrated independence, the struggle against the Huks, jurisdiction over the military bases, the lack of political will to initiate land reform, corruption, political manipulation and electoral fraud, the desirability of foreign investment, the irritation at American advice, the weak economy, the deceit of politicians, and the poverty of the masses. It is a pity that the rediscovery of nationalism and Claro M. Recto's candidature for the presidency receive no attention at all, because these paved the way for subsequent student protest under Marcos.

The terminal years of the Third Republic are presided over by Ferdinand Marcos who not only inherits all the social, economic, and political problems of his predecessors, but also witnesses the Mindanao situation growing out of hand. This is due to systematic neglect of the southern provinces, and to the colonization by northern Christians who take advantage of the Muslims and cheat them of their land which, naturally, gives rise to Muslim resistance and eventually armed liberation movements.

Before moving on to Marcos' authoritarian regime, the obligatory remarks have to be made about the social and cultural evolution of the country. These discussions are of a much lesser quality than the political commentary that is often written in good journalistic style. It seems as if students are trained as newspaper readers, and made attentive to the devices and tricks of politicians, with the president at the center, while cultural and social developments are presented in stereotyped fashion as marginal and non-related events.

The section begins with the observation that all problems are rooted in the long colonial past, a statement that seems to relegate the responsibility to others. The great majority of the very poor at present was already in that condition in Spanish times, the problem of the unequal landownership pattern only aggravating the gap between the affluent and the needy. Yet, during the time of war a class of nouveaux riches got rich by way of trade, and after the war they became part of high society, although they never received high education.[24]

> But it was only a few who enjoyed such good fortune. The greater part of the Filipinos remained in poverty and were without hope. This situation exacerbated the lowering of moral standards and the spreading of criminal behavior. On the other side, in order to flee from poverty and joblessness, many transferred to the cities, such as Manila, to try their luck. This caused urban congestion and the increasing number of squatters. The continuing government policy of pressing for urban development instead of that of the rural communities even attracts more to migrate to the centers of development. Others, like those mentioned, chose to join the communists in the hope of changing their position in life.
>
> The system of education, similar to other areas of Filipino life, is influenced by the Americans; because of its likeness to the American system, American values are cultivated among Filipinos. This is the reason why the educational system is considered colonial. It does not answer to the needs of Philippine society. Related to this is the national problem of the vast quantity of college graduates in subjects unsuitable for the demands of industry. As a result, very many professionals remain unemployed.[25]

In the following section on language and literature, American influence is pointed out again. People seem to be more attached to the borrowed language than to Tagalog. Besides, many people object to its use, because they fear it will weaken their ability of speaking English. Moreover, Tagalog is not representative of the native tongues of the Philippines. In order to avoid this criticism, Pilipino (nowadays Filipino) is replacing Tagalog as the national language. Even so, the influence of English remains stronger than that of Filipino. On many occasions, English is mixed with Filipino when people are pressed to use the national language.

If this were not yet enough, a long list of titles is given, devoid of any context, of which it is said that they exemplify the influence of English in the works of poets and authors, even if they write in Tagalog/Filipino. Even the subjects they choose to write about are influenced by the Americans. Besides, many prefer to write in English.

Also the painters do not find native ways of expression; first they worked in the Spanish style, and now in the American. The exception is Carlos V. Francisco who works in a style of his own. Foreign music is more popular among Filipinos than the homegrown. This compilation of comments concludes with, "The Filipinos received, changed, and enriched the foreign influences on their style of life. The borrowed elements entered the own culture, got a Filipino stamp, and became part of the distinguishing characteristics of the nation."[26]

The word *pandaraya* (cheating, deception, fraudulence), occurs every time in relation to elections and often in commenting on politics in general. In discussing Marcos' reelection in 1969, the text reports how Marcos manipulated, how he played tricks in order to create the right atmosphere for staging the coup that inaugurated his dictatorship. This is all explained in the chapter about the "Authoritarian Regime."[27] Whatever he tried, must fail or be severely flawed.

The Mindanao problem remained unresolved; the land reform program was not correctly implemented and made too many exceptions; labor laws were not respected and low salaries forced many to work in the Middle East, from where they sent the much needed dollars; the educational infrastructure was not attended to and the level or quality of people's knowledge went down; industrial development was financed by increasing the foreign debt; nepotism was the rule and fed into a kleptocracy that, as a system, became known as crony capitalism; corruption was rife and its scale unprecedented; many showcase projects merely served to impress foreigners; human rights abuses were the order of the day; justice was manipulated.

In the face of these excesses, the question was how to put an end to this authoritarianism? The murder of Sen. Benigno Aquino, Jr. was the first step in this direction, inexorably leading, by way of capital flight and snap elections, to the national revolution that became known as People Power while bringing Aquino's widow to the presidency.

The last unit, *The New Filipino,* basically introduces the political system of the Philippines under the New Constitution of 1987. It specifically cites the Preamble which lists the very good intention that is hoped, would be achieved, namely, that the first task of the government is to serve and protect the citizens. This is followed by a discussion of the various branches of government and how they are supposed to operate. The last short chapter begins with the question, *How to Become a True Filipino Citizen?* and introduces the legal criteria surrounding Philippine citizenship, then the rights and obligations of the citizen. The book ends thus:

> The fulfillment of their duties by the citizens is greatly important for the stability and the progress of a nation. They are the true hope of the country. From them emanates sovereignty. They are the government and they also resolve any political, social, or economic problem. Because of this, every citizen should actively participate in contributing to the development of their own nation.[28]

Filipino History and Government

Just as in the DECS book, much information about this text[29] is already revealed by a good look at the table of contents. Of the book's 355 pages, the first 197, or 55 percent are devoted to the pre-Spanish Philippines. This is in sharp contrast with the first that allows for that period 16 percent of its space. Bro. Andrew Gonzalez told me that this emphasis should result in a more positive self-image and contribute to feelings of nationalism. The 95 pages about the Spanish period, inclusive of the time of the First Republic, correspond to over 28 percent of the text, against 45 pages, or 20 percent in the DECS' presentation.

Then, interestingly, the Gonzalez book proceeds immediately to American influences and the preparation for self-government (18 pages, or 5 percent), without a word about the Philippine-American War. The official DECS text appears far more critical, dwelling almost 9 pages (4 percent) on that fight, while further discussing the American period in 27 pages (12 percent).

In the Gonzalez book, Japanese times are treated in 6 pages (2 percent) and no mention is made of resistance or collaboration, in contrast with the other text that devoted 26 pages (11 percent) to the war. Eighteen pages (five percent) are allowed for the discussion of the various presidents, from Osmeña to Marcos.

The last unit, *The Struggle of the Filipinos*, inclusive of the new constitution, is 16 pages (4.5 percent) compared to 56 pages (25 percent) about the presidents and the triumphant New Filipino (27 pages, or 12 percent) of the DECS book. Although both texts have been written according to the official outline, the interpretation of the material discussed is rather dissimilar. In short, *Filipino History and Government* emphasizes the past, with 83 percent of the book considering events up to 1899, and spends the remainder in briefly discussing the present century with a minimum of information about the practices of government and politics, at least when compared with the 64 percent that is written about the twentieth century in the official text. But let us now look at the private schoolbook in more detail.

Pre-Spanish Origins

The obligatory geographical discussion is, in places, very technical and cannot possibly be understood by the age-group the book aims at. The treatment is very lengthy, too, covering 43 pages out of the 197 devoted to the old Philippines. Of interest is that the size of the country is compared to Arizona and New England, in full disregard of its Asian neighbors.

The next 154 pages offer a fantastic quantity of, often baffling, information. During the Pleistocene, five land bridges connected the country with the Asian continent, namely the bridges Borneo-Palawan, Borneo-Sulu-Mindanao, Celebes-Mindanao, New Guinea-Mindanao, and Taiwan-Northern Luzon. This physical connection with the rest is the cause that similar plants and animals are found in the islands. It was also the way by which the first people came.[30] This must have been some 400-500,000 years ago when *Homo Erectus* probably arrived.[31] More cultured groups, *Homo Sapiens,* came later, the Austronesians from Southeast Asia, the Mongoloids from China.[32]

According to H. Otley Beyer, the first people arrived in three waves of migration. The first came 5,000 to 6,000 years ago, and brought people with Neolithic culture. The second arrived in 13,000-500 B.C. They came from Indo-China and South Asia. They brought husked rice (*bigas*). The third wave came from the South, 300-200 B.C., and brought the rice plant (*palay*).[33] After first being peopled by Negritos some 30,000 years ago, Indonesians (this is what Otley Beyer called them) from Indo-China and South China sailed to the Philippines, in two waves, 5,000 to 6,000 years and 1,500 years ago respectively. They had beautifully light brown skin, and were of short, but robust stature. They looked like the people from Indonesia. They knew wet rice agriculture and sugarcane cultivation.[34]

Then came the Malays and the Ten Datus from Borneo, as described in the Maragtas Code. After buying the Negrito lands in Panay, the various datus settled in different parts of the archipelago and became the ancestors of various lowland peoples, among them the Tagalogs. But perhaps all this is merely legend, and investigations continue to search out the true origins of the Malay race in the country.[35]

The discussion of the Filipino communities before the coming of the Spaniards opens with a whirlpool of bewildering facts in which two elements stand out: the old Filipinos had eating habits similar to those of the present, and were exposed to overseas trade.[36] Preferably they lived along the water, be it coast or riverbank, but some groups built their houses upon trees, which is, as in so many other books, illustrated by a naive drawing of a present-day hut straddling the branches of a tree.[37]

Connecting the pre-Spanish past to the present gradually appears as a theme in the text. The Sulod of Panay not only had a calendar of 12 months, but even their first month, *Ulalong*, corresponded perfectly to January. The golden pieces of money they used in trade were equivalent to *pesetas* and divided decimally. The division of labor between the sexes was very much like it is today, and so the conclusion is inevitable, "Many of the economic activities mentioned are still pursued by our present generations."[38]

The islands had a large population, organized in independent *barangays*, that is, family groups or boatloads of original migrants, under a datu. The office of the leader was normally inherited by his offspring but, sometimes, deserving ordinary people could also be elected. In such cases, age, and thus knowledge and experience, was the important criterion. That is why ancestors were also greatly respected. Basically, the political organization of a barangay rested on the family principle. Occasionally, barangays united, because of trading or marriage links of the ruling families, a union that was ritually reinforced by the blood compact of their chiefs. Yet there was also conflict among the barangays because each tended to be concerned with its own welfare only, to the detriment of others.[39]

The government of the independent barangay was headed by a datu who received honor, tax, and service from his subjects. He was leader in all activities, whether in war or peace, all the time caring for and protecting his underlings. Together with the elderly councilors of the tribe, he issued laws that were sometimes written down. Only a few of these documents survive up to the present, because Spanish missionaries or nature destroyed them. The Muslim laws and the Kalantiyaw Code are still in existence. This statement is then followed by an incredibly detailed description of all the things that were regulated by law in barangay society, the working of the legal system, and a few pages about the political organization of the Muslims.[40]

According to the text, society, then and now, is almost without differentiation. The most important principle in life is to be related. The primary unit of Filipino communities was the family, and hierarchical family principles pervaded wider social life, with the fact of being kin to each other assuming crucial significance. The communities were stratified, much as they are today, into the strong and the weak. In modern society we are familiar with *compadrazgo*, but also the old society knew ritual kinship such as the blood compact. Parents were generous to their children and understood their shortcomings; their first concern was the comfort and well-being of their offspring. Small children were especially pampered by their grandparents. Women were not allowed to leave the home unaccompanied; they were chaperoned by a brother or other male relative. People could be insulted easily, which then called for revenge. This, in its turn, was a common cause of conflict. Inheritance was equally divided.[41]

The questionable statement about the old society, in the image of the present, being almost without differentiation, becomes really enigmatic when the next chapter presents us with the standard fare about the four strata of barangay society that are even further subdivided in a range of offices among the highest, and various classes of slaves in the lowest stratum.[42]

The following chapters that describe the life cycle and some beliefs then give way to short, unintegrated and unrelated descriptions of the diversity of the islands' population, from Tasaday to Tagalog, and from the pepper-eating Bicolano to Badyaw.[43] When the Castilians arrived, they found that the Tagalogs had an advanced civilization in which women played an important part. This can be proven by the customary dowry; the control of women over family finances; their right to civil office; their right to property; the equality of rights in all aspects of social life; their freedom of action, of dressing, and of decoration; the presence of priestesses as heads of religious rituals or ceremonies.[44]

Compared to these important women, "The Tagalog male is happy-go-lucky, given to the cockfight and other gambling, but also naturally given to music, fun, and amiable to his fellows . . . They like to fantasize without much self-control. They were keen on their honor." Tagalogs believed in spirits and prayed to their ancestors. Their *anitos* were like the saints of the Christians. Besides, they knew a Creator God, His Messenger-Child, a Holy Spirit, and others, and believed in the last judgment, heaven, and a hell presided over by Satan and his followers, such as witches and vampires. A few Tagalog characteristics that may be good or not so good, are their disposition to *bahala na* (come what may), *pakikisama* (giving in to group), *utang-na-loob* (debt of gratitude), and *hiya* or *amor propio* (self-esteem).[45] So, what's new?

All this is followed by two rather abstruse chapters, the first on "Linguistics," the other on "Archeological Evidence about the Old Filipinos," in which, among others, the custom of jar burial is noted.[46] The last lessons are about foreign contacts and their influence on Filipino civilization. We learn that the Chinese initiated the oldest direct trading relationships, because of this, "the influence of the Chinese on lifestyles and the make-up of Filipino culture is great."

The usual mythology follows. The Philippines was one of the most important centers of Chinese commerce. Chinese chronicles refer to the country as, "The Three Islands (Ma-i), that may well refer to the three islands that compose the Philippines now" (*sic*). The population had singular habits, such as the *suttee* (widow burning). They approached the big, seagoing vessels of the Chinese in their small boats (earlier in the text big Filipino-built boats are mentioned,[47] but the craft had apparently sunk into oblivion). Anyway, this explains Chinese influence on economy, culture, and society, such as the use of the burial jar (!), Chinese food, words, vegetables, and their cultivation around the house.

They also opened the first *sari-sari* variety store. An important piece of information is, almost unself-consciously, introduced, "The relationship with the Chinese was not terminated by the coming of the Spaniards. More than that, it even developed and prospered from the beginning of the colonization by the alien Europeans. The number of Chinese living in the country was recorded at a mere forty in 1571. In 1603, it had reached twenty thousand."[48]

The Hindus were the first to discover the importance of commercial relationships with the people of Southeast Asia. Nevertheless, it was the Arabs who acted to develop these links. They began their commerce with Asia around 800 A.D. When the Chinese obstructed their trading stations in South China, they began to relate directly with the Philippines. During the Sung times, they were welcomed back in China, they stuck to their trading route by way of Borneo and the Philippines.[49] All this speculative information is given to credit Arab traders with the spread of Islam in the islands.

In an ingenuous manner this argument is then enervated, "In the middle of the 13th century, a few places in Southeast Asia had embraced the Islamic faith." Then, from the second half of the fifteenth century, Islam spread in the Malay world, propagated by Arab and Malay missionaries. Coming from Tawi-Tawi, the Muslim chronicles tell us that Makhdum Karim came to Sulu in the second half of the fourteenth century. The Magindanao region was reached in the fifteenth.[50] This is followed by three pages of information about Islam.

In order to appropriate a respectable Southeast Asian pedigree, relationships with India or Hindus need to be invented. This is not difficult, because Indonesian and Indian influences on Philippine culture abound. Some say that India related directly to the islands, while others hold that said influences were mediated by Indonesia. "This latter relationship occurred during the waves of migration of the Indonesians (!). By means of their seagoing vessels they migrated to the country and mixed with the natives."

According to H. Otley Beyer, India had direct links with the Philippines which he proved by interpreting the color of bracelets, and various small images found. Others are not so sure and come up with different explanations. Another medallion "strengthens the close cultural relationship of Hindus and Filipinos." "There are a few Filipino customs that are similar to Hindu customs," such as flower offerings, the cockfight, the *sipa* game, and the *tinikling* dance of the Assamese of India. Also many words have been borrowed from Sanskrit. "Because of this, it is believed that the Philippines received cultural elements from there by way of Persian, Arab, and Hindu traders and travelers."[51]

The alphabet of the old Filipinos is thought to be related to the Brahmi of South India that was also used in the "Asoka Inscriptions" of 300 B.C. Others think that the Filipino alphabet originated from the Tamils. "The Tamils live in Malaya." This script came to the Philippines because of the several migrations that occurred in those times, about 200 B.C. Others hold the writing system to be rooted in Sumatra.[52]

Spanish Times

After so much conjecture, it is a relief to have come to the historical era, to Spanish times. Very detailed information about the first expeditions, and the origin of the name of the country, is followed by the history of Catholicism and the civilizing work of missionaries, while listing the very many, and often colorful, innovations of Philippine life. From Mexico emanate many plants and words, and the Spaniards are credited with bringing many more novelties than any other foreigner, for instance, plants and agricultural practices, foods, clothing, music, dance, architecture, vocabulary, names of places and people, counting and the telling of time.[53]

This is followed by an extensive discussion of Spanish government in the islands, the first part technical, the second focusing on the economy. That not all was well becomes clear in the next chapter on complaints and uprisings against the Spaniards. The list of causes given is plausible and also emphasizes the freedom-loving nature of the Filipinos. Alas, they knew no unity, and the Castilians could suppress them by using other Filipino troops, with the exception of the Muslims, of course. The awakening of nationalism is related to intellectual events outside the Philippines, the emergence of a middle class, the secularization issue, and events in Spain, culminating in the Gomburza execution, the reform and Propaganda Movements. In these latter sections it is of interest that Rizal's role is not specifically highlighted and that, in the discussion of the Katipunan, his famous advice is translated positively: Rizal was not against the uprising. Also Bonifacio receives a low profile, becoming a national hero juxtaposed with Rizal. After their deaths, however, it is Aguinaldo who remains, and who has to deal with the Americans.[54]

The great difference between the first 200 pages in the text about old Filipinos and the Spanish period is that the latter is systematically and historically treated, while the former remains sketchy, speculative, and incoherent. While there is an obvious attempt to manipulate the far-off past as adumbrating the present, it has to miscarry because of the enormous weight of the Spanish influence. It is unfortunate, though, that this is insufficiently realized by the authors, and that the qualitatively best part of the book does not really dig for the roots of present-day Filipino civilization.

Post-Spanish Times

Like the earlier part, the later part is full of tricks and pitfalls. Bonifacio is dead, the Americans come. The Spanish admit having been defeated by the Filipinos and the Americans, and so, "On 13 August 1898, Manila fell into the hands of the revolutionaries with the help of American power . . . This is the beginning of the historically important period of the American occupation and government of the whole archipelago." Aguinaldo's friendly relations with the Americans are illustrated by the signing ceremony of the declaration of independence in Cavite on 12 June 1898 "under the chairmanship of Aguinaldo and Col. L.M. Johnson of the American army." Soon Aguinaldo's dictatorship is replaced by the revolutionary government which is, in its turn, converted into a constitutional regime on the basis of the Malolos Constitution. This document "is the very first republican constitution of Asia."[55]

It is worth repeating the earlier observation that the book seeks to establish the country and its people in prehistory, and that the First Republic is discussed *en bagatelle* under the heading, "The Coming of the Americans." While most recent school texts play up the fight against Spain, and then dwell on the Philippine-American War as a means to drum up nationalist feelings, that war is not even mentioned. The narrative moves immediately on to "The Influence of the Americans," in art, sculpture, architecture, dress, transportation and communication, the language, Philippine English literature, education–the influences are positive and progressive–then, to "The preparation for Independence/Commonwealth." The analysis of the political process leading up to that independence is shallow and short, and the only interesting thing said about the Commonwealth's first president is that he wanted very much to be reelected, and so sought to amend the 1935 Constitution.[56]

The brief observations about the Japanese occupation[57] and the first five republican presidents are factual and not very enlightening, apart from the persistent negative evaluation of the presidencies. Roxas' government was at fault because it failed to suppress irregularities and corruption, such as proven by the War Property Scandal, the Chinese Immigration Quota Scandal, the School Supplies Scandal. It also failed to halt the Huk movement. Pres. Elpidio Quirino had good intentions, but his administration was characterized by irregularities, corruption, scandals, embezzlement of state funds, weak in facing the Huks, the poverty of the masses, and deceit and cheating in elections. Ramon Magsaysay was the president of the people to whose problems he listened. He was the first to pay attention to moral and rural problems. He was also successful against the Huks. His excellent intentions were sadly frustrated by his early death, and so the economic situation could not be resolved.

Pres. Carlos Garcia was a supporter of democracy, an exemplary father, a true Catholic, and a first-rate chess player. He had many good intentions. Yet, "his administration, like his predecessors," was weakened by irregularities and corruption. For most it was "no secret that officials leaving Malacañang had become millionaires overnight, while the poor increased in number and continued to suffer." The only president not evaluated is Diosdado Macapagal. What is listed are the problems he faced, and his intention to strengthen the moral fiber of the nation.[58]

According to the text, the man who resolutely faced all the nation's problems is Ferdinand E. Marcos. Yet, the bad things that plagued the republic for several decades seem to increase. Marcos spoke about a "social volcano" that might erupt at any time, and that indeed erupted after his State of the Nation address of 26 January 1970. Nationalists, reformists, radicals, communists, youth, students, and other activists protested. Instability reigned, the malcontents complained, violence and crime were everywhere, the worst of all happening at Plaza Miranda on 21 August 1971. This forced the president to suspend the privilege of the *writ of habeas corpus*. Thirteen months later the country was placed under martial law that inaugurated the New Society.

This gave the president the chance to be serious about land reform and emancipation of the tenants. At the same time his wife distinguished herself because of her important projects, such as the Cultural Center of the Philippines, the Nayong Pilipino, Pasig River Development, and others, while the Medical Care Program finally got the full attention it deserved.

A Constitutional Convention was convened by Marcos in 1971. This body amended the 1935 Constitution and finalized a new charter a year later. The barangays received a measure of autonomy. All this was approved in the referendum of January 1973. Great progress was made in establishing the national language next to the use of English, while the Education Development Decree emphasized human resource development, a science-centered school curriculum, and bilingualism. Schooling should not be the privilege of the rich only. According to Marcos: "In a truly democratic community, the voice of ordinary people can be heard when their leadership is rooted in common culture. This can only be ensured when those who become leaders arise from the common citizens and cultivate those actions that relate them to the ordinary people."

The pace of population growth considerably slowed down; rapid inflation was reined in; new sources of energy were developed; new deliberative bodies were created in which functional groups were represented. After eight years of martial law this led to the elections of January 1980. "Would the citizens be judicious enough already to vote? Could the elections be clean and without violence? Did the people have enough trust already in the leaders that they will count the votes correctly so that casting the vote is truly meaningful?"

"Like the former elections in our country, also this one was not without the previous irregularities, terrorism, false reports of the outcome, falsified lists of voters or *flying voters,* and many protests." But Marcos promised to investigate all the complaints. Whatever the case, the outcome of the election was a resounding success for the New Society.

Soon thereafter, martial law could be lifted, a period during which many positive changes for the welfare of the nation had been implemented. This great progress is demonstrated by the rapid development of infrastructure; considerable advances in the development of the economy and social justice; increasing yields of rice; a rapid transfer of land to former tenants; the prevalence of quiet and order. Also in foreign relations, and thanks to the great contribution of the First Lady Imelda R. Marcos, great strides were made.

Of course, all these good things could not prevent the military abuses in the South, the incarceration of many political prisoners held without trial, and the return of irregularities and corruption, particularly the massive embezzlement of money in the financial and banking sectors over the last two years of the martial law period. All this, positive and negative, is the background against which the Fourth, or New Republic was inaugurated in 1981.[59]

The final 16 pages of the text, "The Struggle of the Filipinos," begin with the problems the Fourth Republic is facing. The economy slows down; inflation is rapid; creditors threaten; there are shortages of spare parts, raw materials and machinery; factories run at a loss; people are dismissed; unemployment rises; the prices of essential commodities go up; many are hoarding food and other primary necessities; crime increases; human rights are violated; tourism slackens. In this atmosphere, Ninoy Aquino makes his fateful return to the Philippines which inaugurates the period of demonstrations, protests, and "the parliament of the streets." Marcos and his cronies are accused of destroying the economy, of excessive concentration of power, presidential arbitrariness, and unaccounted for wealth and possessions abroad.[60]

By way of rigged and snap elections, the rebellion of Juan Ponce Enrile and Fidel V. Ramos, the EDSA People Power Revolution, Corazon Aquino reaches the presidency, then installs a revolutionary government. Soon a Constitutional Commission is nominated, and the text finishes with a short presentation of the main points of the new constitution. The authors find it important to highlight the following:

> Respect for every individual and guaranteeing human rights; the State recognizes the important position of the youth in the totality of the

its littoral were for long in contact with each other, which had, of course, cultural consequences, as cited by Reid (1988) and Mulder (1996). The traffic in commercial and cultural goods went all ways, and "early Filipinos" participated actively. And then, talking about those days, wouldn't it be very interesting for schoolchildren to know that the first man to circumnavigate the globe was most probably a Visayan? Pigafetta, the "Italian" scribe of Magellan's expedition, is quite explicit in his observation that Enrique spoke the language of the Cebuanos they met. Perhaps he communicated with them in Malay, then the *lingua franca* of a wide, seaborne commercial area, but chances are that he came from the Visayan region indeed.

While for many in Europe, history begins with their ancestors being incorporated in the Roman Empire, or with Christianization, Philippine school history appears to have difficulty acknowledging that the country is a Spanish creation. To do so is both unpopular and unfashionable. Yet it is only by addressing the Castilian period seriously that modern Filipino civilization can be understood. However grudgingly, Spain is admitted to the official text as the oppressor of Filipino freedom and independence, it was oppression and colonizers' arrogance that prompted nationalism and the First Republic.

It was Spain that brought the country into the modern world, that founded a style of life oriented to literacy, town and church, that sedentarized people, that introduced the plow, a plethora of new crops, and building in stone. Even while such contributions are recognized in the Gonzalez book, the importance is not pursued to its deepest consequences, namely that they are the founding stone of the nation.

The quest for fundamentals is, of course, the message of Onofre D. Corpuz's *The Roots of the Nation,* and Nick Joaquin's *Culture and History,* but since the Americans succeeded in substituting the roots in the past by pleasant prehistoric speculation, Spain has become a kind of an anathema, to be blamed for the land problems of the present. As a result, the rise and continuity of the Philippine oligarchy, that strange *mestizo* upper class that to a large extent still owns the place, is never analyzed to its historical origins. Seen in the latter's interests, this is probably more than can be expected.

It may also be that the unpopularity of the Spanish period does not befit the eternal Filipino, the "roots" in a mythic past, or the idea of being a modern, America-oriented country. Neither does it befit the fad of *The Revolt of the Masses* and Constantino's influential nationalism. This is not to belittle the revolution against Spain, the war against the United States, or the role of the common man in those happenings and the possibility of casting blame on the ilustrados. Quite the contrary, but it all results in throwing out the baby with the bath water.

By casting Spain in the role of opponent, the total reconstruction of society hispanization caused is relegated to the wings instead of highlighted on center stage. Perhaps there is a political reason for this, too. The Muslim "Filipinos" must be incorporated in the realm, their resistance against Spain panegyrized, and Islam explained, at the expense of the fact that what is really culturally common to the Philippines is Christianity, especially Roman Catholicism, and the new lifestyle the Spaniards introduced.

Another aspect of this understanding of history is diminishing the cultural importance of Rizal as a super *ilustrado*. The problem is not the relative appreciation of Bonifacio, or whether it is justified to call one from the middle class a "plebeian." The point is rather that all schoolbooks I have seen so far never place Rizal in the intellectual and historical perspective he deserves, that these texts shy away from his historical importance as the first Asian nationalist to expose the debasing nature of colonialism, both for the colonized and the colonizer. It was especially his *Noli Me Tangere* that incited the imagination of ilustrados and urbanites, that galvanized the Filipinos into nationhood.

But it is less this success than his being the predecessor of the long row of Asian anti-imperialists, stretching from Sun Yat Sen to Gandhi, Sukarno, Tagore, and Nehru, and that he reasoned out his anticolonial argument in good humanist fashion. Filipinos, however, seem to take more pride in an international beauty queen or boxing champ than in the intellectual giant they gave birth to. Localized as "our national hero" who did not fight with the gun, Rizal has become sweet and unexciting.

A further remarkable omission that the two texts discussed share with other books in use, is a discussion of the now omnipresent Iglesia ni Cristo. Perhaps there is small cause for wonder considering the Gonzalez book that treats the twentieth century in a very cavalier fashion, apparently exhausted from the unconvincing effort to explore the prehistoric past and the very reasonable, yet culturally inconclusive presentation of the Spanish period. But why is this so in the official text that dwells especially on the current century? The Iglesia ni Cristo is a very successful Filipino invention, perhaps not pleasing to the church of Rome, but at least innovative and national. It seems as if Filipinos are not allowed their history and that American, and other foreigners, meddling in the country's affairs is the essence.

The Presentation of Society

By drawing programmatic lines through history, such as from the free Filipino to the new Filipino with an interval of suppression, or by projecting an archaic, idyllic past as the direct precursor of the present, history is not only seriously distorted in these texts, but it does not provide a solid framework either to explain the becoming and the current state of the nation. It becomes very difficult to elucidate the presence of certain social institutions in perspective, because of this. Former society was stratified, with a valiant datu as its head. That model makes today's dispensation recognizable, a powerful president, surrounded by his clan/family, and loyally followed by his privileged maharlika, or cronies, relatives, and sycophants; below these special people, one finds the freemen, or the middle stratum of society, who pay the taxes; the lowest stratum, the *alipin*, are the suffering peasants and laborers who provide the better-off with food and services.

This reading does not seem to be intended, though. Constitutions are written, amended, redrafted, and framed again, and there must be something important about them, while democracy or, at least, elections, seems to be a worthwhile institution, too. Yet, why this is so, or what the function of this all is, remains unclear.

There is a Constitution of 1935 that is amended because Quezon wants to serve two terms, amended again to accommodate the Americans; then Marcos needs a new constitution, which is followed by a Freedom Constitution, and the present one of 1987. What all this is supposed to achieve is never explained. Also the institution of democracy does not gain much transparency. The perennial observation about elections is that they are fraudulent and violent, and one of the words that most often occurs in describing the political process, is pandaraya, tricks and deceit. Why this is so, and why the performance of the presidents is almost invariably negatively evaluated, is carefully kept in the dark.

There seems to be a problem with land and rich landlords. For this the Spaniards are somehow to blame, but a serious treatment of unequal landownership, its origins, methods, relation to production, position in the political economy, and the merciless exploitation of agricultural labor is not subjected to serious discussion. In brief, and with the partial exception of the rise of nationalism in the second half of the nineteenth century, the books fall short in structural, in sociological explanation.

Governors-general and presidents are discussed individually, not as colonial policy or presidency. Each of them has good intentions, faces obstacles, and fails, with the partial exceptions of Taft, Harrison, Magsaysay, and Marcos during his early New Society. But why failure is so common, how the obstacles are rooted, why corruption is perennial, and why elections are so violent, is not discussed, and so, the principles of scientific social analysis and historical explanation are not introduced at all. The social process is a succession of episodes, its culture vague.

The world beyond private experience is presented as the disorderly arena of politics and legalities. It is the place of artifice, rhetoric and, for the better informed, of English. It appears as a world too big to master, beyond the grasp of a systematic, ideological or scientific, approach, and so also beyond imagination or conscious participation. Based on this, it is very hard to develop a positive culture of the public realm, other than the intentions written in preambles to and sections of the constitutions. The youth should be patriotic and nationalistic, cultivate ethical and spiritual values, have moral character and self-discipline, and so on, so in a subtle manner introducing a moralistic perspective where a historical and sociological one is needed.

The outer world remains an aggregate of unruly individuals who, collectively, face many problems and are left at the mercy of interference by foreigners, especially Americans. It is a runaway world of political tricks and economic manipulation, an amoral area of power play and money that is beyond the possibility of domestication. Predatory practices prevail: colonizers kill freedom and seize territory; landlords terrorize ordinary people; Marcos and his cronies rob the country blind; presidential good intentions are always frustrated; corruption thrives. So, how to arrive in the never-never land envisaged in the preamble of the 1987 Constitution?

> We, the sovereign Filipino people, imploring the aid of Almighty God, in order to build a just and humane society and establish a Government that shall embody our ideals and aspirations, promote the common good, conserve and develop our patrimony, and secure to ourselves and our posterity the blessing of independence and democracy under the rule of law and a regime of truth, justice, freedom, love, equality, and peace . . .

The road to that paradise remains shrouded in mystery.

Excursion Two

Constitution, Democracy and Nation

In Article XIV on Education, Science and Technology, Arts, Culture and Sports of the 1987 Constitution, Section 3 stipulates that:

1) All educational institutions shall include the study of the Constitution as part of the curricula.
2) They shall inculcate patriotism and nationalism, foster love of humanity, respect for human rights, appreciation of the role of national heroes in the historical development of the country, teach the rights and duties of citizenship, strengthen ethical and spiritual values, develop moral character and personal discipline, encourage critical and creative thinking, broaden scientific and technological knowledge, and promote vocational efficiency.

There is no doubt that the first clause is implemented. Some first- and second-grade elementary schoolbooks specify the fine points of Philippine citizenship. In another privately-authored text for the sixth grade, I found the full text of the 1987 Constitution appended. Moreover, in the sixth grade the legalities of the territory and the Archipelagic Doctrine are supposed to be taught, together with the principles of democratic government, of citizenship, the rights and duties of the Filipino national, and international relations. This formal information is repeated towards the end of the first year of high school, when the more history-oriented course reaches "The New Filipino." The History of the New Philippines, that is its course since Marcos, is continued under *World History* (DECS, 1992) in the fourth year, when also the evolution of democratic principles is offered, as we shall see below. A full-fledged course,

"Philippine Government and the New Constitution" (PGNC), is compulsory fare for all in the fifth year, that is in the first year of college or university.

In other words, there is no doubt that a lot of formal and legal teaching about constitution, democracy, and nation goes on, yet doubt seeps in when we scrutinize the qualities that are supposed to be achieved through such teaching. We noted that in all texts reviewed so far, patriotism and nationalism were identified as problems. That these were thought to be absent or seriously stunted; because of this, the aspirations expressed in the second clause of Section 3 must be considered as hopes, and I do not know whether school teaching makes a great contribution to achieving these expectations.

From the ways national community is presented, or history at high school taught, it appears that the teaching of the desired qualities is probably self-defeating. This probability is certainly enhanced by the discrepancy between the expressed ideals and the real-life environment (reproduced in the first two chapters) the students, and their teachers, find themselves in.

The New Constitution is supposed to remedy the excesses and deviations of the Marcos dictatorship; this is very clear from its composition and clauses. It is also expected to bring about national community and the key to it is thought to be the practice of true democracy. According to a widely studied discussion of the Preamble to the Constitution,[63] the lack of unity and oneness as a people not only negatively affected the performance of the Philippine economy, but also demonstrates the government's inability to take proper care of the population's needs. The people are disaffected with the present system; disgusted with graft and corruption, political wrongdoing and official incompetence. As long as the state does not command the respect and the confidence of the citizens, we cannot hope for national solidarity. This unity of mind can only be achieved when democratic ideals and values, such as rule of law, respect for human dignity, freedom and equality, become a living reality. This must, naturally, involve all, which includes the poor and less privileged segments of society.[64]

In de Leon's influential, most widely used text for the PGNC course, he repeatedly dwells on the importance of new practice. When elaborating the "love" mentioned in the Preamble (see end of Chapter 4), he notes that partisan conflicts and political rivalries, military coups and communist insurgency not only divide society, but result in hatred, violence and tensions. What is needed are compassion and concern if national unity and peace–so vital to a strong and stable nation–are to be realized. Practically, this can only be engendered through democracy; it is the means to fulfill the egalitarian objectives of society that have been enshrined in the 1987 Constitution.

Apparently constitution, democracy, and nation are thought to be intimately connected. As we already have seen, the teaching of the constitutional clauses at school tends to be legalistic. Besides, it implies the study of a good deal of highfalutin language. We also noted that, for the time being, the presentation of the nation remains highly problematic. So, what I propose we do is to peruse what has been said about the remedy, and its practical implementation, namely democracy.

In the sixth grade, the pupils study *Ang Pilipino sa Pagbuo ng Bansa* ("The Filipino in the Formation of the Nation"; DECS, 1986-1995). According to this text, Filipinos value and put their trust in freedom, democracy, equality, loyal service to the government, trust in God, belief in the afterlife, and love of their fellowmen. Next to these, they value the unity of the family, respect authority, value property, esteem education, recognize their debts of gratitude, and are given to *bahala na,* that curious mixture of fatalism and resolve.[65]

This mixture of traits is at variance with conventional anthropological wisdom, and smells a bit of propaganda. To start on "freedom, democracy, equality" seems to introduce constitutional ideals rather than to be descriptive of life as it is lived. This is corrected by also teaching that people voluntarily submit to government, God, family, authority, and moral obligation. There are many things in Filipino life that impose on individuals; and thus, many of them show remarkable tendencies to anarchy in the wider society. As a result, the meaning of "freedom, democracy, equality" needs qualification. In contemporary texts, however, freedom, democracy and equality are, all too often, taken for granted. All by themselves, the three are probably supposed to clarify the premise underlying the teaching of the meaning of democracy, namely that the power of the government derives from the individual citizens.

In the book under discussion, this idea is contrasted with oligarchic government. In such a system, power is in the hands of one class of people. The Philippines, though, is republican and democratic. The people are involved in any decision the government takes. It is the people who manage the course of the nation. They do this through electing their officials who serve as their representatives. These officials, including the president, must exercise their power within the constraints of the law.

In a democracy, the law applies to all; whoever violates it, receives punishment. A further quality of democratic government is that people have the right to openly disagree with official decisions. Although these decisions reflect the will of the majority, others may object. Without this right to protest, there cannot be democracy. This is then illustrated by:

> Many citizens, such as parents, students, faculty and heads of private universities object to the National Service Law. They are against this law because its implementation is in the hands of the military. According to them, it is the task of the school to instill in the students the values of citizenship. These citizens are petitioning that it is the school and not the military that is entrusted with education.[66]

The text then reminds us of the 1987 or New Constitution, and of the strict separation of powers that had vanished under the previous dictatorship. The independent judiciary now sees to it that whoever infringes upon the law will meet with justice. Besides, under democratic conditions, the opinion of the citizens carries weight. This is demonstrated by the plebiscite held before accepting the New Constitution. Then, most voters were in favor, which is a clear indication that Filipinos value democracy. Moreover, the very 1987 Constitution proves the primacy of the people in the exercise of power.[67]

Filipino citizens have rights and freedoms that the authorities must respect. They cannot be exiled. They vote and share in government. They may hold public office. Even when abroad, the national government must protect them. They have rights to livelihood, social services and social justice. They are free to travel and to practice the religion of their choice. In a democracy, government recognizes these rights and freedoms. It sees to it that justice is impartially implemented, that property is protected, that health services are provided, et cetera. All this, however, has a counterpart in legal duties and responsibilities for the nation. The republic would collapse if citizens did not fulfill their duties. It could even lead to dictatorship–or to anarchy.[68]

A government not supported by its citizens can never be strong and effective. Citizens are, therefore, under the obligation to lend their strength to the government in order that it can operate properly. They have to be loyal to the Republic and to honor its flag. "Whoever fights the government or lends comfort to the enemy is considered to be a traitor to the Motherland." Whereas people may disagree, they do not have the right to wreck the government. Quite to the contrary, the Constitution clearly states that all citizens must serve the nation. Male students must take part in Citizens Military Training (CMT); employees must be punctual; they must use their time profitably; they should not abuse their position; officials must work for the welfare of all. In other words, people should exercise their power cautiously and carefully, and for the benefit of all, irrespective of their own interests.[69]

In the final analysis, people help the government best if they know and exercise their rights and duties. Membership in civic associations is a way of positively participating in the country's affairs; and so it is to be a useful and gainfully employed citizen. If people honor the rights and duties of others, and when they give just criticism when criticism is due, society and nation will be in good shape. To keep it so, people should be faithful in paying their taxes, and responsible in their use of public utilities. By behaving like this, we give shape to the meaning of our basic law that can be summarized as:

1) Do not do to others what you do not want others to do to you;
2) Use your things properly and do not damage the property of others;
3) Leave the punishment of a wrongdoer to the authorities. People should not judge the misdeeds of their fellows.[70]

At high school, as we have seen in the preceding chapter, history and government of the Philippines are taught in the first year. Interestingly, a certain interpretation of history dictated the presentation of constitution, democracy, and nation there. The last three come as the climax after colonial gloom, debilitated independence, and mendacious dictatorship. They are the magic heirlooms of the new Filipino. In the DECS text concerned ("The Establishment of the Filipino Nation," 1989), it is explained that henceforward the Constitution should safeguard the population from the abuses of a dictator like Marcos.

In the same vein as it had already been formulated by Emilio Jacinto in the time of the struggle against Spain, it is the duty of government to promote the well-being of the people. Its most notable obligations are to defend the state; to establish the family as society's basic institution; to promote the moral character of the young; to promote social justice; to strongly promote social services; to protect labor. Besides, the New Constitution gives a wide berth to human rights and to a more democratic system of legislation and justice.[71]

In the following two pages, the separation and interrelationships of the three branches of government, and the differences between presidential and parliamentary systems, are explained. It all serves the establishment of checks and balances. This is then elaborated in the next 12 pages about the legislative, executive and judiciary establishments. Since the presentation is rather formal, it will take quite some teacher's ingenuity to elucidate this subject matter and, because it all comes at the very end of the text, it must be doubted whether much time is still available to go into these complex matters. I fear that most students will merely be presented with the legal and organizational niceties of the text about the three branches, constitutional commissions, local government, autonomous regions, and national finances.[72]

The last short chapter of the unit, *The New Filipino,*[73] offers the legal considerations surrounding Filipino citizenship, and those concerning the rights and duties of the citizen. As may be expected, all these are given in more detail than a year earlier at elementary school. Again, one needs to be a lawyer to appreciate the fine points of the civil, political and social rights people are said to enjoy. The text is much clearer in explaining the duties: loyalty to the Republic; respect for its flag; defense of the state; support for its development; defense of the constitution; support for the authorities and the rule of law; respect for the rights of others; engaging in gainful employment; registering and voting; defending the weak and oppressed; caring for the honor and identity of the nation; helping those in need. Among the last observations, we still find the importance of active citizens' organizations and public opinion. If the last is really to operate as the "voice of the nation," it should be:

1) Brave in disclosing those actions of the authorities that bring shame to the nation;
2) The product of balancing all the sides of an issue;
3) Always alert.[74]

In the fourth year of high school, when world history is studied (DECS, 1992), we find some additional information about democracy and constitutions. We are brought to ancient Greece and its city states, where citizens' control of government and the rule of law were practiced; the law was there for all, without fear or favor. This situation came about when ordinary people prevailed over the nobility by uniting against them under a "tyrant" who, at that time, embodied the democratic rules. Tyrantship was one step towards the democratic way of government. In the city states, trade and professions flourished [The connection between economy and citizens' emancipation is missed]. It is in Athens that we find the original principles of democracy, the love for freedom. Then follow many details and names before we arrive at Spartans and Persians. Of interest for us is this passage:

> In the time of Cleisthenes, democracy strengthened. He originated (the practice of) "ostracism," or the right given to the Athenian citizens to remove any authority they deemed to be a danger to the state. He also agreed to increase the number of political districts in order to let more

people participate. In this manner, many steps were taken in building a democracy.[75]

In the period of Athens under Pericles, Athenian political institutions are strengthened, and developed in such a way as to provide checks and balances. Important democratic principles were: the equality of all before the law; that every citizen could hold an official position; that all citizens could participate in political affairs. Excepted were women, strangers, and slaves.[76]

The next set of ideas pertinent to explaining democracy brings us to Britain and early modern Europe:

> England is the first among the nations that aspired to democracy. The basic desire fueling democracy is emancipation, and in order to become free it is necessary that all things (*sic*) are equal, especially those things that are related to civil liberty and the common welfare. The first symbol of the birth of democracy is the abolition of slavery.[77]

Then the tortuous relationship between the absolutist claims of kings and the pressure for public participation in political affairs is briefly described. In the seventeenth century it even leads to Charles I's beheading. It is not long after the restoration of Parliament that the *Habeas Corpus Act* is passed, which sets important limits to the abuse of power by king or authorities. In 1689, the Bill of Rights is made law. Thenceforward, the king is placed under the power of parliament, although it remains his prerogative to confirm the members of the cabinet.

The eighteenth century witnesses the emergence of democracy in France and America. The first symbol that democracy prevails is the American Declaration of Independence; there it has been stated that all men are born equal. It was also specified that the government must protect the rights of citizens, and that its power derives from them. As a result, the citizens have the right to change or dismiss their government. In 1789, the Federal Constitution strengthens and promotes democratic life. It regulates the system of checks and balances between the three branches of government, and declares the civil liberties. Then the French Revolution culminates in the Declaration of the Rights of Man and Citizen. In the next century, often thwarted by royal pretensions, democracy gradually matures in the West.[78]

So far, so good. Some basic premises of democracy and constitutional government have indeed been introduced. How are these related to the Philippines? It is true that President Aquino came to power in a peaceful manner, but it inaugurated a period of political and socioeconomic problems caused by frequent military rebellions and the NPA. The same period was characterized by a long series of calamities: earthquakes, typhoons, volcanic eruptions, floods, labor unrest, and assassinations. All of these made foreign capital shy away from the country. In this way, the economy remained weak, and relied heavily on the remittances of 650,000 Filipinos working in the Middle East. The situation is aggravating. Many people have no livelihood and are in dire straits. Prices keep rising and most people cannot buy their basic necessities. At the same time, a small, mainly urban minority, less than two percent of the population, grows richer while more than 90 percent of our people wallow in poverty.[79] The book then finishes with this admonition: "The condition of the Philippines will not change as long as the government does not act to help the majority of the population and as long as it is unable to organize the political aspects of the national way of life."[80]

So, what did the restoration of democracy finally bring? Did democracy and constitutions solve any problems? I do not know whether or not the answer to this last issue is expected to be positive. The book's last question to the student, however, is, "How can the internal problems of the Philippines be solved?"

The matter that remains is, if the students go on to college, the wish is that the ensuing course on PGNC would clarify more about the benefits of having a constitution and democracy, and their presumed connection with nation-building. The book used by most colleges is Hector S. de Leon's *Textbook on the Philippine Constitution,* in which the basic law is reviewed, explained, and commented upon clause by clause. Together with those who found it a good idea to enact that the charter be taught at all levels of formal schooling, the author expresses his hopes as follows: "Much needed emphasis is given to the provisions on the rights of the citizens as it is imperatively desirable that they have adequate knowledge of them so that they may better exercise their rights and discharge their corresponding obligations to others as responsible members of a democratic society."[81]

Later on, it is stressed that active, intelligent and responsible citizenship brings democracy to life, and that indifference may kill it. What this precisely means is not really made clear. According to de Leon, the knowledge and the fulfillment of rights and duties is crucially important, and things like love of nation and painstaking execution of obligations must lead to the desired society. Be that as it may, students are supposed to study the Constitution, which means studying law, and whether or not this learning results in active citizenship is altogether a different matter.

What teachers (most of them are lawyers) have to say on the subject is entirely up to them, and my interviews led me to believe, in contrast with school teaching, that few of them follow the recommendations of de Leon to the letter. Yet, it still is of interest to come with a few quotations from the text in order to illustrate both hopes and despair:

> To be loyal to the Republic. –By loyalty we mean faith and confidence in the Republic and love and devotion to the country. The citizen must be proud of his country, its customs, traditions, language, and institutions. He must share in its glories and feel sad in its misfortunes. It is the 'home of our people, the seat of our affections, and the source of our happiness and well-being.'
>
> A citizen owes, not a qualified and temporary, but an absolute and permanent allegiance which consists in the obligation of fidelity and obedience to his government.[82]
>
> To defend the State. –In the field of love of country, national unity, and patriotism, men can hardly afford to differ for these are matters in which they are mutually and vitally interested, for to them they mean national existence or survival as a nation or national extinction.[83]
>
> To cooperate with duly constituted authorities. –The larger interest of the group and the nation that he must serve necessarily involve his own, and he would be recreant to the claims of those interests if he did not actively concern himself with the affairs of his government. Supine and passive inaction is worse than actual and flagrant infringement of the law of the land . . .
>
> But the law is powerless to deal with that type of citizen, who is wanting in civic courage that he allows crime to be committed under his very nose without even lifting a finger to prevent its execution or to see that justice is done, who is lacking in civic pride that he tolerates the evil and graft in the community without even taking any step looking towards their eradication, who has such a distorted sense of civic values that so long as his selfish pursuits are not molested, he does not even give a thought to (these) . . .[84]
>
> To register and vote. –In our form of government, the conduct of public affairs is regulated by the will of the people (through suffrage) . . . if perverted, or basely surrendered because of money and favors . . . it

serves instead to undermine the entire edifice of our democratic institutions.

The people are the arbiters of their destiny, and if they allow themselves to be fooled, threatened, or bought, they must certainly deserve the kind of government that they get.[85]

In the Philippines, it is not uncommon to see political leaders dragging their constituents to the polls on election day. This shameful spectacle will not take place if suffrage were an obligation. It should be noted that people are more prone to sell their votes if they depend on politicians to bring them to the polling places.[86]

Article XI. Accountability of Public Officers. Section 1. Public office is a public trust. Public officers and employees must at all times be accountable to the people, serve them with utmost responsibility, integrity, loyalty, and efficiency, act with patriotism and justice, and lead modest lives.[87]

The Constitution sees the historic weakness of our national life in the absence of a national language . . . It is evident that the use of national language by all Filipinos will serve not only as a vehicle for achieving our goal of national identity and unity, but also facilitate communication and understanding and promote the Filipino people's collective participation in nation-building.[88]

There is much truth in the observation that the numerous social and economic problems that confront us today, including that of graft and corruption, can trace their roots in the weakening of the family as a basic social institution. In the final analysis, the good of society is best achieved through the good of its nucleus–the family. If this vital cell of society is fragmented or decadent, so is the country.[89]

Comments

The Constitution itself, and the commentary provided by de Leon, present us with that curious mixture of realism and idealism Filipinos display. To state in the Constitution that civil servants must be honest, or patriotic, seems, to me, at first glance overdone. On second consideration, however, it probably hints at real problems. And so it is with the other commentary referred to above. Whereas the Constitution has been designed to remedy problems, it is people, and especially politicians who have to do the implementing, which is, most obviously, another piece of cake.

In the ultimate analysis, we are stuck with a document, the 1987 Constitution that, by itself, cannot do a thing but bore students. Murdering rebels are apparently loyal because they are sometimes rewarded with high positions. Marcos' stalwarts and cronies are in every office of government. Do people like this? I do not know. The people speak with God's voice. From them emanates power. Government is of, by, and for them. Again, I do not know, but to me it sounds mystical. What we, what students see is people in power who try to do very much as they please. Really, to explain or visualize what, or where, "the people" are, is indeed very difficult. Are they the government, the state, the nation? In the various texts reviewed these concepts have not been clearly differentiated. So, is rebellion against the order of the state the same as treason of the Motherland? Perhaps not, as long as you can become a senator because of it. Then, finally, can the conscientious practice of democracy be expected among people who, in vast majority, are poor and struggling for survival? Can such practice build a nation?

After interviewing lecturers, the weakness of the PGNC teachings became more obvious. These teachers do not necessarily agree with de Leon's commentary, but they operate in the same vacuity resulting from an overemphasis on law. Their remarks, like de Leon's, are awfully *ad hoc*, reminding of newspaper columns. What remains is the letter of the law. Of course, the law should and must be implemented. The government is the servant of the people; it derives its power from the people; people must be loyal to the government. And, as they must be aware, they also recognize that the government is weak, that there is an absence of order and discipline, that even the Supreme Court is wishy-washy and that its decisions often are controversial. After all, law is a game, and litigation a habit.

It is as if the law is an entity unto itself, something free-floating, hovering over society, and being divorced from it. While in grade and high schools modest attempts still were made to connect it with the practice of life, with Philippine culture and with the history of democracy itself, the teachings at college level appear to have been separated from real life. Why it is so difficult to implement law, especially a charter imbued with ideals and high hopes, remains unclear, and does not seem to entice deeper comments than those offered by the newspapers lecturers also read.

What is the use of grumbling about a weak state, feeble nationalism, or indifferent citizenship when these are not being understood in their historical development? When complaints have been divorced from their social embeddedness? How can we understand democracy in the Philippines if we do not consider its origins in different histories and societies? Its institutions are imposed and, as some will have it, have been distorted. I think they have been reformed, or call it adapted. They have been remolded by Filipino practice, whether Filipinos themselves like it or not.

Therefore, if the teachings are to come alive and acquire meaning, they need to be transferred from the sphere of law to the historical and sociological context of Philippine life and culture. After all, the very charter is very much a product of practice and experience, and the hopes that these inspired to do better. Yet, hopes are hopes, and patient is the paper you write these down on. Perhaps that constitution, democracy, and even nation are no better. They exist in law.

5

"We, Among Ourselves"

ESPECIALLY AMONG people who have, through education, been most exposed to "western" culture, who spoke Spanish, or speak English, the quest for roots, for "Filipinoness" cannot but be expected. Unconsciously they experience an uncanny situation–the cleavage between their home life and the public world in which they operate. Over centuries, that public world has been colonized and been culturally subverted by the transplants of foreign religions, alien languages and strange impositions. Those most exposed to these became children of two worlds, developed double identities, and it became only natural to them to ask themselves who they were and are.

Towards the end of the nineteenth century, this became apparent among members of the Propaganda Movement. They were Spanish-educated, but not accepted as equals by the colonizer. They were second-rate citizens in their own country. But then, did they know their own country? What were their origins? What were they heirs to? To investigate these topics, the scholarly Jose Rizal consulted early Spanish sources, and even annotated Antonio de

Morga's *Sucesos de las Islas Filipinas,* which had originally appeared in Mexico in 1607. At the same time, Pedro Paterno was beginning to speculate about original Filipino culture and religion; he was probably the first to be struck by the we-had-a-civilization-of-our-own syndrome that is still affecting certain people today, as we noted in discussing the Gonzalez text in Chapter 4. Others–again, there still are many exponents of this line–such as Isabelo de los Reyes, studied popular culture. Subsequently he became known as the father of Philippine folklore studies.

The production of literature in Tagalog, and the so-called subversive plays of the early American period, signaled a heightened national consciousness, and the desire to give shape to country and culture. All the same, the Americans were amazingly successful in smothering the early enthusiasm. Already in 1910, original Filipino civilization and anthropology became safely respectable subjects at the newly-founded University of the Philippines (U.P.).

The sea change brought about by the occupation was future-directed towards progress and modernity, to democracy and perhaps even independence. History and origins did not seem to matter any longer to the new generation of Americanized intellectuals who only appeared to become aware of the ambivalence of their cultural being and the ambiguity of their origins in the late 1950s and the 1960s, a time sometimes dubbed as the "Second Propaganda Movement."

From then onwards, we notice an ongoing quest for identity and its roots in the past, for nationhood and self-confidence. This search surfaces in various shapes and forms. We have seen that school is supposed to play an important part in instilling "Filipinoness," but also that the teachings on the far-off past and national community are not always convincing. In the newspapers, we detected that bizarre tendency of self-denigration, which sometimes degenerates into self-flagellation, such as we shall still observe in our Excursion to "This Godforsaken Country." Fortunately we can also take in more serious lines of inquiry. Certain authors concentrate on the long Spanish period in which, according to their insights, the bases of modern lowland Christian Filipino civilization were led. Their telltale titles reveal what they hope to accomplish, *The Roots of the Filipino Nation* (O.D. Corpuz), and *Culture and History: Occasional Notes on the Process of Philippine Becoming* (Nick Joaquin).

To locate roots and becoming in the Spanish era is definitely unpopular with many contemporary historians. They are convinced that the prehispanic Filipinos have more to offer to themselves, and to the world, than the foreign institutions imposed throughout the colonial past. They grant that this has shaped the surface, the mask Philippine society presents, but hidden behind it is the true Filipino whose roots go much deeper and whose basic identity has been formed in the far-off past. This view, therefore, emphasizes continuity and evolution. Sometimes it is combined with a Marxist approach in which modes of production prevail over cultural becoming. Others, such as Amado Guerrero (Jose Maria Sison) and Constantino present us with Marxism-inspired analyses in their own right.

All this shows that considerable questing is going on, and that the prevailing images of Philippine culture and society provide many authors with the challenge of developing a more positive picture, Azurin even proposing to "reinvent the Filipino." Whether or not that can easily be done must be doubted, but the imposition of different interpretations on history do result in alternative scenes.

The first nationalist historian to stand out because of the originality of his views is Agoncillo. He recast the history of the Philippine Revolution through denying the acculturated *ilustrados,* strangers in their own land, their rightful place in history and through accentuating the *masa* (masses) as the mover of revolutionary history. Constantino remolded Philippine history in a Marxist framework that is not only strongly anticolonial (including internal colonialism), but also teleological: History unfolds itself towards a purpose, towards emancipation from a shackled imagination, from false consciousness.

In the 1970s, we witness the early attempts to construct knowledge about the Philippines on a particular Filipino basis. Then Enriquez began to develop, on the basis of "values" and interaction terminology, what would become known as Filipino psychology. At the same time, Salazar reached his preliminary conclusions about how history should be written from within: Philippine history by Filipinos written for Filipinos in Filipino. His aim was, and is, to provide understanding of and insight in national matters in terms that are relevant and immediately accessible to the native public.

These efforts matured when, in the 1980s, the idea of the study of Philippinology established itself at the College of Arts and Sciences faculty of U.P., Diliman campus. This discipline aims "to report and explain about Pilipinas to Filipinos in their own terms and with a view to strengthening Filipino nationality." This *Pilipinolohiya* comprises a broad stream of cultural studies that explore the roots of Filipino being. Among its exponents we find Jose, who mainly concentrates on folklore; Reyes, Hidalgo and Patajo-Legasto, who focus on language and literature; Covar, who attempts to develop a Filipino view of man. Nevertheless, the most important and influential ideas are nurtured in the history department and aim to present the Filipinos in their own right, free from foreign stains and as the actors of their own history. In this chapter we shall pursue this course, and see what alternative images of history and society these ideas give rise to.

Salazar's "We, Among Ourselves" View of History

In several of his publications, Zeus A. Salazar explains his notions of a meaningful historiography of the Philippine people. He points out that the Tagalog word for history, *kasaysayan*, is built on the root *saysay* which implies the idea of "making sense." This sense is grasped by those for whom kasaysayan is meaningful. In the old situation, it would be the sense contained in epic stories and mythology. This is the sense that has been and that is developing within a society itself, and is expressed in a single language. It does not originate from the outside, but is grounded in the own experience. Under those conditions, it is truly "ours" (*pantayo*); it is a coherent worldview relevant to the members of the group concerned.

Such worldviews provide for social cohesion. In the Philippine case, however, this integrity came under the attack of colonialism when the Spaniards imposed their point of view on the natives. They became an objective of Spanish historians in the islands, at the same time that they absorbed a good measure of strange religion and culture. These "they" were the intermediary class of leaders, teachers, priests, and other assistants who mediated Spanish ideas to the populace at large, and through whom the colonizers learned to understand the local society.

These precursors of the modern intelligentsia learned to explain themselves in terms comprehensible to the foreign outsider. They stopped seeing themselves in their own pantayo terms, and thus lost their cultural wholeness; they even came to see themselves through the foreign-looking glass. This latter point of view Salazar calls *pangkami* (i.e., *nous-autres* versus "you"), and is characteristically expressed in languages alien to the Philippines.

Does this mean that the pantayo view, the "view of ourselves among ourselves," has been annihilated? No. According to Salazar, ordinary people have been little affected by the centuries of cultural colonization. It is the intellectual elite who, consciously or unwittingly, cultivate the *pangkami* view. These are located on the one side of the "great cultural divide" that separates them from the masa whose consciousness still is of themselves, is pantayo, and rooted in their kasaysayan, in their language, in their own culture. It is this consciousness that represents the national community (*bayan*), the country's essence.

Modern Filipino historiography should transcend the great cultural divide. Its task is to make the *historia* of the elite and the kasaysayan of the masa meet, which can only be done through the use of one language in which to narrate history in the context of Philippine culture. This will result in a discourse among Filipinos that comprises all segments of the society. Such a discourse is a kind of a closed system or closed circuit in which society and culture fuse, as it occurs in the ideal of an undifferentiated community. It will unite Filipinos in the "we among ourselves" view.

From the way Salazar put it, it is clear that his historiography has a program and a purpose. It contains the promise of united nationality. It is to demonstrate the–still unfinished–becoming of the Philippine nation. It presupposes that there are such things as a shared spirit, or world of values and ideas; a common language, and a particular civilization. And, if these are not in place, they need to be created.

The greatest obstacles to this project are those who have been acculturated to the West, and Salazar never tires of lashing out at the self-colonization of those who mentally dwell at the cosmopolitan side of the great cultural divide. It is the latter who stand in the way of the development of a truly national civilization that roots in the Philippine community. They keep cultivating their ties with foreign lands, and fail to develop a deep understanding of the psychology, culture and worldview in which Philippine history is grounded. Needless to say that this understanding, which is part of the common experience and the collective consciousness of the masa, must be brought to the surface by the unfailing efforts of the new Filipino historiographer.

Up to this day, however, there are two, mutually separated cultures in the land: the so-called national culture of the elite, and the communally-rooted civilization of the ordinary people. The situation is not hopeless, though. The members of the ruling class have also been born in the country, partly been educated by simple servants and thus, they suffer from cultural schizophrenia.

If they would discover their true personality, they would rid themselves of their affliction; then they would be true Filipinos. They should inspire themselves at the little tradition of popular culture, take pride in it. This would rid them of their inferiority complex in regard to the foreigner. Anyway, the masses, and their civilization, will prevail; it is, therefore, inherently "good" that it is the masa who shapes history. Subsequently, Filipinos may look forward to enjoy and participate in their community-based national culture that sprouts from their spiritual essence and rooted history. Then they are giving shape to the "we among ourselves" view.

We may note that this further elaboration add dogma and mysticism to Salazar's historiography-with-a-purpose. Foreign imports of culture, with the exception of Islam, are vilified and need to be overcome. The links with the world outside need to be cut. The true "view of ourselves" is one of isolation. The real Philippines can only be discovered through focusing on the Philippines by itself. There, within the country, we find an inexorable course of history that Salazar's periodization brings to light as the gradual establishment of nationhood.

From the dawn of history unto 1588 is the period of community/ communities (*pamayanan*) that, in the latter centuries, develop into petty statehood. The second period runs up to 1913; it is the time the country (bayan) is being formed. This is followed by the development of the nation-state (*bansa*) that gets us into the present.

Similar to school history, the modern historiographer is unfazed by the complexities of the present. After all, he knows where history is going, which enables him to describe the scenario in detail up to the elections of 1992. Thus, the grant of independence of 1946 inaugurates the period of experimentation with the nation-state. Its independence is deceptive. In 1954, this simulacrum of self-determination demonstrates itself in a full-blown identity crisis. By 1963, the systemic crisis finally results in social protest and the will to fight.

In 1972, the quest for sovereignty sets off on the wrong foot, and leads astray through the counterrevolution of martial law. In 1978, this clearly shows in the crisis of national integrity. The Aquino assassination of 1983 brings the country to the brink of revolution. In 1986, the quest for sovereignty gets onto the straight path. Whereas the crises of state and society, of economy and culture persist, love of country, nationalism and the national spirit have begun to flourish. Finally Filipinos are on their way to find themselves in a shared view of themselves.

It is not apposite to here discuss the value of these influential ideas. I think that I have been fair in abstracting the principles of "our own view of ourselves" from Salazar's writings as they have recently been collected by some of his students (Navarro, *et al.*). From people following these principles it may be expected that they develop a fresh image of Philippine history, culture and society; an image probably at odds with that resulting from conventional teaching at school. This is precisely the question Salazar's co-faculty Jaime B. Veneracion addresses in his book *Agos ng Dugong Kayumanggi* ("The Flow of Brown Blood," 1990), which is a revision of standard history written for secondary-school teachers. Let us, therefore, inspect what we finally see when taking Veneracion's point of view.

Agos ng Dugong Kayumanggi

Veneracion is true to most of the principles developed by Salazar, and introduces his work as:

> Our book emphasizes the most important problem of our time: the forming of one totality of people/community (*sambayanan*). In critical times each of us looks for direction on the basis of personal solutions for the problems of adjusting to the environment. Many groups want to break away. The government itself is separated from the citizens and a vast segment of society has the outspoken desire to bring it down. The existence of one community still is theoretical. In the perspective taken it becomes clear why this is the problem and it is around this theme that our historiography should revolve. For a long time we have been tied to the themes that foreigners made for us. It is always they and their accomplices, the elite (or the powerful families) who are the main characters of our national history. What should be noted in our time is the *bayan* (country, nation, the people), because the real motor that drives progress and change is located in the totality of the people/community (*sambayanan*).
>
> The *bayan* (community) that we shall highlight, exists in all the regions of the Philippines: in the Christian plains of Luzon, Visayas, and Mindanao, in the Muslim area (*kamorohan*) of the Lumad of Mindanao and in the tribal populations (*kaigorotan*) of the Cordillera. In all regions there also exists a great divide–the ruling classes and the mass (*masa*) or ordinary citizens. This great separation will appear in the kinds of dwellings, food, and vehicles, in the schooling of their children, in the language used (English for the elite, dialect or Filipino for the *masa*), and in many other things. The dominant culture is definitely

different and this becomes the reason for the acute decline of all of us as a nation.[1]

Just the same, the author maintains that there is a "broad unity of the totality of the people."[2] Thus, whereas he sees national history unfolding itself in different places, such as the mountains, the plains, and the coast, and at different times, he assures the reader that the experience of the majority is one as they all are victims of the oppression by a small ruling class. This points to the fact that a single bayan (country, community, nation) can be integrated by developing justice and progress.[3] These opinions derive from the author's idea that the social sciences enable us to relate surface reality to underlying structures[4] and thus allow for interpretations that go deeper than mere historical facts: "Because of the complexity of historical happenings, they can only be interpreted within a structural framework."[5] Consequently, subjective perceptions based on one's belonging to a family, class, or culture, can be overcome by understanding them in wider perspectives. Then the "objective" view will appear:

> While man is evolving, there is the fight of the oppressed classes to obtain a higher level of humanity–to be at the same level of prosperity as the power-holders. In that way the oppressed classes play a greater role in the making of history. No change in the status quo that is especially advantageous for the ruling class, can be expected from the latter. On the other side, the victims of oppression have the motivation and reason to fight for the progress of their class.[6]

With so much in place about the principles of scientific interpretation, the Filipino point of view and the question of periodization still need elaboration. *Ang pantayong pananaw*, or the indigenous point of view, is not meant to explain anything to foreigners, but revolves around the relationships that form the country: the Muslims, the colonized Christian *Indios*, and the Igorots of the Cordillera. It studies the connections between these groups through time. Emphasis is thus given to the inner dynamism of the country in order to direct the attention to "the true goal in a meaningful future."[7] This future is the formation of a sambayanan, a national whole, arising from the small native communities through the bayan, or township, such as the Christian pueblo (from 1565 onwards) and the Muslim *kampong* (from 1280 on), to the formation of a bansa, a nation, because of the interaction of the various component peoples (Indio, Igorot, Moro). Inexorably this will culminate in the national whole.[8]

This brings us to the substantive text. In the considerations of prehistory and the period of the small communities, emphasis is given to maritime traffic, migration, exchange and the existence of extensive trading relationships among the more recent inhabitants of the islands.[9]

Before the Spaniards arrived, the settlements, strategically located on waterways, were linked through commerce. First of all there was the exchange of goods between downstream and upstream locations, and in certain places settlements grew powerful and large, such as in the Manila area, in Cebu, Butuan, Sulu, et cetera. Such settlements were under the control of powerful families who taxed trading and productive activities. Especially in the southern Philippines we find extensive trading networks, not only between interior, agriculture-based centers, such as Buayan, and coastal settlements, such as Cotabato, but also linking the southern islands with the Moluccas and the trade of Indians and Chinese. It was only when the Spaniards built fortresses in Zamboanga and Cotabato that the Moros lost control of the trading routes; yet, those in the interior, particularly at Buayan, remained actively opposed to the colonizing power.[10]

The Bayan

The second part of the book is about the bayan, the *polis*, about organized urban life with which the Filipinos formally enter the period of civilization. In that transition, the people were facing foreign concepts and domination that were ingeniously and selectively adopted by the original culture.[11] Anyway, a bayan is a center of commerce and politics, and the word does no longer imply the unity of all. It is the place where the officials stay. When riches accumulated as a result of higher production, social relationships grew more complicated. People became divided in classes, with some having the power to make others work for them, and relationships were no longer based on being relatives of each other. We find powerful leaders and their followers/subjects (*sakop*).

> It is difficult to understand the original social classes because we are used to divide on the basis of juridical, legislative, and executive positions. We also divide ordinary people according to their roles in production, landownership, and suchlike. Yet, such positions are not so apparent in our native society. There are leaders who hold the power of life and death over their subjects, yet a subject who is "oppressed" can look for his own (another) leader. The free *Maharlika* (nobility) can be

the rowers of their leader's boat or cut rice in the fields. Also the *alipin* ("slave") has the opportunity to rise in society or to remain the slave that will be buried together with his dead master.[12]

In trade or war, the leader must be able to accumulate a surplus that assures that many followers will be attracted; in that way the datu becomes popular while binding his clients by way of the *utang-na-loob* (debt of gratitude).

> But we can note that here begins the conflict between the classes in the great *barangay* and confederations because of two prevailing kinds of relationships: a system of dependence and a system of slavery. Slavery results from tribal warfare and debt peonage–institutions that weaken the foundation of family relationships in the *barangay*. The dependency that prevails between the *datu* and the members of his household is formed along the pattern of the elders versus the younger ones. The lord became the advisor of the serfs and slaves. Even today the lord of the household is called *kuya* (elder brother) by the servants. But in other places, such as Negros Occidental, the master is called *Señor* or *Señora*, which is a Spanish feudal influence.[13]

Even so, in spite of feudal and class oppositions, life in the original communities was characterized by the striving for unity among members of the same clan. They expressed themselves in an indirect manner, thus avoiding conflict and establishing strong inner bonds. If conflict surfaced, it was reduced to a laughing matter, a joke, and this is why the prevailing sentiment in the community tended to unity and mutual help.[14] To keep it like this, the economic organization of the early communities founded on the redistributive principle in which rich and well-known people shared their blessings and kindness with the others, for which they received praise and prestige in return.[15]

In religion, the greatest honor was given to the *anito*, the collective soul of the ancestors. Originally, the anito gave life to all and protected the living; it was omnipresent in the activities of the people. Also praised and respected were the *ninuno*, or forefathers and senior relatives. Ritual sanctified traditions and customs, emphasizing the positive aspects of social relationships while covering up their contradictions. Mutual free help in communal affairs, known as *bayanihan* was the moral basis of the group. The *catalonan* ("shaman") and the headman were the intermediaries between the living and the ancestors. Occasionally, prominent leaders underscored their prestige through adopting foreign religious titles, such as *Sultan* and *Rajah*.[16]

In the final analysis, it can be said that the complete picture of the early community is an inventory of culture sprouting from the water. The material foundation of the beliefs and customs of our ancestors originates from their adjustment to river, bay, and sea and in the acknowledgment of the enchantment/mysterious qualities of the mountains. With the arrival of foreign cultures, the mountains remain the center of our original civilization.[17]

Colonization

The pueblo, introduced by the Castilians, became the Indio bayan. It centered on church, market, and town hall. Such townships were connected and surrounded by small communities, the *visitas* and *sitios*. These contrasted with the bayan where hierarchical relationships were immediately apparent. The village communities did not have a clear division in classes. Next to these were the frontier settlements, the *estancias* or cattle ranches, whose residents defended the proprietors against the encroachment of rice farmers. Beyond these were the communities of the *tulisanes*, or brigands. They were out of the reach of government and normally had no Christian names. Sometimes they descended on the townships, and gave whatever they had obtained to the poor. They opposed the government and its policy of resettlement known as *reduccion*; many of them were victims of excesses and oppression.[18]

The year 1572 (*sic*), when the Spanish *conquistadores* took Manila, is important in Philippine history. The northern reach of Muslim influence was rolled back, and clear centers of competing power arose in the colony. On one side, the strong sultanates of Sulu and Magindanao were impelled to gather their strength to attack the coasts in all corners of the Visayas and Luzon. On the other side, the Spaniards established strongholds at Cotabato, Zamboanga, and Borneo. In the fight against the foreigners, the ethnic groups of Mindanao gained in political sophistication. The small, scattered tribes of the Cordillera did not react in the same aggressive way as the sultanates in the South. That is why their original cultural life could continue.[19]

While still in Cebu, Legazpi became aware that Manila was the most populous and richest settlement in the archipelago, attracting Chinese, Arab, and other Asian traders. This was reason enough to conquer this town, in 1571, and to make it the center of the colony. The Spaniards had no doubt that their actions were legitimate. The population and their leaders were placed under the authority of the king of Spain who ordered the Spaniards to study the culture of the natives and to demonstrate the barbarism and uncivilized condition of the *salvajes* whom they desired to "save." The Spaniards exploited the cultural weakness of the natives by convincing them that the foreign colonizers would defend them from enemies. In many places of the archipelago, the population requested the king of Spain to be their monarch, because the king of Spain freed the Indios from the demons, and from servitude to the former ruling class of datu. In this way, one good deed for the natives justified the ruthlessness of the colonization.[20]

In their early years, the Spaniards concentrated considerable forces in the South and up to Brunei, but the Muslim southerners also tried to regain their interests in the North. An interesting side effect of the deployment of Spanish power was that it united former enemies in Sulu and Mindanao, and that it sped up the Islamization process in Mindanao, especially in the time of Sultan Kudarat. The Spaniards' handicap in setting up their colonialism was their shortage of soldiers and personnel. That is why they deployed their forces only where it was necessary. Part of their strategy was to set the various tribes against each other and to exploit conflicts.

Whereas the desire to Christianize the natives was given as the primary reason, the true motive of the Castilians was economic. According to their mercantilist views, the easiest way to make money was the exchange of goods between Mexico, China, and India. Chinese goods were collected in Manila, then sent on by the galleon to Mexico. That boat (*bapor*!) left from Cavite by way of the San Bernardino Strait (*sic*); that link was a fortified commercial route. The outlying parts of the archipelago merely functioned as barriers against their enemies–the Portuguese, the Dutch, and Chinese pirates.[21] Anyway:

> Colonialism is like a fish trap. When the trap has been built and the fish is fenced in, it is not important which of the fishes was the first to be caught and cooked. Similarly, the occupation of locations in the Philippines depended on Spanish priorities and needs, and as a result nobody throughout the archipelago could escape from the colonial experience. Different forms of violence were experienced by the natives, becoming a mercenary soldier or a victim of war. There is no place where the population did not become part of the mercenary army or suffered the misfortune of being attacked by it. The similarity of the matter is that the natives were victims of colonialism . . . The colonial influence prevailed and pervaded in the lives of the natives, especially in their behavior and

habitation. The natives were forced to imitate the colonizers' urbanity, an imitation of a consciousness devoid of self-respect.[22]

The Spaniards relocated and concentrated the population. This was not only to facilitate government, but also served to break the power of the datu over their related or patronage-bound subjects. The big house of the datu was replaced by a bigger symbol of power still–the *kumbento*, or presbytery. According to European thinking, civilization can only prevail in a town, and the Spaniards impressed on the consciousness of the natives that they were not civilized because they had no towns, and that the foreigners were offering a high civilization. This is why the lifestyles of the natives changed under the policy of resettlement.[23]

The former datu became known as *principalia*. They were the privileged accomplices of the new masters, sometimes "giving" or "selling" extensive tracts of land to the religious orders, in contravention of the needs and interests of their subject population. Oral traditions, such as storytelling, lost out because of the breaking up of the group of relatives and the formal expositions in church. As an expression of urbanity, the message of the church stood in contrast with the "barbaric" customs of the natives; subsequently, the old stories were replaced by hagiographies and the *Pasyon*. Anyway, because of the ease of, and eagerness for conversion, the depth of Christian understanding must be doubted.

The traditional elite fared well. The catalonan cooperated with the priest in administering the sacrament of death (*pahesus*, or extreme unction), and the principalia collected taxes and organized public religious celebrations; because of these duties, the principalia were given a bad name by the people.[24]

Up into the 1660s, the Spaniards were faced by many revolts. The motivation of the first type of them was the restoration of the old socioreligious order that, in spite of the prevalence of slavery, was less oppressive. The native priests, or catalonan, played a major role in these revolts. A second type was led by the former ruling families who were eager to restore or improve their position. A third type of rebellion surfaces in 1745-1746, and was the result of new agricultural relationships and excessive exploitation. The catalonan or former datu do not play a role in these later disturbances; from then on, it is social and economic conditions that explain the revolts.[25]

For most of the seventeenth century, especially during the days of Sultan Kudarat (d.1671), trade flourished and more or less stable conditions prevailed in the Muslim South, but Moro power scattered and degenerated in civil war towards the end of the century and into the next.[26] The establishment of a colonial center in Luzon gave rise to a steady theme of our history, namely, the bloody relationships between the Christianized regions and those of the Muslims and Igorots; the resulting problems persist into the present. On the whole, under early Spanish colonialism, the integration of the country remained weak. Townships developed in separation, each according to their inner dynamism.[27]

The opening of roads led to the development of wheel-carried transportation and horse-breeding, also to circulating markets and trade in imported goods. As a result, the value of land went up, land rent replaced the head tax, and the hacienda, producing export crops, came into being, together with the owner-dependent tenants. It was the non-ordinary people who became the owners and, gradually, much land fell into the hands of the friars. They let it be worked by laborers, or farmed it out through the intermediary of a trusted *inquilino* (tenant-overseer); the system opened the way to many abuses.[28]

In discussing the changes in the principles of leadership, the author informs us that datu exercised their power through *pakikisama*, that is through goodwill and cooperation; through appealing to family ties, and through creating utang-na-loob, or debts of gratitude. With the coming of the Spanish officials, the former became *principales*. They were incorporated in a patron-client system, which was the philosophy of governance of the Spanish Empire. In that view, the king was the client of God, and those who were under the king, as the representative of God, were his clients. The representatives of the king were, therefore, the patrons of the natives who should be honored and obeyed. The power of the principales founded on their talent to move between the indigenous sociopolitical hierarchy and that of the foreign colonizers.

The position of the former datu was beefed up by royal law. Whereas they had lost some power because of the abolition of slavery, they received other privileges, such as the right to collect taxes and tribute. This placed many in debt to the principales, so relegating them to the position of "slaves." By means of new titles, such as *Don*, money, and Spanish dress, the former datu obtained two sources of power, firstly, the language and support of the foreigners and, secondly, the utang-na-loob and the pakikisama (pliability) of their original sakop, or subjects. They remained popular among their followers and became the brokers in the colonial-native relationship.

Religion changed. In prayers the Spanish taught, all became mere servants, and everybody could be equal to others. Heaven, and gratitude to God, offered security. This was different from the fear-inspired spirit-world of old. In

Christianity, death is the invitation to come to God's kingdom, and the suffering on earth is a test of the determination to go there. A concept of the old belief system that entered into the new religion, is the asking of forgiveness (*kapatawaran*). The *tawad*, or "discount" in a commercial transaction, is a way to obtain a favor by supplication. In their original religion, Filipinos entreated the ninuno and anito through honoring and praising them in order that they grant protection from the spirits. This belief entered Christianity: processions, the kissing of images, and confession were the new ways to negotiate and ask for God's blessing. The best known native custom that was incorporated in Catholicism is the ceremony of the veil and the cord at marriage.

The English interlude (1762-1765) may be seen as the conjuncture that stands at the beginning of a new economic order. It opened the Philippines to world trade and the production of export crops. Of course, earlier the mercantilistic monopoly had been broken, and lively trade existed between English merchants from India and the Spanish colony. Seen this way, the occupation of Manila merely dovetailed with the commercial interests of certain members of the English bourgeoisie. The latter were also very active in the Sulu sultanate where they obtained local, and especially Chinese products. As a Spanish reprisal, the sultan was put in prison in Manila, but the English freed him there. As a reward, the latter surrendered his possessions in Palawan and northern Borneo to them.

The British relaxed excessive oppression at the haciendas and in taxation. This breathing space stimulated the native population to drive out certain friars and to rise in revolts. These uprisings, of which those of Diego and Gabriela Silang in Ilocos, and of Francisco Dagohoy on Bohol are the best known, demonstrate the qualitative difference from the earlier rebellions. The latter aimed to drive out the foreign civilization, while the eighteenth-century movements articulated themselves in the colonizers' idiom, and further expressed the desire for participation, and recognition of native human dignity. The revolts of this second type were not against colonialism per se, but sought to address abuses. This is instanced by the very Catholic reasoning of Dagohoy, and the reforms and European aristocratic titles desired by Silang.[29]

Towards a Nation

After the British occupation, we learn that the Spaniards tried to restore their prestige by introducing reforms that slowly awakened the Indios to the idea that they form a community. The government fostered migration from

Spain, while the country also served as a place of exile for many subversives of the revolutions in Latin America and Spain. In that way liberal ideas were introduced. The newly arrived became critical of friar domination in politics and social differentiation on the basis of color. Opposition originated from the native priests who occupied the parishes that were abandoned by the Jesuits in 1768; because said parishes were isolated and unprofitable, they began to imagine a community separate from the colonists.

Another factor contributing to nationalist consciousness was migration between provinces, including Moro slave-raiding. After all, the practice of slavery was an important ingredient of the Moro economy that persisted well into the early twentieth century, but that also had as a result the mixing of people from throughout the islands. Anyway, for those concerned it was often more enjoyable to be kidnapped by the Moros than to suffer from Spanish oppression, a point that is then illustrated by the fate of those deported or forcibly resettled by the colonial authorities. All these population movements brought the various ethno-linguistic groups into contact with each other. Also the practice of sending rebels into exile to, for instance, the Marianas, where they deliberated together, must be considered as an important step towards the emergence of national consciousness.[30]

The political weakness of the South, agricultural development, the collapse of the galleon trade, and the Philippine integration into the world trade resulted in the consolidation of the colony. The prosperity of the nineteenth century is reflected in the big stone cathedrals built then. The period also witnesses continuous land-grabbing, and disdain for the rights of the occupants, that resulted in vast haciendas. Combined with technological innovations, three groups of rich landowners emerged: the friars, Chinese-mestizo merchants, and certain native families. Because of increased commercial activities, the towns (pueblo), and the Chinese, were thriving.[31]

The "Filipinization" issue sets the Spanish regular clergy and their economic interests against the native, secular priests. The friars' greed and discrimination destroyed their prestige and triggered off reactions like the establishment of the *cofradia* of Apolinario de la Cruz ("Hermano Pule") in Lucban. Although the government smothered this movement with blood, it was unable to disband the tulisanes. The tulisanes even increased in number, possibly as a result of the complex social contradictions resulting from new technology and novel agrarian arrangements. By the middle of the nineteenth century, they became the carriers of the ideology of armed opposition that inspired some of Rizal's characters; for instance, Kabesang Tales. They came to be seen as native heroes, precursors of the Katipunan. The seeds of the propaganda and revolutionary movements of the last two decades of the century had been sown.[32]

The theme of contradictions is important in Veneracion's considerations on patriotism and nationalism. He elaborates this distinction with linguistic exercises on the Tagalog words for country, community and nation. Anyway, nationalism seems to be defined as the striving for political independence. Patriotism is the ideal of the ordinary people, and aims at rights, such as equality of opportunity. As a result, the elite's purpose of the Revolution of 1896 was independence; then they could run the affairs of state. The masses, however, expected that political change would lead to unity, that injustice and absence of opportunity would give way to a prosperous society, characterized by brotherhood and equality.[33]

Be that as it may, it is especially in Europe that the student-children of the rich *inquilinos* have to come to grips with their "otherness"; they were the first to think in terms of nationality; they imagined a wide community, of old known as Pilipinas. They trusted that what they thought would be the opinion of everybody in the Islands. They knew what would be best for all. This is the reason why they expressed themselves in Spanish; they were explaining "Filipinoness" to outsiders, which is at the root of the pangkami view. In their desire to explain the situation in the Philippines to Europeans, Paterno wrote about the high "Malay civilization" that was destroyed by the Spaniards. This is also why Rizal wrote his commentary on Antonio Morga (*sic*). He wanted to demonstrate that the Philippines had its own properties and civilization before the Spaniards arrived. Any recognition of the fellow brown men was used to proclaim that this race was not lagging behind the truly civilized nations/races.[34]

In the Christian towns a lavish lifestyle patterned after the colonizers developed in which literature replaced oral traditions. The shape of culture expressed the dominant ideology, such as in the *moro-moro* (stage plays) in which it was impressed on the young minds that the fight against the Moro was a holy duty. Balagtas held another view of the relationship of Christians and Muslims. The friendly relationship he depicted in his *Florante at Laura* may be seen as the first seedling of nationhood. His allusions to freedom and independence are unmistakably a call for the redemption of the brown community, and had their influence on Rizal's thinking; besides, the latter's

Noli Me Tangere shows the sociological environment of nationhood at Capitan Tiago's party where all kinds of people unknown to each other meet. "What happens in the novel is similar to what occurred in Filipino society then. The reader will be able to feel that he is not unique in his condition because the factual contents in the novel are his very reality."[35]

In this way we can understand why Rizal is considered the father of nationalism; he expressed it very clearly in the constitution of La Liga Filipina as to unite the whole archipelago as a living and unique body. But what influence could he have on the native mass? They were kept at bay because of the Spanish language. The mass had a different understanding of the purpose of the Philippine Revolution. They were striving for unity to establish the nation, and so, in the Katipunan, the *ilustrado* principles, such as sovereignty, were combined with the patriotic principles, such as equality. Naturally, these were expressed in the native language.[36]

> These are only a few proofs that the happenings overseas had an effect on the thought and consciousness of the people. The very difficulties of economic life are not the reason for their restlessness. Towards the end of the nineteenth century, there are many indications that it is the consciousness of the people itself that changes in the direction of accountability, towards the desire for a just society after going through all the travails.[37]

The Katipunan was conscious of the role and need for historical awareness in order to discover our nationhood. This corresponds with the tradition of the Propaganda Movement but in the Katipunan it was more connected with the improvement of the living conditions of the natives, and not just an intellectual discussion about identity as a civilized people. Two well-known poems of Bonifacio are then adduced to illustrate the "ideology" of the Katipunan; they tell about love of country, of love for the true and caring *Inang Bayan* (Mother Land).[38] To earn her love, sacrifice may be required, which is amply demonstrated by the popular Pasyon that relates Jesus' life, and that holds a recognizable and liberating message for the masses. The Pasyon makes sacrifice and death that redeems understandable; so, the death of Macario Sakay fitted in with others, with Christ, the fathers Gomez, Burgos, and Zamora, and Rizal; in the eyes of the masa, martyrdom is really part of heroism. Little cause for wonder, therefore, that the famous leaders of the patriotic revolution were rooted in the culture and the thought of the *masa*. That thought is expressed in their oral literature and served the styling of the popular leaders.[39]

Towards Independence (rather than towards nationhood)

Soon the momentary unity the revolution inspired gave way to class-based self-interests; patriotic and nationalistic aims drifted apart; because of the influence of Masonry, the patriotism of the ilustrados and the middle class weakened and decreased in the 1930s. Political leaders based their popularity on nationalistic feelings, that is the desire for a state independent from America. This nationalistic feeling did not consider the welfare of the common man.[40]

In their striving to erase the memory of the bitter resistance against them, and by separating non-Christians and Muslims from the others, the Americans were most successful. The study of the various tribes in the Cordillera they initiated caused the people there to doubt their nationhood, because the research stressed the differences rather than the unity of the national tradition. In looking for opportunities to exploit natural resources, the Americans gained the sympathy of the landed class. Most members of this elite collaborated with them, in the expectation that they would slowly gain political power. Besides, many ilustrados believed that American help was needed to achieve independence; they easily forgot their history, that is the democratic and civil rights tradition of their predecessors. Ilustrado leadership often combined Masonry, internationalism, and liberal ideas; they were naturally anti-friar, such as the Protestants, the Aglipayans, and also many Catholics. This anticlericalism, and the newly instituted liberal education, often resulted in pro-Americanism.[41]

In Mindanao and Sulu, things were different. During the second part of the nineteenth century, Spain had succeeded in bringing the South under its authority; the sultans and datus had no choice but to cooperate. When Spanish might crumbled, however, everybody scrambled for power. Although the northern revolutionaries called for unity between them and the Muslims, also in fighting the Americans, the sultans had their own ideas about freedom and were not well disposed towards a Christian government. Soon they compromised with the Americans. As a result, the power of the sultans was reduced to impotence; they lost their prestige in the eyes of the people. The datus of Magindanao became American collaborators, with the exception of the upcountry datu of Buayan. The reason for Datu Ali's opposition was that the abolition of slavery destroyed the "feudal" basis of the "sultanate system," or datu power. Anyway, in 1905 he was betrayed by his fellow datus.[42]

Initially, the Americans saw Mindanao as a separate territory. While envisaging the eventual independence of the North, they intended to keep the southern parts because of their natural resources. This inspired the Muslims to aspire to a Bangsa-Moro state and attracted American capital. Colonial policy thus led to the separation of the elite from the people. Those who opposed were labeled bandits. The middle class was pacified by being offered positions in government, while imprisonment threatened those who rejected the Americans.[43]

The American occupation deeply affected Philippine life, although we must be careful in our evaluation of the period. The usual rhetoric about public health programs, for instance, should be taken with a pinch of salt. Cholera epidemics were largely due to the weakened health caused by war-time conditions and reconcentration; besides, health measures were convenient in separating the guerrillas from the population.

Education aimed at creating English-speaking colonial bureaucrats; it was a means of social mobility for the middle class. English became established as a language of literature that had western individualism as its theme. Some of those who came back from study in the States became propagandists of American culture. The resulting American orientation gave rise to a "colonial mentality." Yet, unintentionally, the cultural confrontation resulted in the discovery of the origins of Filipino personhood. At the same time, free trade destroyed handicrafts (weaving) and small industries in the Philippines.[44]

Road, and especially rail transportation were vigorously promoted and opened vast regions for development and trade. The mixing of people settling the frontiers of Mindanao laid the foundation of Filipino nationhood. Although the vast friar estates became available for redistribution, these and other lands, even in homesteading areas, soon fell into the hands of the locally powerful, including former revolutionary generals. Because of the prevailing share tenancy system in Central Luzon, many small farmers migrated to Nueva Vizcaya and Cagayan valley. Mechanization further stimulated the one-sided capitalist exploitation of land and people.[45]

The introduction of the two-party system created the new national pastime of politics. Henceforward, and instead of religious celebrations, interest in town became focused on political life. Politicking brought the *padrino* system. As an attaching of clients to leading patrons, it is very similar to the Datu-sakop relationship of earlier days. In order to be appointed to a high position, the recommendation of a politician became necessary. It operated on a bigger scale than the concept of belonging to a group of relatives of the original barangay; now it covered the ethnic group. The American custom of rewarding political loyalty with high positions is demonstrated at the career of Claro Recto who became judge of the Supreme Court and chairman of the Constitutional Convention.[46]

The rich provincial families flocked to Manila for the ostentatious display of their wealth at balls and yearly beauty contests. By organizing these on the birth and death days of heroes of the Philippine Revolution, they may be seen as ritual expressions of the national ideals of the urban middle class. Meanwhile, the popularity of Tagalog theater faded as cultural life was drowned in an abundance of American entertainment.[47]

The national comedy show, such as enacted by Manuel Quezon and Sergio Osmeña could not cover up the restlessness and protests resulting from the fact that no social renewal was in sight. On the contrary, social injustice was aggravated by the ruling dispensation. Often, agricultural protests took the cloak of religious movements; they also expressed themselves politically, as in the Sakdal movement. The latter stressed the need to expel the American imperialists in order to solve the land problem. Consequently, they pressed for immediate independence. They held that nationalist politicians, such as Quezon and Osmeña, were betraying their original stance by accepting the Commonwealth, which delayed the liberation of the country. The radical vision of Sakdal leader, Ramos, refreshed the listless patriotism of the masa. The failure of the *Sakdalista* uprising, however, made this movement give way to the socialist and communist parties. As a result, the Commonwealth government was being directly confronted with the social crisis. In response, Quezon announced several programs aimed at solving the problems of share tenancy and industrial relations. These ran against the vested interests of landlords, including the Church, who played up the communist threat, and Quezon changed direction. As a member of the landowning class, Quezon was in no position to push for radical solutions. Due to the economic dependence of the ruling class on the USA, his vision about independence became blurred, which was exacerbated by the threat of a Japanese attack.[48]

The Pacific War must be seen in the light of the long imperial rivalry between Japan and the USA. After the first year of occupation, the new masters inaugurated Philippine independence in connivance with the traditional ruling class, but also by linking backwards with the Philippine Revolution and the Sakdal movement. Because of their fascistic sympathies, and fired by fear of the "Red Plague," capitalists, Dominicans, and the Church lent support to the new dispensation. Yet, government officials used their position to weaken the Japanese by stealing and corruption. Law and order broke down. Guerrilla leaders took over from the old ruling class, but most often their newly-won power served their self-interest only. Even so, the people in the countryside profited from inflation and from being beyond the control of the landowners.

During the war, relative prosperity prevailed in the countryside. It was the people in town who suffered, and many evacuated to the provinces.[49] In the final analysis, though, the war wrought tremendous destruction, material and spiritual, resulting in a social collapse, while conflicting ideologies of the different classes remained.[50]

The war produced patriotic liberation forces, such as the Hukbalahap (Huks). Others set on the Americans as saviors and liberators. Japanese cruelties made the latter popular again; forgotten were the excesses of the first decade of their occupation; besides, colonial education presented the Americans as liberators and did not stimulate the will to be free. So, in the end, they yielded the enduring gratefulness of the Filipinos, while neocolonial intentions were kept hidden behind the "special relationships" that were supposed to tie the two nations together. All the same, economic change gave rise to progressive groups, such as the PKP, or Partido Komunista ng Pilipinas (Communist Party of the Philippines). In the American period, communist and socialist thought became part of Philippine history.[51]

Community?

The final part of *Agos*, covering the period since the war, is called Sambayanan (community). It opens on a programmatic introductory statement:

> *Sambayanan*–meaning one nation, one country: our aim in the future. Up to now, this is a principle; it is not an actual reality. Our nation is divided in many domains, in material property, in opportunity, in consciousness. The historical divisions run along region and tribe: those in the Moro territory; those who were dominated by the Spaniards, called Indio; those in the mountains and forests, called Igorot and Lumad. Yet, in every tribe and territory exists the deeper division in classes, with the elite exploiting the broad mass of poor people. This division can be seen in the type of housing, of vehicle, of grave, and in the language spoken.

On the one hand English, expensive cars, Forbes Park; on the other (hand), tabloid newspapers, jeepneys, Filipino or dialects. This division is not just limited to the Christian areas. It is also apparent among the Moros in the relationship of the sultans and *datus* with the ordinary Moros, and in the victimized tribes.

The evolution of a national community is a long historical process. It can appear as a cultural process, such as in the development of a national language, of colorful legends, songs and poems. More basic, though, is that it found on an economy based on the equality of the citizens. Government cannot realize this. Such as happened in other places in the world, the evolution of community began in the consciousness of the *masa*, and its drive of achieving its historical mission of change and development.[52]

The interpretation of the early postwar developments is clear from the suggestion that it was a movement towards authoritarianism. MacArthur trusted Roxas up to the hilt, in spite of the latter's collaboration with the enemy; other wartime leaders were suspected, though. This weakened the leadership, because they were afraid that America would withdraw its blessing; as a result, they did not protest the Parity Amendment and the Military Bases Agreement. In this way, the sovereignty granted became meaningless; the Philippines remained a colony. The Democratic Alliance refused to give in to American pressure, and thus they were expelled from Congress. This forced them into armed resistance. In 1948, under the auspices of the PKP, the Huks of Central Luzon took up their arms again. Their armed struggle collapsed in 1954.[53]

Meanwhile, mainstream society, propped up by the Church's conservatism, was firmly in the grip of Cold War propaganda. Old politicians, who had collaborated with the Japanese, could make their comeback because of divisions among patriotic and progressive leaders. The most famous is Recto who, later on, propagated a nationalistic view the Americans disliked: if the Philippines were to progress, security, sovereignty, the economy, and political power should be in Filipino hands. Recto, however, could not prevail over American intentions. At the same time, the Church, because of its anticommunism, could regain the position of social leadership it had lost in the revolution against Spain. Recto's nationalism was elitist because he did not connect with the consciousness of the masa. This nationalism-in-English is known as "*barong Tagalog* nationalism"; it did neither include the Moros nor the people of the

Cordillera. Among the latter, American colonization even continued by way of missionaries and their schools.[54]

The perennial plagues affecting Philippine (under)development are venality, political weakness, and American meddling. The country remains dependent on agriculture which circumscribes industrial activity. Under the aegis of Pres. Carlos Garcia's "Filipino First" policy, some industrialization occurred because of protection. The Board of Investments (BOI) of 1960 initiated big, capital-intensive projects that resulted in large-scale corrupt manipulation and international debts. Garcia's policy did not succeed because of economic recession; the big national projects failed because of bad planning. Agricultural relations remained excessively exploitative yet, because many members of the ruling class obtained interests in industry and trade, planning for land reform, both under Macapagal and Marcos, became a possibility.[55]

Whatever the planning at the level of the state, the Philippines will follow its own method of development. A "New Society" will arise. This means radical restructuring through continuing the Revolution of 1896, which was basically a national-democratic revolution. Everybody will be called on to ally with the nationalist and patriotic principles. This appeal for a new society is reflected in the slogan, *Isang Bansa, Isang Diwa* (one nation, one spirit). The little people and the oppressed ethnic groups must be truly free, which means free from oppression and suffering. Then real independence will prevail.[56]

In spite of these high hopes, ordinary people still seem to have to travel a long road to their freedom. This became most apparent when, with Marcos, authoritarianism, and with it deceit and protest, came to fruition. During those days, students entered, for the first time, on the political stage; they claimed to embody the national conscience.

A plethora of protest movements arose, such as the Moro National Liberation Front (MNLF), the new Communist Party of the Philippines (CPP) with its armed wing the New People's Army (NPA), the Cordillera Peoples Democratic Front (CPDF), and the Cordillera Peoples Liberation Army (CPLA). With all these in place, and by adding his own cunning, Marcos succeeded in creating the right atmosphere for declaring martial law that, after an initial positive reception by sections of the Church, the business community, the Americans, and a considerable segment of the citizenship, soon degenerated into abusive military-backed dictatorship and crony capitalism. In order to keep the citizenry happy, the regime initiated certain giant showcase projects that miscarried: a land reform program; a Miss Universe contest and other festivals, while it was sly enough to co-opt a broad range of intellectuals.[57]

Veneracion then raises the question whether Marcos should be explained by his hunger for power and riches, or whether he is a reflection of deeply-rooted Filipino ideals and values? The author opines that Marcos' ambitions and original Filipino values were in harmony; besides, the quest for quick solutions to grave political and economic problems was attractive. In a society rife with clannishness, Marcos brought to life again the tradition of the datu-sakop relationship, known in government and business as the patron-client bond, in which connections and recommendations are more important than individual competence. This system gave rise to new social contradictions because, while some got rich, all those unconnected suffered, while the callousness of government made most people lose hope. This situation prepared the way for Marcos' fall through People Power, and brought the citizens out in protest ever since the murder of Ninoy Aquino.

The succeeding pages have been written by a participant in the events rather than by a detached historian; they describe the happenings of February 1986. We are reminded of the role of the mass media and the fact that People's Power (*sic*) also emerged in certain places in the provinces. To explain why the "people power revolution" happened, the author details the points of view of Enrile, the Church, the Americans, Manglapus, *The Manila Times* (Amando Doronila), and the Marcos loyalists. No attempt is made at integration or synthesis. Instead, the narrative jumps to the coup d'état of November 1986, the description of which is called "conjunctural analysis."

This jargon seems to stand for the necessity of exhaustive information gathering because all elements are related to each other. Anyway, Enrile is the bad guy whose drive for self-preservation prevented him from executing meaningful projects that would benefit the masa. The cabinet reshuffle resulted in the dismissal of the patriotic ministers. The ideology of people power weakened; it became totally irrelevant with the Mendiola massacre of 22 January 1987. Said ideology was concerned with human rights, national reconciliation, respect and sincerity. In its stead, military means began to take care of "order" again, separating the president from her moral responsibility to the people, and so from the possibility of achieving the unity of the Filipinos.[58]

In conclusion, Marcos may be seen as reviving the tradition of a long presidency that was begun by Quezon. In having a democracy without a party, Marcos himself became the party. It is not just his stealing that makes his contribution to Philippine history mean; after all, all politicians are dishonest and corrupt. Marcos' great disservice was that he dismantled the state, the belief in the rule of law and equality. The state became violent and arbitrary.

After his overthrow, however, it was not the revolutionary forces, but a "rainbow coalition" that succeeded. In the final analysis, the military and the Church profited. There was no prestige any longer in having opposed Marcos.[59]

Lamentations bring the book to its conclusion. There is the danger of coups d'état. These differ from the revolutionary change of government that also aims at remaking the state, which nowadays means to bring down the ruling classes in order to be replaced by a state of proletarians and farmers. Coups d'état, though, are executed by a faction in the military in alliance with certain interest groups among the elite. This is illustrated by Marcos' "New Society" that substituted the old oligarchy for the president's "cronies"; in 1986 we witness similar happenings, but this time in reverse. All the time the military gained in political weight. Needless to say that representative institutions and respect for constitutionality weakened. The extraordinary way the Aquino government came to power expanded the role of the military while their plotting remained largely unpunished. The government appeared to be hostage to them.

Other problems are the long-standing revolutionary insurrection and the government's "total war policy" that gives rise to armed vigilantes and militarization of the countryside. Naturally, this pulls the violation of human rights in its wake. Such political problems relate to economic ones. The deepest root of the ongoing rebellion is in the economy. If there would be social equality, if the poor were not oppressed, if greed did not reign, there would be no revolutionary movement.

The gap between the haves and the have-nots is blatantly visible, and the oppressed classes are forever cheated. This is readily apparent from the steady rise in prices that is part of the capitalist system. The deepest cause for this is the government's need for money which increases taxes, furthers public borrowing, and stimulates the printing of money. The regular reason for insurrection is located in agricultural conditions that the government has tried to remedy by way of, very expensive, land reform programs. Then, almost half the government's budget goes to servicing foreign debt, at the same time that the economy is largely controlled by foreigners; besides, good dollars are spent to import luxury items that do not agree with the needs of the masa. Moreover, foreign "aid" and cheap imports stand in the way of national production. Added are the American bases, their negative influence on Filipino morals, and the nuclear arms question; the destruction of the natural environment; disrespect for constitution and law; the establishment of paramilitary forces (CAFGU); the expanded role of the military, and its excessive influence in government. In conclusion, the promise of democratic space, created by the "EDSA Revolution" has not been fulfilled; the role of civil society has been severely restricted again; civil rights are under threat; apparently, such rights, and freedom, need to be fought for.[60]

The summary conclusion claims that a few of the roots of current problems have been discussed; at present they are aggravated by indifference and inaction. History flows on, though, and all take their part in forming the people into a national community. Filipinos originate from a great race that challenged the seas, resisted nature, and remained its own through 400 years of colonialism. The long history of our race, beginning 250,000 years ago, and up to the ethnolinguistic groups that compose our nation, constitutes the foremost basis of our becoming Filipino. Culture and history: these two concepts are the origin of the identity of our Filipino becoming. This culture and this history, in their complex totality, is the blood that must flow on to our succeeding generations.[61]

Image

From the excerpt of *Agos,* we may safely conclude that Veneracion faithfully follows the main principles of the "we among ourselves" school of history. The school holds that programmatic, purposive history can be written. Because of this, it has the gall to boldly rush into the present where the narrative, much like the school texts, gets bogged down in the complexities and problems of the here and now. The "revolutionary forces" could not yet overcome the ruling class; the "proletarians and farmers" could not yet unite their patriotism with nationalism; the national community in which all are equal is not yet shaping the state. Military might and armed confrontation still reduce civic rights to rubble. All this is rooted in the capitalist economy in which the haves oppress the have-nots, and in which "democracy" does not lead to their emancipation. The fight is not over yet.

The problems and complexities of the present are recognizable enough, and so is the appalling position of the poor. It is also clear that the latter do not move history. No wonder their "patriotism" is "listless." They have other things to trouble themselves about–survival for one. Perhaps they have always been miserable and exploited. This, at least, is another principle the author defends. From the earliest days of social differentiation, the rich and powerful profit from the underclass. Give people power, such as revolutionary generals, wartime guerrillas, collaborators and former scholarship students, and they turn corrupt and self-serving. This is law in Philippine society. Marcos exemplifies it. Hunger for power and riches is normal; these are shared through patronage–which is a tradition as old as datu-ship.

The author does not claim that the "EDSA Revolution" was an affair of the masa; and we may doubt whether it moved history at all. An exploitative elite made its comeback; breathing space for the common man was illusory; social divisions continued to be in place like ever before. So, what happened to the drive for national community? Well, according to the final conclusion, concepts, such as culture and history, will take care of this. I like these metaphysics. Veneracion has not only been explicit about the part "structure" plays, but in his historiography concepts, too, play the parts of driving forces. "Nation," masa, "ideology," "belonging to group," "colonial empire," "community," and quite a few others, become actors on his stage of history. I think it is a service to demonstrate how changing economic circumstance results in new social configurations; but when concepts and vulgar Marxism become blinders, nobody will see the wood for the trees. As a result, all, especially the teachers for whom the book has been written, will err.

The image of the present–the author is right in his depiction–is bewildering. For a book that pretends to be history, such confusion cannot be the problem. It is the task of the historian to clarify the past, and it is indeed a risky venture to come too close to the present; it is foolhardy to predict the future. Nevertheless, all of us would like to know how the present is conditioned by the past.

With his observations on leadership, the author may have hit the mark. Patronage may be the principle of social organization that is perennial, from the old days up to the present. This principle is naturally at odds with class organization, democracy and equality; it is vertical, per se. Thus, this bares one of the basic contradictions of the text. The author wants to analyze according to classes, yet cannot dismiss the persistence of patron-client relationships. The way he has depicted the ensuing relationships is also full of contradictions. Datu and principalia become good and bad guys all at once. In the idyll of prehispanic society, leaders were benign. Yet, they were also superiors, and thus exploited others. Under the Spaniards they remained popular, at the same time that they were given a bad name by the people. Sometimes, I think, Veneracion writes as it suits him.

The prehispanic past sees the early development of class-divided society.

Even so, people avoided conflict, and made it a laughing matter. Religiously, though, life was not so nice. People had to live with a fear-inspiring spirit world, and could be at war with their neighbors, too. The coming of the Spaniards, therefore, was not so bad. They freed the Indios from the demons, and from their servitude to the former ruling class of datu. By concentrating the people in townships, they made civilization possible. They taught a religion of hope. They unified the country, and finally, because of their discrimination and abuses, they stimulated the sense of nation, which the Americans subsequently undid.

Whatever the accuracy of the information, I appreciate a certain evenhandedness in Veneracion's narrative. The principles and dogmas he subscribes to are repeatedly mentioned, but do not dominate the analysis. He does not go out of his way to substantiate the we-had-a-civilization-of-our-own view. He is amazingly positive about the Spanish "civilizing mission."

He strikes a good balance in relating the American period. Yet, his perspective of the Filipinos being on their way to fulfill history through reaching national community prevents him from tracing clear lines through the immediate say, twentieth-century past, and make him bend over backwards to make us believe in the essential unity of history and experience that ties the one-nationhood of Igorots, Lumads, Indios and Moros. All are supposed to be in the same "fish trap." It was pleasurable to be slave-raided by the Moros. American anthropology made the people doubt their nationhood. Such weird statements apparently result from the daft dogma of confining Philippine history to inter-archipelagic connections, and from being blind to anthropology, apart from improbabilities such as "cord and veil" and "forgiveness." Next to patronage and authoritarianism, this is about all we get to know about cultural continuity.

The masa shares the unifying experience of being oppressed. The masa moves history. The masa will make the nation. So, how to explain the complexities and differentiation brought about by modernity? While I appreciate his few and possibly apposite points about the institutional Church, Veneracion does not elaborate the subject of divisions and dividedness, other than the idealized elite-mass opposition. Yet, in his treatment of early independence, he mentions such players as the government, collaborators, corrupt politicians, the Church, wartime guerrillas, the masa, the Huks and the Americans, later joined by students, the military, and business. Can all these be classified as either elite or masa?

This ingenuous opposition takes the view off substantial cultural and structural developments in Philippine society. Very visible epiphenomena, like the thriving Iglesia ni Cristo, cry out for explanation. What are the effects of massive education? Where do the current middle classes hail from? The development of early and current middle classes is one of the most spectacular phenomena of modern times, the Philippines possibly coursing ahead in their evolution if compared with other countries of the Southeast-Asian region.

One would like to know much about who these people were and are, what kind of ideas they articulated and currently carry, whether they absorbed the Chinese population, or whether the latter should be classed by itself. Also, how do these new people affect political culture, social thought, and gender ideology? These middle classes stand in need of serious historical treatment if we are to understand the present and its connections with the past.

Many essential things are omitted, and there is more to tell about modern history than the military's growing visibility or foreign economic influence. The cleavages within the ruling class–the author most often speaks of ruling classes–are only alluded to, yet are extraordinarily important to understanding the course of modern history. So, probably, is migration–as a perspective and a practice. There is, indeed, a pressing need for systematic school texts explaining the complexity of the present, not through summing up social problems, but through the open-minded analysis of the dynamics, whether economic, social, political, or cultural, that shape and move the social process. That, at least, is the promise of the social-scientific method the author professes to embrace.

In conclusion, by attempting to structure an image based on two opposing classes, the author forces the issues so much that a picture arises that is distorted to a degree as to be difficult to recognize. In this picture, the economy and twentieth-century politics are the prime movers of history. Important as these may be, they cannot demonstrate the inexorable thrust of Philippine becoming, "The Flow of Brown Blood," from Palawan cave man to national community. This is so because this thrust is not characteristic of the present, in spite of the activities of various liberation fronts.

Twentieth-century history, also in the Philippines, is not so much characterized by class struggle as by the advance of technology and communication, by migration and urbanization, by education and the rise of middle groups; it is moving away from relative self-containment to globalization. This movement is "resisted" by people seeking for identity in morally particularistic bonds, such as those offered by religious, sectarian and civic associations, gender, ethnicity, patronage, and the family, while a minority is well up in cosmopolitanism. I fear the sambayanan, the national community is not in sight, and few are the people who want to imagine it; world history has passed that station.

By myopically focusing on the territory of the Republic, and so isolating it from its Southeast-Asian and global environments, by using an extremely narrow-minded framework in which contradiction and oppression are the key words, by paying scant or no attention to the actual systemic forces and the cultural heritage, by refusing to use anthropological data and insights, the book fails to realize its promise of a systematic accounting that prepares the reader to mentally grasp what is going on. On the contrary, history appears to break up in assorted problems that are presented in journalistic fashion, devoid of line or synthesis. Consequently, the programmatically promised relating of the present to the past while revealing the emergence of new conditions, begins to shake with the onset of the American period and breaks down during the era of independence.

The resulting picture is blurred, is an image of confusion that is integrated neither by social science theory nor by ideology. Even the chosen historical perspective does not lend it cohesion. So what? Early on, the author clearly stated that the most important quality of the view from within is to write in Filipino. With that claim I have no disputation.

6
Society in Fiction

NORMALLY, THE IMAGERY authors evoke of life in contemporary society provides a stark contrast with the ways the national community is depicted in school texts. This is not so amazing. School teaching tends to have a high ideological content, and depicts ideal circumstances: life as it should be, at least, as far as it is imagined and proposed by the dispensation in power.

In a dictatorship, such as Indonesia, social studies have been entirely structured along the ideological lines the population is supposed to go by. This image is contradicted by the writings of independent authors. While the social-critical trend among Indonesian writers has, so far, not well-developed, in Thailand there is, at least since the war, a very lively tradition of fictitious critical scrutiny of society and its institutions.

In the case of the Philippines, we have noted that school textbooks tend to idealize much less; that there is an absence of national doctrine; that the interpretation of history since independence is indeed very ambiguous; that school texts are informed by an ill-reflected sort of realism. Because of these peculiarities, Filipino authors, although providing contrast and juicy details, are more in line with general perceptions of and information about life in the wider society, if compared with their Indonesian and Thai counterparts. In other words, the writings produced in the Philippines reaffirm the images that are constructed at school and in the newspaper. Naturally, their authors have more freedom and scope to do so, but generally confirm "what everybody knows."

As observed, the social-critical tradition amounts to more than it does in Indonesia, but lags far behind what Thai authors have produced over the past five decades. Moreover, many writers do not seem to be drawn to the present, but are fascinated by critical junctures in Philippine history. Often novels are set in the time of the revolution, or even deeper down into the past.

The sixties, then up to the declaration of martial law, keeps many a pen moving. The late eighties, basically the post-Marcos crisis, has been highlighted, too. Yet, apart from the numerous writings of F. Sionil Jose, few novels address general conditions and, up to this date, I have not found anything that squarely addresses life, and its sundry problems, in the 1990s. Be this as it may, let us now first review the few titles I thought relevant because of their social information.

Bulaklak ng Maynila[1]

The novel offers a view from the ivory tower of the "Diliman Republic." The author, Domingo Landicho, is a professor of creative writing and literature at the University of the Philippines, where he also accomplished his Ph.D. degree in Pilipinolohiya. His novel is set in one of the poorer quarters of downtown Manila, that is the Magdaragat Slum of Tondo. There, and on the sidewalks of Quiapo, most of the action takes place. It is not ill-written, the narrative is conceptually weak, freighted with improbabilities and, worse, inaccuracies; besides, it is somewhat boring because of the endless repetition of overused metaphors and hackneyed phrases. Happily, however, I am not a literary critic, and what we are interested in are the author's basic conceptualizations of life in Manila's underbelly, on which he opens with a chapter on the "Iron Entrails" of city life.

There is no shortage of works dealing with the lives of the poor. Landicho's book is just one of the latest exponents of this genre. Among his precursors, we find well-known authors, such as Adrian Cristobal Cruz (*Ang Tondo Man May Langit Din,* late 1950s); Edgardo Reyes (*Sa Mga Kuko ng Liwanag,* 1960s);

Ricardo Lee (*Si Tatang at mga Himala ng Ating Panahon,* 1970s); Jun Cruz Reyes (*Utos ng Hari at Iba Pang Kuwento,* 1970s). While some of these authors treat their subject more convincingly, it is Landicho's merit to bring us up to date, in the sense that he may reflect the touch of optimism that was largely absent from the earlier trend of social realism. True, Cruz's novel is colored by good hopes, too, and opened a window on life in the slums; then, however, in the 1960s and 1970s, perceptions changed. Life in the underbelly became harder, as it were. E. Reyes' novel is about extreme exploitation, degradation and perversion.

Lee does not even situate many of his episodes in the confines of slum life: many of his stories are about street children, preyed upon by, and preying on, child molesters. J.C. Reyes, too, situates his underdogs in the hard realities of city life at a time that these were aggravated by the rule of martial law. Whereas the said authors placed their characters in social context, situationing has become much less clear in Landicho's narrative.

The focus of *Bulaklak ng Maynila* is with individuals and their motivations, even though certain personages may readily be understood to stand for certain social conditions. The story centers on Ada, the flower of Manila. When we first meet her, she exits from the slum to greet her parents on her way to school. They are Roque and Azun, who have just installed their sidewalk merchandise.

They are quarreling; it seems to be Roque's habit to come home drunk every night, and with no money left to pay their debt to Timo who grows fat on financing the street vendors. In the eyes of the latter, Timo is a good man; he helps them survive. So do the police; by selling their protection, they cooperate with the vendors in making a living. Sometimes, the police even pose as vendors when they "sell" jasmine garlands to the jeepney drivers. It is an elegant way to collect their *tong*.

Elegant are the ways of Timo, too. When he makes his round, Azun has to beg his lenience. Timo advises that she drops by his house on her way home. When his suggestion is seemingly ignored, he stresses, "I shall be waiting for you." Later, in the evening, somebody knocks at Azun's door. Ada is already asleep. Timo forces himself on Azun. "I love you," he says, "Don't worry about your debt." Azun protests, her defenses are weak, however; soon, she is excited; happiness flows through her veins. She gives herself freely to Timo. Then another rap at the door is heard. Then it is the turn of the drunken husband to force himself on her. She fantasizes about Timo.

When Ada tends her mother's sidewalk stand, she is harassed by a group of teenagers who pose as buyers. It finally leads to a fight in which Ed, a cigarette vendor, takes her side. When the group feels threatened by other vendors and spectators, they make off. By that time Azun has arrived to teach Ada a lesson:

> "The customer is always right"
>
> "But they offended me"
>
> "Such is life on the sidewalk. We are poor. We have to live off it. Let's appreciate that. Together with the suffering it brings."
>
> "Why must we always be made to feel inferior?"
>
> "Hold it!"

Later on, Ed drops by to console Ada. He touches her. "I love you." Late into the night, she feels a smarting pain. Her mother will explain that she is a woman now.

At school, Cris waits for Ada. He has a crush on her. As a mute, he considers himself an upcoming artist. He lives with an aunt, and has some spending money. He also wants to get to know the family of the poor girl. Azun, too, has two men in her life. Somehow, Roque, more drunk than ever, heard the gossip about Timo's clandestine adventure. It becomes a noisy and threatening scene. Armed with a kitchen knife, Roque challenges Timo. When finally taken home, he avows:

> I am a bad husband, yet, what do I get in return? So, when I pass the sidewalk, all of them are glancing at me. That one? Haha . . . I also love you. Such is life. But I tell you, it won't be long like this. Imagine, those children, those protégés of mine whom I employ as beggars, they have a nice income, and from my share of it . . . we'll rise. So is it. The poor depend on the poor. That's what I always say. Be patient, but then, what happens? It's ridiculous. It's very irritating.

Explaining herself to Ada, Azun maintains that people often do, and have to do, things that they do not like themselves. Often people are mere victims of circumstances. "I always tried to be a good wife to your father." Before she knew him, she–coming to the city from the Visayas–had been lured into prostitution; her marriage brought her to the more self-respecting life of a sidewalk vendor. Be that as it may, the relatively affluent and influential Timo, on whom much of the neighborhood depends, is serious about his desire to possess Azun. The point is that Roque stands in his way.

At several places, the author inserts "observations" about "the residue of society," the beggars of Quiapo. These observations revolve around Angelita, a blind girl who lives with an old beggar woman. The strong point of Angelita is her voice; she can sing beautifully. This not only attracts money, it also attracted publicity. People interested in beggars reported about the two as the "Madonna and child" among the poorest, and for a while this contributed to their livelihood. Those, however, who made the scoop and wrote the story are the true winners. When you are really at the bottom of the pile, there is little to hope for but alms. Even so, they live complete lives; they are born, live and die on the sidewalks. Still, they have their modest hopes. They even sing.

After school, Cris is waiting for Ada. Although she is expected to go home, Cris succeeds in taking her for a ride. At a certain moment, they are in a park. There, far from the noise and stench of town, they start petting and necking. Cris maintains he loves her. He has money, too. In a cab, he takes her to his aunt's well-furnished place. The aunt is not very interested in meeting Ada. She is at the point of disappearing into her daily night life. Her estimate of Ada is, "She still has milk at her mouth. Mind you, Cris, she is green indeed." Even so, before Ada is in a taxi again and on her way home, she had got to know what it is to make love–delightfully exciting, then leading to inexplicable loneliness.

A change in the district's administration, or new owners, can make a difference in the rules, and the rumor of such events causes a stir among those who occupy the sidewalks. The newly powerful always seem to start on clearing the streets, demolishing shanties, and thus to regularize and "beautify" the environment. Soon such measures boil down to payoffs to the police; but there are limits to what can be creamed off from the poor. After all, the sidewalk is their livelihood, the shanty is their home. Even so, they always need to be alert to sudden clean up campaigns when the police raids their stalls and goods. This goes for the beggars, too. They can be rounded up just like that, and thrown into jail.

The vendors' only resort is Timo. They are fully aware that he lives off them, yet they need him even more than he needs them, and thus they must grant him the liberties he takes, such as with Azun. Now, with the change of guard in the district, they need him very much, because Timo is the lifeline connecting them to local and urban politics; besides, the politicians concerned are very conscious of the voting power of the slum dwellers. In this way, everybody depends on everybody else.

The police has the law to maintain, the others have the bribes to relax it. The politicians have the power to regulate, yet need the votes to stay in power. Laws and regulations aplenty–these are there to serve individual purposes, not the common welfare. Yet, those on the low-end of the pile are often hit hardest. It often seems as if their humanity is denied. They have no choice but to go with the flow of fate.

Roque remains keenly aware that he has been duped. He remains suspicious, peevish, and is very piqued whenever Timo is mentioned. Moreover, his situation did not improve when the police rounded up the beggars and watch-your-car boys upon whom he depends. He needs money. One night, he sneaks out of the house. The next day he is among those accused of breaking into the house of and killing a Chinese. In spite of the police being almost immediately at the scene of the crime, Roque escaped, but at night, when he dropped by to see Azun, he is arrested. At that time, too, the police seemed to know his whereabouts.

It boils down to a plot hatched by Timo. Two of his protégés talked Roque into joining them in the burglary. The police had been forewarned. Because he stabbed the owner of the house, Roque may expect a life sentence. At the same time, Azun is deeply indebted to Timo, and harassed by his runners. Even the house where she and Ada live is claimed back. In spite of her knowing that it was Timo who got her husband behind bars, she has been left with no choice but to move in at Timo's. Then the man forces himself on her again. But he is an experienced lover. He does it nicely. He is not drunk like Roque. She likes it. Does it matter? No, we are merely driftwood, pushed on by the stream of life; we have no choice. Seemingly, life goes nowhere.

Does this mean that people have no honor in life? That there is no dignity? The author wants us to think there is. Although Azun mentions said words, it is Ada who has been destined to give them shape. While Azun floats inexorably into Timo's net, Ada decides to go it on her own, to seek her own keep. The first person she turns to is Ed. He lives in a poor hovel, and is burdened by the task to see to a Christian burial of his aunt. On her way back, she meets with a butterfly of the night who dances in a club. Since Ada is beautiful, she is invited to join the show. It is a success. With the money so earned, she helps Ed defray the cost of the burial. Then she is picked up by Timo's assistants, and brought "home" to where Azun has taken the place of lady of the house. Sneers Timo: "Honor . . . dignity! You hardly know what you're talking about. A while ago, I saw your daughter, dancing almost naked in front of people. And now you want to talk about honor? You are just talking wind."

Well, if honor, dignity, loyalty, and suchlike, are unaffordable luxuries to Azun, these remain Ada's preoccupations. Living at Timo's is like living in a golden cage. Yet, Azun has taken to it, she identifies with her new affluence and power; she begins to look down on former friends and associates. Thus, when it is clear that Ada still sees her cigarette-vending friend Ed, she is read a lecture by Azun, "We are on our way up. Everything changes. Such is the law of life. I want you to have a future."

To win Ada over, Timo promises to make her Queen Helena of the *Santacruzan* festival. This elates and confuses her. Anyway, it brings Cris back into the picture; he will be the Queen's consort and, as an upcoming actor, Timo pays him well for the job. At the lavish reception following the procession, Timo becomes increasingly drunk and boastful. When the party is over, Ada still meets Ed. Then her mother comes down to persuade her to come in and sleep. In the sitting room, Timo has fallen asleep. When he wakes up, he rapes Ada. (The author still finds it necessary to write, "She could not feel the least of pleasure at Timo's indulgence.")

The next day, she runs away. With little money to buy food, she is easily persuaded by a Chinese shopkeeper to enter his keep, and do the washing. At night, he tries to rape her. "He is like an animal in heat. He regularly forces himself on me. I hope I'll be pregnant. Then I'll be his missus." The older servant's words do not console her. She makes off into the night. Back to the sidewalk to sleep. Back to the club. To dancing.

In this way, she meets Ed again. She settles down with him. In their poverty, she is happy. Even when confronted by Timo, she sticks to her new life. Instead of dancing, she now does the dishes at the club. Still, Timo looms large. One day, Ed is killed in an "accident." She continues to live in his hovel. She defends her honor and dignity, "even if it is in quicksand." This is illustrated by Cris; he did not make it, and slides back into despair. Basically, this is also where Azun has arrived. Timo's infatuation with her has faded away. She, however, has no way to go, "I buried my memories. I merely live today. If I allow for the past, I'll be destroyed. Clear your head. Banish your thoughts, throw them out like stinking garbage. We're mere victims." Yet Ada does not accept this type of reasoning.

In the last 70 pages, the author wants to construct a whole world again. Timo turns against Azun; he wants Ada. This leaves Azun totally dazed. She is consoled by Mang Tomas, the old sidewalk shoe repairman. He calls himself her father. He takes her to his hut. (Mang Tomas has four adult children, living in different parts of the country; his two sons are an accountant and a civil engineer, respectively). Slum demolition–the dwellers are too scattered to oppose–brings Ada into Mang Tomas' hut too.

When Timo comes there to rape her, he is stabbed to death by Azun. This shocks her out of her daze. Her cause is being hailed by feminists. She's acquitted. Angelita, the blind beggar girl, wins a song contest; is invited to sing at other occasions. Ada receives money from Ed's uncle. Cris turns to God. Azun and Ada visit Roque in jail. Angelita is promised an eye operation. Mother and daughter go back to their original house. In the end, all is well.

Image

It is not that the book is not full of improbabilities, but if we just concentrate on the first 250 pages when all sorts of miracles do not yet happen, we find, in spite of some ideological messages to the contrary, lives in which the main motivation seems to be to follow fate and personal inclinations, and in which everybody seems to be taking advantage of everybody else. The poor live off the poor; the police lives off the poor; the shrewd exploit the poor; everybody uses the little power he has to his own advantage.

The book is ostensibly about honor and dignity. Ada, Manila's flower, is the exemplar. "The novel is about the dehumanization in which Ada grows up, yet the path taken does not get bogged down in the quicksand of pessimism, but leads to the victory of the human spirit that holds on to dignity, love and hope" (back cover). To do this, Ada the schoolgirl needs to be abused, first by a young adult "boyfriend," then by her "uncle," then by a Chinese–but she will wash dishes instead of dance, suffer poverty and injustice, and inspire love and hope in others.

To do so, the author needs anti-heroes and villains, Timo, the vendors' patron, is familiar to many Filipino novels. He is the one wielding power and influence; people depend on him. That he grows fat on their sweat does not matter; the one you depend on, is good. But he is only good as long as nobody is in his path. When contravened, he becomes dangerous. He is used to getting it his way. If he has set eyes on Azun, he will get her. If Roque is an obstacle, it will be cleared. If he wants to show his might, he does so. His tentacles spread everywhere. He degrades Azun in every respect, disposing of her husband, taking her in, being served by her.

The only thing Azun knows to do is to forget about honor, about the past, about herself, and to be comfortable in her newfound position. When

Timo lays his violent hands on Ada, Azun is shocked back to "honor." Killing him gets her into the headlines; she becomes a feminist cause; her acquittal is also an acquittal of her past: she loves Roque again, in spite of his permanent drunkenness, irresponsibility, and pimping of the poor.

Of course, the author is right. There is honor among the poor. They have their rays of hope, their dreams, their loves. After all, they are human too. We need these things in life. It is what keeps churches in business. Yet, in spite of his wonderful ending, the obstacles and odds on the way to the good life are almost insurmountable. Escaping is there for a few; for most, being poor and downtrodden is the life of everyday. The only way up is to sell yourself to the devil, to a patron–with destructive consequences. In practice, honor may lay deeply hidden in the self; it is not a common commodity where the law of the jungle–the author repeatedly assures us that the city is a jungle–prevails.

Shifting Sands[2]

This novel about love and idealism does not really address the life and working of Filipino society, yet needs to elaborate a little on the circumstances in which loves and idealism can thrive. As far as love goes, these are of a personal nature, and have much to do with private experience. Idealism, though, is evoked by social challenges. These can be found in prevailing poverty, injustice, landlordism, the use and abuse of power, the callousness of patrons, and suchlike. All these, and the perceptions surrounding them, are often mentioned in public discourse, and it may be useful to see how they are presented as the backdrop of *Shifting Sands.*

Most of the story is set on Isla Blanca, a white-beached tropical paradise on which we find a small community of fishermen. The island had been appropriated by the Spanish grandfather of the present owner, Mr. Villarama. He is the principal provincial tycoon, monopolizing all sorts of business. Politicians depend on his favors, and the votes he can muster because of all the people dependent on him. This, in turn, enhances his opportunities. The pursuit of these opportunities is his life, more than anything else.

The people of Isla Blanca, like so many more throughout the province, recognize Mr. Villarama as their patron. Half their catch goes to him. He reciprocates by sending supplies to their parties, and a particularly joyful occasion is the yearly celebration of his birthday. Unofficially, he supports the volunteer doctor working on the island. He even had a costly waterpipe built at the latter's instigation. Yet, on a certain day–similar to umpteen other occasions–he shows his true colors; the island is to be developed into a world-class tourist resort. This, he argues, will be to the good of the population.

The residents do not agree. To them, the island is holy ground. Villarama silences the main protester, not by killing him, as it has been feared, but by "buying" him. When the advance construction party arrives, fishermen's huts are cut down without mercy. In the melee, a youth is even hit by the bullet fired by a security guard. Villarama always gets his way. It is no use opposing.

The tycoon's influence runs so deep as to touch the underground. Naturally, he opposes his daughter's choice of her husband-to-be. This suitor, like other idealists, is a product of U.P., of a privileged background, but making the honest choice to side with the poor, and to change the structure of Philippine society. He is an active member of the (underground) liberation forces. As such, his comrades do not take his marriage to Miss Villarama for granted. Neither does her father. Suspicions against the future groom–such as being a deep-penetration agent (DPA)–are kindled, thanks to Villarama's intercession with the armed forces and their real DPAs. This is similar to what happened and happens a thousand times over; the revolution eats its own children. Tanya's fiancé is butchered by his very fellows.

Mr. Villarama is the exemplar of power, pure and simple. Power gets its way, it bulldozes, is persuasive, bribes, smiles, is absolutely amoral, and ruthless. As a result, respect for power seems to come "naturally." Lovers and idealists oppose–to no avail. Power, at least as far as the male goes, is sex. The chain of women, conquered, bought, and subdued in Mr. Villarama's way seems endless. Yet, did it bring happiness? The author comes back at him (he is close to 70 then) by having his wife run away, by leaving him with the shambles of "family life." Will he finish his days as a lonesome, unhappy man? I doubt it.

Image

The only clear social picture we get from this novel is the one about power, how it originates–in land-grabbing, or in befriending the "right" people, be they friend or foe–and how it maintains itself and expands in relation to politics and politicians. Loyalty and morality do not belong to its qualities; ruthlessness does. This image of an outer world, possibly encompassing an inner one of love and idealism, is pervasive and surfaces in many writings, not only fictional, but in the press as well. It incites idealism, and powerless rage.

Migration Literature

Beginning in American times, Filipinos have been moving in numbers across the globe in search of greener pasture. Early on, many went to those parts of the United States where their manpower could most readily be deployed: to Hawaii's plantations and Alaska's fish canneries. Some of them wrote about their expatriate existence, about being caught in between homesickness and dollars: Carlos Bulosan (*America is in the Heart,* 1946) and Bienvenido N. Santos (*You Lovely People,* 1955) are prime examples. Others focused on the loss of identity of returnees, their feelings of alienation when confronted with "home." This problematic surfaces in Juan C. Laya's work (*His Native Soil,* 1940) and in one of the novels by N.V.M. Gonzales (*The Bamboo Dancers,* 1959). Anyway, the flood of Filipinos on their way to the American dream is relentless. Many of them are highly educated. Many among them write. In the group of currently States-based Filipino writers, we find Linda Ty-Casper, Ninotschka Rosca, Paulino Lim, and Epifanio San Juan, Jr.

Sometimes, such authors write directly about the experience of life in the Philippines. Often they touch on the subject of exile, of being in strange lands, of the desire to be back, of the difficulty of being back. To many, after having broken away, homelessness and separation become a way of being. Ties with dear others become tarnished, unraveled, unreal. Distance becomes the theme, its hazards the subject.

Meanwhile the flood of people leaving the country has reached fabulous proportions. In a way, life at home has become surrounded by the global village, a wide stretch of "public" land that does not seem to clearly belong to anybody; where Filipinos are being abandoned and where they are on their own. Their anchoring point is the far-off homeland; their experience is one of exile. It seems as if everybody has relatives, friends and acquaintances in the position of being a migrant, a temporary or a permanent overseas Filipino worker (OFW). This has thus become a shared point of view, a common way of seeing the world. No wonder, then, that this has become part of the indigenous literary tradition, and a topic of scholarly research.

The America-inspired literature demonstrates considerable continuity. It is of Filipinos who may venture back from time to time, but who are really States-based. The later waves of migration aimed at temporary work, in the Middle East, in Hong Kong, Singapore, Malaysia, Japan, or on foreign, often Norwegian merchantmen.

Women constitute a very large segment of the migrants. They work as nurses in Canada, entertainers in Japan, mail-order brides in Australia and Germany, domestics in Hong Kong and the Middle East, factory labor in Taiwan; and many of them had to add the injury of being abused to the insult of their deprivation and loneliness. As it may be expected, this has given rise to regular reporting and discussions in the newspapers about the miserable conditions of work; about rapes and suicides; about the killing of cruel employers, and the subsequent trials and executions; about the powerlessness, or the unwillingness, of Philippine foreign representations to interfere for the sake of their nationals; about the insatiable greed of the agencies living of the export of labor. These themes resurface in the literature on women in exile, such as the stories in *Mga Hibla ng Pangarap* ("Strands of Hope"),[3] about which it has been said:

> Government calls them heroes for their contribution to keeping the country alive with their dollar remittances. And indeed they are. But they are so in ways that have nothing to do with our common conception of heroes as knights in shining armor out to rescue damsels in distress. They *are* the damsels in distress. No, not even damsels, though they are truly in distress, as this collection of often bitter, always moving, stories shows. The sign in a Hong Kong elevator banning dogs and Filipino women from its premises is the least of their worries. They have quite enough to do just being *seen*. Are they really heroes, or martyrs to the cause?[4]

An important problem surfacing in many of the stories is the fact of being morally abandoned by the people they work for. Those staying behind find new lovers; some husband-fathers rape their daughters; some live leisurely off the remittances; others turn extremely jealous. Wives remaining behind get into comparable problems. Children have to do with half- or broken-homes. Misunderstandings flourish. Secrets are kept. Bad news is revealed. Emotions are stirred; love turns into treason; trust becomes suspicion. People reach out for and miss each other, and so it is in another work of Irah B. Borinaga.

Distant Echoes: A Modern-day Novella[5]

Her main character is Carmina Morales who left the Philippines for the States some ten years earlier. Then she also left her children, ranging from approximately ten to eighteen years old. Her marriage to Luis was no longer viable, and for the sake of extending her stay in Chicago, she married a gay American. This enabled her to pay for the family house in Manila and the higher education of her children. The book opens when Carmina is on her way "home."

The narrative and the plots relate the distances that have grown between her and the children; the lies that need to be told to keep illusions in place; the secrets kept in order not to cause worries and anxieties. The children are living their own lives, and the mother feels guilty in regard to them. The children convey that she does not need to, that all is well, that they appreciate her economic efforts. These children are not of one kind, though. While they know each other, they also have their private ideas and experiences that are not supposed to be revealed to the others. But Carmina is on the receiving end all the time.

Naturally, there is much pleasure in being "reunited," and even in meeting with her "former" husband, and eventually, his new partner. Such occurrences evoke endearing memories and short-spun feelings of togetherness yet, in the end, people appear to have grown far apart, the pleasure of each other's company being short-lived, or rather, superficial. Motherly advice and ideas do not connect any longer with the adult lives of the children. They have their own experiences, reach their own conclusions, find–and must find–their own ways, often through trial and error, through tears and comfort.

There is no longer a place for a "motherly" mother. Everybody's die has been cast; Carmina has become homeless. She returns to Chicago. Her actor-"husband" went to New York, and is in no hurry to join her. Meeting her friend Cielo, who married, or rather, picked up a much younger Filipino husband (with a family of his own in Manila), they get soaked together. Cielo's relationship is breaking up; Carmina is just back from facing hers: "I'm a fool. A real hundred-percent fool." Cielo shook her head bitterly. "I am, too. We both are. But life must go on," Carmina declared. "Right?" "Yes, of course!"

The Yawning Gap[6]

A contemporaneous picture of the quest for justice in the countryside is given by Crescenciano Gonzaga in the *The Yawning Gap*. The main protagonist is confronted by his father: "You are going to fight the mayor? He has not been defeated yet in any of the cases he has brought before the court. Are you not aware, my son, that money talks and that power begets power?"

With these words the worldly wise father-tenant admonishes his son Mario, who has taken it upon himself to defend Gorio, one of the mayor's dependents who has been accused of stealing and slaughtering a carabao. During their interview in jail, Gorio explained his case to his defense counsel, the young and bright Mario Polistico. Seven years earlier, the mayor had convinced Gorio to develop a six-hectare plot of land, and to turn it into a coconut plantation. When the trees would yield, Gorio would be recompensed through the grant of full ownership to one half of that cultivated land. When he came for his share, the mayor started to procrastinate, then accused him of stealing one of his carabaos.

It is abundantly clear that Gorio could never have done this, and that the mayor is looking for a way to be able to dismiss the just claim of his tenant. Yet, mayors are not used to losing cases in court. To complicate matters, Mario also happens to be engaged to Elisa, the mayor's daughter.

The case against Gorio is an obvious fabrication, blatantly illustrated by the very court proceedings when the case is tried. When judge, prosecutor, and accuser team up, the verdict becomes a certainty no common sense can defeat. Thus, Mario's NPA friend Tano has to stick to his vow–this type of justice will seal the mayor's fate. During the victory party at his house, the mayor is indeed shot, and of course, Mario's establishment enemies conspire to get him behind bars because of it. It is Tano who rescues Mario from jail; he is being given a teaching chore at the NPA camp.

Conversations between the two old school friends clarify the undesirable condition of Philippine society where a few–the rich, the corrupt, the powerful–command the lives of the poor who are systematically oppressed, exploited, denied justice, or what have you. Political power appears to be the key to the good life. It naturally combines with selfishness. The two friends have no trouble in agreeing to this much.

How to fight and change the system is the bone of contention. Tano believes in armed confrontation. Mario espouses the sense of justice and the power of good example, schooling, development, and democracy. This course can only succeed if leaders shed all personal and selfish interests. In other words, what is needed most is change in individual attitudes and values.

Mario's ideas, religion, sacrifice, true love, the honesty of Pres. Corazon Aquino, justice, a few shining examples in the higher echelons of the civil service, and an awakened conscience of the nation are obviously what the author sets on. These are even made to penetrate Tano's mind, and thus, after some severe setbacks in the field of battle, he decides to surrender with his remaining men. They are ambushed by another NPA unit; more blood flows. Will the Philippines ever reach peace? Will justice ever prevail? Or is it opportunistic politicians and their money that will keep the country in their stranglehold? Are love and idealism really powerless?

Fiesta People[7]

Although recently written by Josefina Protacio, the story has been set in 1971, at the time of the Plaza Miranda bombing. Just the same, I found it extremely recognizable, reflective of Manila today as much as of the Manila then. Granted, no light rail yet, Rizal Avenue still attractive in its big-city ways. Then, as now, the traffic jam remains familiar, and it made me think of my up-to-then worst experience of gridlock, in 1969, in Manila. Then as now, high-rise buildings were going up; the churches of Quiapo and Baclaran were attracting those in need of blessing; people were enjoying, and preying upon, each other. However this may be, such details are, by themselves, insubstantial. The book's timelessness has little to do with its temporary setting that, anyway, does not play much of a role. Its relevance has everything to do with some perennial themes of Filipino life; with family, with politics, and with youthful disgust–call it idealism–of these two core institutions.

The story opens on a scene at the US embassy. Filipinos queue and scramble to get ahead of everybody. These days, everyone seems to wish to leave; off to Saudi, to Germany, Hong Kong, off to greener pastures. Away from what the author describes as the "shitty, stinking system"[8] where power and money have their way and where the dastardly poor can merely demonstrate–to no avail. Even so, Danny Singson sticks around; getting out is not the cure. He will show them his principles. Eight years in college–three courses, finally finishing in Arts–should get him a job, but as his father, a small-town physician in Mindanao, observes:

> You don't want to find work; you want work to find you. You're looking more and more like Juan Tamad, waiting for the fruit to fall. But believe me, Danny, there is no fruit to wait for anymore. Everybody's out there, plucking the tree clean.[9]

Juan was lazy, but he was smart. Vice and virtue are but two sides of the same coin: this was the moral Filipinos had been raised on. If you can cut corners, why take the long route? If you can get an influential friend to lend your son a job, why make him join the line to the smug bureaucrat's desk?[10]

Is Danny beyond those with influence? Not at all. His uncle is Senator Singson, his father's younger brother. Yet, Danny wants to go it alone, pawning his belongings until becoming so poor, he has to beg for the coin to buy him a jeepney ride. He is a rebel without a cause. He wants to get his parents off his back. He disdains his friends who use their connections. He does not want to play the system. What he positively wants, however, remains unclear.

Danny is contrasted with his law-college friend Benjie, who had to drop out when his father was killed upon winning a lawsuit against a governor. This started Benjie in life. Selling his father's estate–the bone of contention–with that very official, he got a price ten-times better than was originally offered to his dad: "I could have asked for more–after all, I've got him by the balls–he did not quite expect my father to have a law student for a son." With the money, he established himself in the antique business. By courting the 35-year-old daughter of an upstart tycoon, who had three kids from two previous affairs, his business was capitalized to capacity. Benjie invites his old friend, "Danny, drop by if you care!"

Native business acumen, that is, playing the system, is regularly contrasted with the sly and patient ways of the Chinese. Such as old Sia Peng who, besides crucial shops, "also co-owned with a Japanese a lumber concession, and the talk was, together these two aliens bribed local inspectors to pass good logs off as bad logs before shipping them to Kobe, cheating two governments with the transaction."[11]

Danny's dealings with the Chinese are concerned with his confrontations with the pawnshop owners, who treat him condescendingly in spite of his being well-dressed. Later, he told Danny accusingly: "You must be rich." But the look on his face said, "So, why pawn things if you're this rich? And why travel to Japan? Rich people don't go to Japan, they go to America or Europe, New York, London, Paris, Rome."[12]

The Filipina wife of the pawnbroker, though: "knew perhaps she had to tread on tiptoe when dealing with compatriots. The wrong tone or facial expression could very well bring about an awkward scene, a loss of face for every one. Too much *amor propio* being bandied around when her people could hardly afford it, was the expression Danny read on her face."[13]

The book is spiced with a thousand-and-one observations of Filipino life, especially in the big city, but also of relationships with relatives, with the powerful, and the powerless. The Chinese remain Chinese, in spite of Filipino citizenship; at school, pupils are made to memorize Lincoln's Gettysburg Address. Connections get you through Customs; obligations need to be repaid or are, at least, expected to be so; teachers pilfer school property; using English "puts one a class above the *bakya* crowd; blood ought to be thicker than water; abortions are a rather common occurrence; it is only idiots who do not use their connections; Chinese eateries have very dirty restrooms; water pressure is perennially problematic; everybody, certainly the professionals, wants to leave the country; the police routinely torture suspects in order to make them sign confessions; the city is festive and fecund of violence; you pay "car-watch" boys, if not . . .

> Really, this city isn't Chicago of the East for nothing. Shoot-outs, robbery, rapes, kidnapping. And small wonder, when movies, comic books, and television these days glorify nothing but sex and violence . . .
>
> Opinion columns, if not ranting about government corruption and red tape, are always pontificating on society's general malaise but as usual coming up with no cure. . . .
>
> On top of the social volcano, they quote the President often. But what do you see? Society editors hobnobbing with the rich, gloating over the beautiful people they meet at cocktails . . . What double standard. So bogus. So–well, so Catholic.[14]

The city is double standard, too. Ermita's honky-tonk pleasures are paired with its decay; the rules authorities impose are ignored by public and police alike; the church is not really beyond a little mumbo-jumbo; conversation, communication is drowned out by jeepney radios on full blast; policemen pick their teeth over their post-lunch San Miguel beer; small people are too proud to admit to their poverty. Danny's principles are never going to make a dent in the practical ways of others.

A sort of a divide seems to split society. There is the elite–self-seeking, going its own way–that stands apart from the others. They are Manila's Four Hundred. For them, the Cultural Center of the Philippines has been built. For them, foreign philharmonic orchestras are flown in. They keep the poor out, wall the slums off, and fence themselves in luxurious subdivisions where the grass is always green, whatever the season, whatever the drought. There, or at the fine hotels, they throw their parties, do their politicking, make their deals,

You reward someone for integrity, for honesty, for other basic Filipino values that, I know, this administration no longer appreciates.

You mean that there was no 'gentle persuasion' by you or your family whatsoever?

Absolutely no, Senator Singson looked at his wife, however strange that may seem to you.[23]

Then, the senator's wife hastens to explain: "Well, I thought that it was a hasty and nasty deduction. We are not a family of criminals. We are a God-loving, hardworking, and law-abiding family. Of course, we have enemies, *political* enemies who would jump at any opportunity to smear our name. Luckily, God has always been on the side of truth. Our side."[24]

Requiem for a Rebel Priest[25]

The America-based author, Paulino Lim, Jr., situates his story in the Aquino period. Since the focus of the book is on individual motivations impelled by time and circumstances, the image of society remains vague. The book primarily evokes an atmosphere, and the author is quite successful at that. The disillusionment that set in soon after the euphoria of People Power has been palpably described. Indeed, Marcos was out, but his legacy lived, and lives, on.

If the Left was initially welcomed back into the fold, the "fold's" condition seemed to be that it accepts its dictates. Soon democratic space contracted. The talks with the NDF/NPA were a hoax. Before the temporary armistice came to an end, the army was attacking again. The end of January 1987 saw the massacre of peasants at Mendiola Bridge. Land reform consisted of unreformed words only. Landowners ran arrogantly high. The so-called Freedom Constitution was riddled with loopholes. Corruption thrived. Abuse of power had simply been "decentralized" and delegated to whomsoever could grasp a piece of the pie.

The positions of government and NPA polarized like never before; between February 1987 and sometime in 1989, the communists reached their maximum strength, and lorded it over vast tracks of the countryside; they also posed a real threat to cronies and officials in the city. The military was restive. Six coups against the widow-president created more anxiety among many than could be aroused by the NPA; weren't the latter dubbed, "Nice People Around?"

In between the extremism from all sides, and the rapidly decaying infrastructure that presaged the near-terminal brownouts and water crisis of 1992-1993, there is no cause for wonder that Aquino's human rights record is worse than just appalling.

It is these things that set the background of the book, together with: the hunger in Negros (1985-1986); the civil war in Bicol (1987-1988); the renegade nuns and priests joining the guerrilla; the excesses of the rich and the venality of anybody in power; the squalor of Manila; the shameful behavior of Pinoys in America; the breakdown of law and order; the hesitant, then rightist-again position of the institutional church; the travesty, or hypocrisy, of faith; the polarization of society; "unjust social structures, corrupt bureaucracy, (and) capitalism"[26]; the inroads of foreign (U.S.) consumer culture; the nationalists' opposing of English and colonial miseducation; the sham of democracy in a country where most people are poor; the extremes of social injustice; the exploitation of Filipino labor abroad; the sphere of half-lies and pompous English; the rapacious private schools; the low educational standards; the demonstrations against American bases; the fear of the military; the depressingly dirty surroundings in town; the endless civil war; corruption in every nook and cranny of society.

Yet, all of these things, recognizable as they are, have not been integrated to result in a structured image of society. They merely hint at the atmosphere of the Aquino years, years that were colored by hopelessness, pessimism, and self-denigration; years in which self-mockery and faithful fatalism functioned as the best remedy:

> Here, we laugh at storms, earthquakes, corruption . . . a way to keep our sanity. We also pray, that keeps our faith.[27]
>
> If victims are left in its wake, the fatalistic Filipino mind sees this as the unraveling of God's will, as punishment and atonement for sins, like calamities of earthquake and tidal wave.[28]

Sin: A Novel[29]

Similar to F. Sionil Jose's *Mass* and *Ermita,* this novel is critical of the country's elite, their extravagance, perversions, arrogance, conceit, and boundless greed. This time, the author singles out the Spanish *mestizos:*

> Look at all the successful businesses and organizations in this country. They are all Spanish mestizo, or Chinese mestizo–not Indio.

> My father and my grandfather believed that the Indio is inferior, that his brain is not big enough for creativity or management. It is us, mestizos, with our mixed blood, who will bring this nation up from the dungheap.[30]

The lead character is CC, a man of unlimited means and an equally unlimited sex drive. In the ruthless pursuit of his aims, all possible honors have been bestowed upon him: he is Mr. Ambassador; sugar baron; nationalist entrepreneur; honorary Spanish citizen; bearer of "The Order of Lapu-lapu." He hobnobs with "The Leader," although he is not so close to him as his father was to President Quezon, or as his grandfather to Aguinaldo. This intimacy with power was the key to wealth; wealth that brought more wealth, and influence, and power.

An effective means of ingratiating presidents, politicians and high officials is catering to their libidinous needs. His father knew how to please President Quezon, then provided the Japanese top brass with beautiful mestizas, and was finally recognized by MacArthur as an outstanding guerrilla leader, in spite of having sought a cabinet post in the Second Republic's puppet government. These days, CC recruits female talent from around the globe and, after testing them, releases them as bait, as rewards, as incentives. Of course, he would not like to be called a procurer, much less a pimp but, as in all business, in all pursuit of power and gain, the end justifies the means.

What is the sin of the book's title? Is it in the most steady of CC's relationships, that is to his sister with whom he also sires a child? Or is it with the callous exercise of privilege to which lesser mortals have to submit? Or is it in the unbridled drive for power and wealth? Is it the machinations to subvert people's morality in order to make them follow his bidding? Perhaps the sinfulness is in arrogance, conceit, and being blind to the suffering of others. Maybe it is in the weaknesses and venality of others, who can be bought all the way, form ordinary journalists to the justices of the Supreme Court.

When new history writing casts a doubt on the origins of the family fortune, CC is emotional in refuting the claim that his grandfather misappropriated money that changed hands at Biak-na-Bato. Grandfather was an honorable revolutionary, and a democrat at that: "Whatever my grandfather did was for a larger cause and why should he be blamed if, in the process, he also profited?"[31] Anyway, he was farsighted enough to quickly learn the language of the Americans, the language of dominance, while "All those noisy Tagalistas, if they believe their nationalist cant, are doomed to be left by the roadside."[32]

The novel oozes with Spanish mestizos' disdain for nationalism, the

Tagalog language, native blood, and is outrightly insulting regarding the putative qualities of the Filipino. They are an improvident lazy lot, and imminently corruptible at that. It is the mestizos, whether Chinese or Spanish, who see and grasp the opportunities. War offers such chances. It teaches men how they can rise above the misfortunes of others.

The mestizo oligarchy is the most obvious reminder of the colonial past, and they mean business. The nationalist noises–they are mere irritants: "I often wonder if there were any Indio leaders in the Revolution at all."[33] As a group, they are protective of each other, and careful to marry among themselves in order not to sully their Spanish bloodline. They are the driving force behind Philippine politics and economy. Their loyalty is primarily to themselves; their native soil is a field of opportunity that thus needs some maintaining and investment, but culturally they are obviously overseas. As a result, their "nationalist" activities consist of collecting rare Philippine books, antiques, and Chinese porcelain; of building up Makati and Quezon City; of running shipping lines and investing in tourism. At best, such activities are set off against a complete contempt for the native population.

The novel's main character sums it up:

> If there is anything Indios cannot accept, it is the searing truth about them, their perfidious character, their ostentation and boastfulness. Who will believe their pronouncements, when everything is hot air, when no sooner have they proclaimed their virtue then they turn around and do the opposite? These Indios–they are stupid, and their country–thank God for exceptions like myself–is silly.[34]

Alibangbang[35]

The problem with short stories is that they allow for impressions of an atmosphere but, because of their brevity, cannot aspire to sketch life's and society's complexities. If I yet review a few of them, it is because the authors and their introducers hold these particular stories to reflect the mood of Filipino life in the later 1980s.

According to Efren R. Abueg's comments on Roland Tolentino's work, it is only the most recent writers who finally succeed in evoking the true shape and content of Filipino awareness. This consciousness was put soundly to sleep by the long period of colonialism and imperialism; now it stirs again. It is too early to say, though, however much this coming to life will stimulate the material and spiritual conditions of the Filipino public. After all, to incite the spirit that has not moved for 400 years is no minor endeavor.[36]

Tolentino and his generation are said to explore reality. They carefully dissect it, peeling off layer after layer of the mask behind which life in these times hides. They bring people and their motivations to life. Yet, often the environment in which their characters operate is fraught with violence, terror, intimidation, competition, and exploitation. Existence is a gloomy experience. It is cruel. People take advantage of each other. There is no way out. Debt simply accumulates. People express all this in their sadness, in their being without hope, in their loneliness, and in the religious frenzy of charismatic sects and the megalomania of the elect.

> The nice world is for a few only. The great majority lives in fear and darkness. For the courageous types, it is possible to flee from the world–when you will kill, or kill yourself, or turn crazy, or let yourself float on the stream of fate without purpose or direction. Nobody in your environment cares, neither do your fortunate fellows, nor God, that is why:[37]
>
> On the day Mother's husband died, the birds were humming. The dust scattered. The sun shone. The sky was clear. And God, and all the Saints were on their thrones in heaven.[38]

According to Abueg, Tolentino hits the nail mercilessly on its head. His is a severe attack on the political and social atmosphere of the times that stimulates the reader's self-awareness and sensitivity to social and national conditions. He definitely has a point if it is true that hopelessness and surrender to circumstances are as widespread as he thinks; if the forces that affect people's lives are as ruthless as depicted in the lengthy title story, "Alibangbang." It is set in the period that President Aquino unsheathed the sword of war against the communist rebels. This was a time of extreme militarization, human rights' abuses, and rape of nature.

In order to gain expressive power, the author resorts to a phantasmagoria in which social forces often are represented through mythological creatures. The NPAs are the *aswang* (harmful spirits) the *kapre* (malicious giants) want to eradicate. As the "booted ones," the latter unleash a reign of terror at the simple-minded population. These are a poor lot indeed. They wallow in ignorance and poverty. They are dirty and grotesque. How did Mang Asyo get his wife, Impong Sion? Their fathers were buddies, given to the cockfight and liquor. On a day they are drunk together, they bet on who of the two can pee highest:

> Impong Sion's father began; roaring with laughter, he gets his water up to Mang Asyo's father's throat. Mang Asyo's father merely smiled while he released his formidable cock–big like a gourd–reaching up to his breast. "Ta-ti, tati, tati, tatita, shuw," whistled Mang Asyo's father, while beginning to piss at Impong Sion's father's muddy feet, and then up, towards his balls and his navel, towards his chest and throat, into his mouth–which still causes surprise up to this day–until his eyes could merely blink because of the pain induced by the acrid fluid. Impong Sion's father did not have the twenty pesos.[39]

As a result, Impong Sion is brought over to Mang Asyo's place; ever since, she is abused. She is made to draw the cart as if she were a carabao; she's whipped like a riding animal. Her body is one of the places in which Mang Asyo releases himself. She is supposed to care and cook for him; to massage and console. When Mang Asyo finally perishes, she doubts whether she is able to go it alone.

Life among the suffering masses is heartless. Partly, they inflict this brutality upon themselves. Then they are victims of pretentious landowners who reward their labor disdainfully: Impong Sion is given Ma'am's old panties and bras. Most disturbing of all are the Booted Ones who terrorize them, rob them blind, exploit their labor, rape their daughters and who, in the end, just kill them.

These Booted Ones protect, in the name of saving and serving the land, the rule and realm of Gob who, in league with Gook, preys on the forest and natural resources. The land is being denuded; the trees are cut; the natives (tribals) are made slaves; the peasants are pillaged and despoiled. Even development is introduced. This entails experiments with upgrading bran and straw to serve as human food. And when Gob visits, he is moved to tears, and promises to take the suffering of the people to his heart.

It is not worthwhile to specify all the instances of dehumanization, frenzy, gullibility, degradation, terror; the vigilantes, civil surveillance, fanatical sects, and private armies. If there ever was, compassion has been lost. If there ever was, civilization has ceased to exist. Nature and cupidity, accidents and stupidity reign supreme. The author illustrates it through newspaper headlines: "Colonel Boots Ambushed"; "Donya Paz Sinking Kills 3500"; "Colonel Boots Honored by President"; "Typhoon Sisang Kills 320"; "Payapa Renamed Colonel Boots

City"; "2500 Aswang Surrender"; "Natives to Be Relocated"; "Human Rights Activists Are Aswang Too"; "Landowners Accused of Economic Sabotage"; "Illegal Strikers Disbanded"; "The President Shares Coke and Buns with Dimasalang Families ('I shall do everything within my power,' says a teary-eyed President)"; "National Maritime Safety Week Declared. Sponsored by Donya Paz II."

Still I am not sure about Abueg's introductory comments when he writes that Tolentino's work succeeds in evoking the true shape and content of Filipino consciousness. What we are confronted with is a society gone berserk, from which civility has ebbed away, where civilization has been abandoned, where nobody cares about anything but himself.

In the other stories, too, we meet with the merciless preying of family members on those who have some income; with drunkenness and murder; with religious megalomania and charismatic fanaticism; with loneliness and terror. Is that what is meant? Perhaps the author explains himself best through one of the mottoes to his collection:

> Constabulary Maj. Roberto 'Bobby' Ortega cleaned up Baguio City of muggers, drug pushers and other criminals . . . He would trail a holdupman–his favorite prey–observe while the criminal committed felony. Catching his quarry redhanded, Bobby would pounce his prey by shooting him on the spot. I once asked Bobby how many criminals he had killed this way. "One hundred fifty-five," came the quick reply. Then Bobby showed me an album of photos of criminals who became his victims . . . I asked him how he felt after killing a criminal. "Like I had an orgasm," Bobby said.[40]

Pitada[41]

As a book, Tolentino's and Eli Guieb's collections of short stories belong together. They have been published back-to-back in one volume. Their stories deal with the same period. Expectedly, though, they report on it in a different manner. Tolentino's is more society-focused, painting the atmosphere of a social context eroded by unreason. Guieb concentrates more on individuals, their feelings and motivations. Of course, these are social products, as much as the author's imagination is–and Guieb, in his introduction, is the first to assert so.

The general introduction to Guieb's work has been written by Jun Cruz Reyes. According to this author, society is in a permanent crisis. Why? Because of change. Everything keeps changing–and since the process appears to be speeding up, the certainties of the past fade at an ever accelerating pace. This throws individuals back upon themselves or–as it occurs several times in the stories–into collectives that function as old-fashioned families, or communities, in their attempt to dominate the individual members.

As it happens in Guieb's narratives, persons need to free themselves from compelling relationships, at the same time that they need these bonds in order to achieve their emancipation. Live-in partners need to be complemented by extra-live-in lovers, because everybody is special, and nobody can serve all individual needs. Parents divorce. Children run away, join university, then The Movement. They need this activism to learn to see social conditions, then to act on these. But if they strive for self-realization, they need to divorce themselves from the movement, too. Even the bonds between brothers and sisters are questioned; these, too, are not a matter-of-course, and frequently it is even desirable to cut them. Sometimes it is necessary to cut the line to life itself.

It is clear that alienation and separation, dissatisfaction and vague hopes, meaninglessness and uncertain emancipation–after all, we remain tied to time and circumstances–are the staple of rumination. These individual experiences are seen as reflecting "the times," "a period of doubt." How to realize self-confidence in the stream of happenings, and yet, is there anything else an individual can rely upon? This seems to be Guieb's message; it has been illustrated by individuals and personal relationships. As a result, however much it has been claimed that these are products of time and conditions, these conditions themselves have been taken for granted, and thus the social image remains vague.

The collection does what may be expected of short stories: they paint an atmosphere. They illustrate the mood of a society where bonds are disintegrating, where relationships cannot be taken for granted any longer, where individuals have to fight their lone battles. In brief, the human condition in a vague Philippine setting.

Image

The image of the public world, of general society, the authors evoke is, to me, shocking. They seem to have compressed in single volumes what can be read in a newspaper in a year. Besides, said authors are absolutely open about the excesses characteristic, in their view, of life in the wider Philippine setting. We have noticed that even the schoolbooks demonstrate a good deal of realism, and that existence in the country is seemingly surrounded by appalling, dehumanizing conditions.

The question is, whether they are exaggerating. Are their accounts experience-near? Are they recognizable, or mere products of morbid imagination? Sometimes the general reporting about Philippine society strikes one as pathological; things must, apparently, be portrayed in a negative manner. Such befits the prevailing picture of politics, but is politics the same as life in the islands? Or is the social volcano about to explode?

There is no denying that there is a lot of violence all around and, with it, a lot of anxiety, but I also observe many people living peacefully and going about their affairs in a routine, in a normal fashion.

The thing that, perhaps, best transpires is the chronic state of anarchy in which life labors in the country. It is an irregularity that is expected and with which many people seem to feel at home. Of course, it is not nice to be preyed upon by military and police; it is objectionable when an open-air *karaoke* opens right in front of one's house; it is unfair to have to bribe a politician to land a job as a teacher; it stinks when all cars belch smoke; it is ridiculous when public projects are projected as political beneficence, thanks to Congressman Kuwan, but such is life. It is the flourishing of *jueteng* in a jueteng-free environment; it is the elderly, oh-so-friendly immigration official asking for a fee to super-express process the fast-lane service; it is the taxi without meter; the vendor without change. It is, perhaps most of all, the absence of civil responsibility in an wider, anonymous society where everybody minds his own business, and his own only.

Life beyond the private sphere is perceived by most as unsafe and predatory. Has this always been so? In the school texts we noticed that the American period is pictured as the exception: then there was regularity. Now it is anarchy; things do not stick together any longer. Meanwhile, this decay also seems to affect interpersonal relationships which–widespread myth, or consensus, has it–were reliable. The family was the fortress of Filipino life, from which one made forays into more general social space, in which one could maintain oneself through networks of relationships.

A very interesting point shared by most authors, although not all of them address this problem, is not only that they give a negative evaluation of relationships in the public, in the political and businesslike world, but that they question the validity of bonds in the inner circle. It seems that the fortress of the family has also been affected. Guieb and Tolentino were very explicit to this point. Sionil Jose's relationships are self-serving to the extreme. In *Fiesta People,* family is reduced to politics, and ingratiating bonds are business, pure and simple. Contrary to the author's wish, this is what transpires in Landicho's novel, too: all right, there are people of integrity, there are people capable of giving love, but the normal thing to do–the expectation–is to seek the personal advantage. The migrant literature is bitter about this.

There is more to say about the perception of society that colors the narratives we briefly reviewed. I was basically struck by the persistent negativism, by the conclusion that Philippine society is missing a moral basis, that it is, at best, a market where bargaining positions are informed by relative power and, of course, money. In such an amoral environment, irregularity is deeply ensconced; it has become the norm, and because of it, people can live with it. That does not make their judgment, and even self-perceptions, friendly, though, as we shall see in the following Excursion.

Excursion Three

"This Godforsaken Country"

Throughout December 1993 and January 1994, I set myself the task of collecting the "we"-statements I found in the editorial and opinion pages of the *Manila Standard, Philippine Daily Inquirer,* and *The Philippine Star*; I also read the weekly *Philippines Free Press.* These "we"-statements do not project a rounded self-image. Most of them say something about the perceived state of affairs in the outer public world that people experience as beyond their grasp and with which they identify to a limited degree only; identification is, however, indicated by the use of "we," "our," "us," "this nation," "the Filipino," and so forth. During the period of collecting data, the economy had begun to show signs of recovery, and a moderate sense of optimism pervaded. In spite of this, the inexorable self-bashing continued, juxtaposed with moralistic advice about how to do better.

Generally, the perception of the national character, or the Filipino in the public world, is negative, and so is the perception of the public world itself: The Editorials comment: "Our society has really gone to the dogs," or "What do we Filipinos have today? You answer that question and you cry." These compete with the following lamentations of other columnists and editorial writers:

- "This God-forsaken country";
- "This vice-ridden land";
- "This chaotic republic";
- "The country's unending crisis";
- "Our floundering ship of state";
- "As a nation of underdogs, we . . .";

- "This country is truly one of the most murderous in the world"; and,
- "Our culture of violence/corruption/political idiocy," etc . . .

Of course, not everybody wants to see it this way, yet the comment of a letter-writer about newspaper columnists; "having . . . the unnatural wish to see us all fail" is very rare indeed.

To explain the dominant perception, or "The present crisis in our national life," the authors either blame it on the way society and state are governed, or on the negative values and traits that, if changed to their positive counterparts (say, corruption *versus* honesty) would augur the good life, bringing order and prosperity. Let's concentrate on the political aspects first. Positively stated, "It is our singular blessing that being such a disorganized people, we have no method in our madness; so we are still quite a distance from self-destruction."

This observation concurs with the comment about a very confused situation: "They are running this place like our country is being run by its government." Why is this so?:

- "Our politicians try to tear the country apart";
- "Our lousy system of justice";
- "It is a good thing that Justice is blind. In the Philippines she wouldn't like to see what's really going on";
- "A government that stakes our lives to the dictates of foreign creditors";
- "Our businessmen bribe";
- "Corruption has seeped to the top of our law enforcement system";
- "Years of corruption and a tunnel vision has kept our economy in an infant state";
- "Here, in this lousy, graft-ridden, incompetently governed country";
- "The country's image as lawless, anti-American, anti-business";
- "The eminent corruptibility of our officialdom";
- "We have a crisis in leadership";
- "Our beloved president, who does best when he does nothing";
- "What we've got is a nation over whom nobody presides";
- "Our insensitive leaders . . ."; and finally,
- "Can we trust our officials to keep our heritage intact? Of course not."

It seems that the negative perception of politics and government has a deeper cause, namely that the people are failing in their democratic duties:

- "We're in a bad fix . . . but in theory, at least, we are not helpless. In a so-called democracy like ours, the ultimate power rests in us–the people."

- "The Filipinos have developed a somewhat confused concept of this thing called democracy . . . most Filipinos believe that when you have freedom of speech and of the press, freedom of worship and periodic elections, the requirements of democracy are substantially complied with."
- "Our problem is that we regard politics and government as a spectator sport. We simply cheer and condemn, while the politicians and officials provide the entertainment";
- "What we have is a fiesta democracy";
- "Do we have democracy? What we have is skull and bones dressed up to look like Glorietta";
- "We . . . spending money on fraudulent elections and referendums, outright stealing and expensive junkets";
- "We Filipinos have never had the knack for organization";
- "Our professed ideology is that we need to be free in order to prosper."

This last comment very much leads to giving free rein to "The Filipinos' undisciplined nature," and "The Filipino daredevil attitude." From all this logically follows:

- "This God-forsaken country's near-terminal case of poverty, population boom, environmental decay, agricultural and business failures, and vanishing social values";
- "In our country where justice is selective and where law-enforcers are involved in crimes."

A generalized, but sweeping, picture is painted–"Most Filipinos cater to mediocrity and sensationalism and succumb to their baser instincts." This balances with, "We seem unable to attain class," and "We aren't taken seriously by foreign investors," also because of "Our national notoriety for being always dependent on foreign aid." Yes, "As a nation of underdogs," "We are outclassed" by "others, who take their politics and religion seriously, and who have a certain degree of commitment beyond our nature to make," while "we unknowingly show a 'poverty' consciousness by our excusing, blaming, begging."

Looking at this picture from the lighter side is Raffy Recto. He "slams those critics who keep describing the Philippines as the 'sickman of Asia.'" On the contrary, he says, "we have developed a land vehicle which has six wheels and flies . . . A garbage truck without a canvas cover." Or, "The Philippines will rise . . . but we will rise into becoming Asia's biggest Smokey

Mountain (a notorious garbage dump). A Mt. Everest of discarded speeches and minimum wage laws."

Are such "jokes" told "because we have become such hidebound cynics in self-defense against all the lies we know we're being told?" Probably, if the questioning of the Ramos slogan, "The Philippines can," is "jokingly" answered with "Garbage can."

Naturally, not everything is bad, and I also found a few positive statements, such as:

- "Our police authorities have shown competence";
- "We complacently conclude that certain of our officials do exercise a measure of vigilance";
- "After all, isn't it time we regained some trust in our country's judiciary?";
- "There is still hope for the Filipino (upon observing that not all public utility vehicle drivers are traffic rule violators)";
- "Filipinos are known to be intuitive problem-solvers";
- "We are all one and the same race of peaceful Filipinos"; and,
- "No one beats the Pinoy in adapting to anything. Try to stop him from coming up with his own version of any popular song."

More deeply insightful is the observation, "There is a part of our nature that draws us powerfully to examples of self-denial that may be beyond us; the part that finds nobility where weakness and solitariness have combined with courage." This agrees with, "Filipinos are great hero-worshippers." Then, in spite of "Our hospitality," often abused by foreigners, "a trip to Hong Kong, since 'Inveterate shoppers that we Filipinos are,' brings into contact with a place where 'Filipina' is the equivalent of maid . . . it does not mean that we have to perpetuate the lowly jobs. We have self-worth."

Moreover, "The Philippines has much to offer the global community; the world takes much inspiration from (there follow the names of artists thought to be at par with other internationally known names)," and so, Ruffa Gutierrez, "a Filipina (second runner-up in the Miss World contest), was proving once and for all, that we are not a country of domestics."

The opinion of foreigners, or the image of the country abroad, inspires many writers. "Many Filipinos abroad have given their countrymen a bad name," and many of them are supposedly domestics. Not everybody agrees; in protesting "The 'negative image' that domestic helpers, mail-order brides and entertainers are supposed to have given the Philippines abroad," the writer asserts that, "It is these incarnations of cartoon characters that we have for public officials . . . that give us a bad name abroad." This jibes with the observation that "When members of Congress show unabashed contempt for our President, to the point of insulting the office he holds, we should not be surprised if foreigners look down on him and the people he represents."

According to many, culture seems to be the culprit. "The Filipino is talented but wanting in many other virtues," which can be illustrated by "Our *walang paki* (do not involve yourself where you have no business), *maka-sarili* (care for yourself only) populace"; "Honesty, it seems, is lacking in the Filipino character"; "Filipinos are indeed stubborn . . . They only think of what feels good at the moment. They only think about the present . . . Their unconcern makes them even more stubborn"; "We do not have the right values" yet, "We are too frightened to change." So, is it that "The Filipino needs to be shaken out of his lethargy, his complacency, his smugness?" Max Soliven seems to agree: "Our problem is not to restructure or even 're-invent' our government. It is to reinvent our approach to life and politics. What I see all about me is disunity, name-calling, pomposity, selfishness, greed and overweening ambition. Truly, *kaya natin ito*. We can do it. But we won't progress until we overcome ourselves."

According to a columnist, it would be beautiful if we could, "Turn back the hands of time to those years when values ruled the roost in Philippine society," but alas, they do not seem to rule now because of "the weakness in our culture," and "the malaise of Philippine society." Ours is "a culture more concerned with how we look to Washington than to ourselves," "an impotent culture" where "our idea of originality is to follow the ways of a stranger" so making us "the mental colony that we are." "How advanced is the decay of our culture" from which "social values have vanished?" Even "Intelligence is undervalued in our society. The measure of smart is what you get away with"; and so, "Do we have a damaged culture? Yes, we have." "We're a country in which there is too much mischief and malice, and too little discipline and consideration for others."

The last quoted observation implies a remedy: there should be less of the first and more of the latter; people should look at themselves critically, and turn negative traits into positive ones. Easier said than done. In one column, the historian Agoncillo was quoted as having said that "Self-deception is the worst tragedy of the Filipino as a people." This agrees with other opinions, "Why is the plain truth so difficult to establish in this country? Is it because we Filipinos are such gulls to believe every rumor we hear?" and "The Filipino is afraid. We stay away from the religion issue. We are victimized because we soft-pedal, because we do not dare unsettle hurt feelings."

This type of beating around the bush was also shown by "The Filipino lawmakers, unaccustomed to tough and fearless talk from national leaders (Mahathir) on such sensitive issues (domination by and relations with western countries), who were stunned." Dodging the real questions and problems seems to be endemic, "Ah, we Filipinos! How easily are we duped!" which is corroborated by "many Filipinos believe or want to believe we are a land of miracles (EDSA 1986; Marian apparitions; faith healing)." Well, hope for miracles combined with "the deterioration of our moral values" may lead to "the Filipinos' propensity to put down each other" which may be the result of "the Filipino male's psyche of machismo and self-centeredness" from which naturally follows "our lack of unity as a people" and the "sense of community service that is also so rare in Filipinos today." Indifference to each other and recklessness created, "What folly this is that we have now made New Year's Eve too dangerous even to go to Mass." Apparently there is more than a problem of firecrackers in keeping the public world in order, "How can people respect our policemen when we have such misfits in the service?" It is almost as if wider society reflects "Our prisons (that) are run as vice dens."

7
Culture of the Public World

IN THE INTRODUCTION, we have noted that a fully fledged public world had come into existence in the last two decades of Spanish rule. By imposing a state, the colonizers created a countrywide public sphere, dominated by political, administrative and religious institutions. For their smooth operation, the latter needed to co-opt the native elite who became known as *principalia*. Heavily mixed with commercially inclined Christianized Chinese, and with some Spaniards, members of this elite proved to be astute entrepreneurs.

In conjunction with the economic activities of the colonial state, they created a modern, world market-oriented economy. In the second half of the nineteenth century, their highly educated offspring gave rise to a vocal civil society that formulated citizens' demands and nationalism. Principalia status, entrepreneurial background, education and civic demands fused in The Great Malayan, Rizal.

This situation of a colonial state, an agricultural economy, and a small elite persisted into the period of independence. The continuity of this arrangement is probably best symbolized by the hundred-peso bill issued in

1986. It depicts the transfer of sovereignty: a conspicuous American flag is lowered while the Philippine banner goes up. The message seems to be the American legitimization of the Republic and its ruling class. Henceforward this, binational and bicultural, elite will sail the ship of state, with Washington's blessing. The United States was sure to have left it in the right hands. President Roxas was MacArthur's hand-picked choice. To assure future favor, the constitution was amended, military bases were granted, and duly elected representatives were expelled from parliament.

Of all things, independence was not the fruition of nationalism. It was not a product of struggle. It was an agreement between the government of the United States and members of the Philippine elite. It did not inaugurate a period of nation-building. Apart from the resistance of the Huks, it did not lead to popular mobilization.

Nationalistic or organized masses do not tally with the interests of the ruling class. As a result, the continuity of colonial education was not seen as problematic. It had to wait until the 1960s before nationalistic demands were articulated and before popular mobilization–students, communists, Muslims, trade unions–occurred. Initially, and well into the 1970s–and for many to this date–Filipinos took pride in being the only Christian nation in Asia, in being the Asian "showcase of democracy," in being the third largest English-speaking nation, in being western, even globally oriented. They were relatively prosperous and well-educated; in Asia they held themselves to be superior. They shared in the great tradition of the West.

The official culture of the public world is western. It is constitutional, democratic, Roman Catholic. Its legal system is in English. So is the serious press. Public school is bilingual. Global fads and fancies are easily–often eagerly–adopted. The appearance of things is western indeed. Some of this is real, some of it is make-believe, some of it is mere veneer. The point of it is, of course, that it all is Filipino, and that we have to take in how people live with it, how they interpret and understand it themselves.

From the images we reviewed in this study, we noted the prevalence of a certain vagueness, of a certain confusion about life in the wider society. Somehow, public life does not seem to articulate well with the private sphere. In relation to the former, school texts even maintained that the country and its people lack identity as a nation. Often public life could best be described through the metaphor of the market. National community appeared to be indeed problematical, and even nationalistically-inclined textbook writers or U.P.

professors were unable to make us believe in the birth of a solitary nation any time soon. History did not connect with the present, and yesteryear's ideals turned stale in short time. Writers' devastating honesty was especially disarming.

As a reaction, certain people dig for roots. Others seem to invent them. School is supposed to remedy the deficit of nationhood. The national language must be developed and taught. Nationalists at U.P. founded the esoteric "we among ourselves" cult. Prophets of moral recovery teach righteous modern values, such as less family and more public spirit. The Church wants to clean society of traditional politicians and corruption, and of effective family planning. Is there a prospect that these brave causes will be fulfilled, and that we are headed for a different culture of the public world?

There are, certainly, many people who aspire to renewal. They hope to see an end to traditional politics. They would like to see people become serious about religion. They expect a nationalist revival. They want Filipinos to be proud of their country and citizenship.

Others are less idealistic and more practical. They work for the emancipation of the underdog. They agitate for equality–especially for justice. They deplore the fractiousness and fissures that divide the nation against itself. In brief, many voices can be heard, but the most impressive of these is the voice of the silent majority, the voice of indifference to all such issues.

Of course, the majority as well would like to see less crime, less violence, more law and more morality. But they do not think that things can change that easily. More importantly, they have, or rather are adjusted to the situation, and go about their own business. The "problem of nationhood" impresses them least of all, although they may feel disturbed with what many hold to be the country's reputation abroad.

I have argued that it is critical public opinion, and thus an active civil society, that brings the public world to life, that makes it modern, and that operates as the opponent of politics and state power. Most likely, such a civil society is generated by old and emerging middle classes, through education and urbanization. This is not to say that lower classes, and even the people in the countryside could not articulate demands on the political center. They do. But they press for survival, and a fair deal. At best, they will indirectly affect thinking about the public world.

The culture makers are, historically and in fact, members of the middle classes. They are teachers, journalists, artists, labor leaders, politicians, clerics, civic activists, ideologues, academics, authors, officials, business leaders, and even military men. They infuse their ideas into the cacophonic discourse carried on in the public world. They influence and create public opinion.

At times that discourse is lively, controversial and idealistic. In the time running up to the revolution against Spain and, via dissident theater, well into the American occupation, public opinion was vigorous. Then the debate dies off; what remains, in spite of some socialist discussion in the margin, focuses on power and personalistic politics. Cultural, national and historical issues are relegated to the wings. The nation becomes progress and future-oriented.

In the late 1950s, first nationalist, then progressive debate is revived. A new communist party is founded that soon mobilizes impressive muscle. Many priests and nuns radicalize. Grassroots propagation, stimulated by Marcos' blatant dictatorship, flourishes in spite of repression. Nationalists invent Philippinology. Ninoy Aquino is murdered. Agitation and restlessness intensify. Businessmen start demonstrating.

The middle classes mobilize at EDSA. A new constitution! Simultaneously, the firm repression of the Left, of the countryside, of labor, of human rights, resumes. The American bases still lead to nationalist protests. Then energy seems to have been spent. What remains is confusion, disappointment, the hangover after so many expectations. President Aquino did not quite make the grade. President Ramos' peptalk–We can do it!–Rizal Year, Centennial, and EDSA rhetoric failed to galvanize the nation. Survival is everybody's preoccupation. Idealism, high hopes have been replaced by indifference. Care for yourself. Money permitting, consume. Find the money in the Middle East, in Japan, anywhere overseas.

When people think about the public world, they think of politics, of politicians' popularity, of their entertainment value. Left, right, middle–do they matter? Traditional politics remains firmly in place. They also think of the economy, about money, prices, inflation, perennial low performance, unemployment, and labor migration–mostly to foreign shores. People are hardly taught, hardly learn to think about alternatives. There is little informed debate in the press; it highlights politics, *ad nauseum*. Even the schoolbooks propose a public world in which politics reign supreme. Through the ahistorical and anti-sociological treatment of the twentieth century, history and society silt up in a muddle, and no intellectual tools are handed down to develop systematic comprehension of the wider world. Often moralism substitutes for reason. To save the country, we need a moral revolution!

The historical consciousness of college students is next to nil. Their ability to analyze social events is not much greater. Their identification with the nation is weak. Quite a few of them are religiously active. Many worry about their job prospects. Most are confused. They vote, for an actor or another star, another popular person. Will he or she make things better? And how? Vagueness prevails; hopes are hazy. The focus of this generation, if any, is with work and career. They are driven, so to say, by the economy. Will they earn money? How to land a job? Study to prepare for just this. As a result, there is little space left for social discussion. The relevant thing is to make your way through a field seeded with competitors.

These characteristics of the present generation stand in stark contrast with the student idealism of the 1960s. Then, study still was a privilege. Nobody really worried about career prospects. Social, political, national and other questions were debated. Marcos' arrogance invited demonstrations. The world could still be made. Students' conscience and awareness were to make the difference. Leftist thought held a powerful appeal. Then things started changing. While martial law kept debate alive, albeit underground, the world moved on into an increasingly technocratic era.

The economy needed more skillful people. The educational establishment responded. From 272,000 students at the tertiary level in 1960-1961, the total moved up to 1,460,000 in 1990-1991. This extremely rapid rise went, expectedly, with a relative decline in standards, and strong demands on the job market. Now, nobody is amazed any longer by college graduates finishing up as domestics in Hong Kong. The real story, though, is that this quantum jump corresponds to a new culture of the public world. The vast masses trained at college are socially inattentive; besides, they were produced in a period of beginning and maturing mass culture, of consumerism and television. They grew up with comics rather than with books.

The loud-stark protests of the progressive fringe carry hardly any political weight, and whether they are understood by the vast majority of the new people who make up the educated middle classes is a moot point. The jump from almost 300,000 to 1,500,000 indicates the vast number of people who are rapidly upwardly mobile, at least in terms of education. They do not connect to an older tradition of critical study. They, together with all the other migrants to the cities, have left something behind that is not awfully relevant to their new situation and, having arrived where they are, they need to create sense in life. They are in need of new culture.

They do not need to worry; in this era, the problem of creating meaning has been taken out of their hands. Mass culture is being made for them, in shopping mall and through television, by Colonel Sanders and Jollibee, through pop songs and fashions, advertising and lifestyle magazines, international sports and violent video. Their world is being made by the economy in which they have been assigned the part of consumers.

It is money that drives the public world. Business, commerce, work, survival, corruption, rent-seeking, profiteering, shopping, the good life, wages and prices, impel affairs in the wider society. Instead of public opinion, advertising fills it. Problems are problems of the economy. In the same public world, politics is both business and spectacle where popularity seekers become presidents. Politics is hardly a matter of partisanship; it is a conversation piece and, importantly, a source of patronage. As a result, patronage-seeking is logical political behavior at all levels. Politics is less about good governance, and more about benefits. Politics, therefore, is operating as any other business. It is deals and counter-deals; it is a market.

Altogether, this provides a weak basis for the flourishing of civil society. Most educated people have very little feel for history, for questions of continuity and identity. What school contributes to this is, as we have seen, on target: history leads to confusion, and the great national happenings are safely on the other side of the watershed event of the American invasion. Then the new colonial masters established order, progress and regularity that go lost during independence. Then, too, the past lost its relevance for the present.

Thus, apart from leaving a historical void, school contributes little to positive cultural construction. Of course, it provides a nationwide curriculum all have to pass through, and this creates a certain cultural homogeneity, but compared to what one can witness in neighboring Indonesia and Thailand, there is almost no propagation of a national doctrine or pointed nationalism. On the contrary, the nation is reduced to a legal framework, and society to politicking. Interestingly, it is with the political game that people most identify.

What Filipino politicking has been able to achieve is to maintain social hierarchy. It still is a few powerful families firmly on top who provide scant guidance for the population at large. On this point, I have little to disagree with the U.P. nationalists. Elite and masses live in two separated worlds. They are two nations in one state. Between these two, however, rather vast middle classes have developed, of civil servants, of small and medium businesspeople, and of professionals. Most of their members appear to be content with their role of consumers. In the vast anonymous urban space they operate in, they exemplify the sociological idea of society as a place where everybody minds his own business, pursues her own interests. Society is a market. In the market, only money counts.

The Church and the churches upbraid this situation. Perhaps that their advice to vote for the right man, for a capable and impeccable candidate is an appeal to active citizenship. All the while, however, they preach morality; and morality individualizes. If all individuals are virtuous and law-abiding, society must be in good shape. In other words, those who preach ethical solutions for social ills, preach an anti-sociology which refuses to consider social hierarchies and other structural impediments to justice and equality. This has not always been so. During Marcos' days, and still well into the Aquino dispensation, vociferous, social-activist priests and nuns, including some bishops, addressed the questions inequality raises. Inequality leads to injustice, and thus to sin. If anything, the Church is opposed to sin, and should fight it. As a result, it is morally justified to reprove the rich and advance the emancipation of the poor. Now the heyday of this liberation-theological movement has passed. The members of society struggle on.

All the same, the Church is a player in the public debate. The interlocutors are not just exponents of state and politics, of the economy, and an underdeveloped civil society. At times, institutionalized Roman Catholicism is quite visible, and Cardinal Sin's opinions feature regularly in the news.

I do not know what the power of the pulpit really means–religion is very much a quest for personal blessings–but among important segments of the middle classes, appeals for moral reform have a pervasive influence. The locus of reform, as has been observed, is individuals, or their families. These appeals share with the righteousness that emanates from other sects and churches. All of these flourish, and are obvious enough, but their attractiveness and admonitions address the private sphere of life. They are publicly visible–such as the mass–but the target of the enterprise is private: blessing, power, salvation.

Of course, churches can be political and economic players; then, however, they operate like any other participant. The curious role they have in the public debate is their emphasizing the private sphere. This takes the sight off the public world proper. In church and school, that public world becomes the province of immorality. People should be good; society is in a mess. Well, perhaps, it is just messy.

The government belongs there to see to a minimum of regularity, but since it is intimately connected with politics, we cannot expect it to be a neutral player for the benefit of the common good. In this set of perceptions, then, people will take pride in the morality, regularity and cohesiveness of their family life. In other words, the real or suspected crisis of family life is the worst menace to the Filipino social imagination. It is also the problem of the churches.

The family is supposed to be the bedrock of Philippine society. According to the constitution:

> Article II, Section 12. The State recognizes the sanctity of family life and shall protect and strengthen the family as a basic autonomous social institution. It shall equally protect the life of the mother and the life of the unborn from conception. The natural and primary right and duty of parents in the rearing of the youth for civic efficiency and the development of moral character shall receive the support of the Government.
>
> Article XV, Section 1. The State recognizes the Filipino family as the foundation of the nation. Accordingly, it shall strengthen its solidarity and actively promote its total development.

To this, Hector S. de Leon still wants to add:

> The unique value of an institution of this kind to political society is so immediately evident that one of the first duties of the State should be to protect and strengthen family life . . .
>
> There is much truth in the observation that the numerous social and economic problems that confront us today, including that of graft and corruption, can trace their roots in the weakening of the family as a basic social institution. In the final analysis, the good of society is best achieved through the good of its nucleus–the family. If this vital cell of society is fragmented or decadent, so is the country.[1]

My experience in the Philippines seems to confirm that this opinion is widely shared among Filipinos. To them, the family is their hold in life. As might be expected, they know, and experience, the discrepancy between ideology and practice, yet hope to live up to the norm where wider society appears to be indifferent and anonymous.

The wider society, the public world equates with politics and business. People need it, have to deal with it, yet hope to be able to withdraw into the emotional security of their private spheres. The predominant image of the public world may, therefore, be well reinforced by the contrast it affords with the idealized family. The contrasting images somehow confirm each other, and deflect from positive action in the society that is, after all, no better than a market. This results in a kind of cultural shortsightedness that confines the relevant world to family, relatives, patrons and community.

It is the *barangay* of old kept alive into the present. Its surrounding territory was the realm of nature, a place to hunt, to make forays into, an undomesticated area stretching among the own, and other communities and clans. As an everybody's and nobody's land it was a shared and a hostile realm all the same. It was not a place to commit oneself to, to take responsibility for. It was there to use, to profit from, at the same time that in it one was at risk.

When a state was forced upon the scattered populations, it was a colonial one. This means that it was low in legitimacy in the eyes of the subject people. If one could get away with it, there was nothing morally wrong in taking advantage from it, or to avoid its impositions. The public sphere, so to say, was something to defend oneself against. In essence, this did not change when the Americans took over. To profit from the state, or to sabotage it, even became an act of patriotism during the Japanese occupation.

A little later, a neocolonial elite became the legitimate heir to the colonizers. They saw the land somehow as their private property, to be exploited for their personal benefit. As a result it is hard to perceive the state as the caretaker of the common good or the public welfare. Whereas it undoubtedly does its best, the ideas of common good or public welfare have not developed beyond most rudimentary comprehension, and in the hands of a state run by traditional politicians who seek their own interests, the state, like in colonial days, offers little to identify with or to participate in. The public world, in other words, does not inspire commitment.

If there is some devotion, it is not to state or nation-state. If there is, it is directed to the land in general, to the *Heimat*, the place of birth and home. It is devotion to the motherland, to *Inang Bayan*, to Mother Land. This attachment is both vague and more particularistic. It is like the bond with family and relatives. It is the privatization of the nation that poses Heimat in contrast to the public world of society at large.

It appears to be tough to be committed to the state, to be a proud citizen of the republic, and that not because of present performance, but because its tradition is so unconvincing. This, compounded with the confusing school images of the whole and its history; with *kadiri*–nauseating–politics; violence and crime in the press; injustice, arbitrariness and fate in fiction, give rise to indifference and cynicism. One is part of it all, but reluctant to identify with it. A regional or communal identification is more comfortable. The lack of opportunity the land offers fuels a steady stream of migrant labor and outright emigration. Of course, one remains Filipino at heart, the more so while abroad, but takes little pride in citizenship of the republic.

All this agrees with an outward orientation reminding of Rizal whose shop floor was the world. This orientation was strongly fostered during American times when we saw considerable labor migration abroad and to the frontier in Mindanao. During that time many thousands went for study to the United States–as they still do.

The global perspectives this opened are with us today. They form part of the fabric of Filipino culture that does not view the person as being confined to the nation-state. In a way, the Filipino public world spills over into a much wider arena in which millions of Filipinos meanwhile play their parts. As a result, interest in and attention for the own society and its public affairs remains–apart from politics–underdeveloped. It is viewed as being in a state of mild anarchy in which, nevertheless, people know how to find their way. They joke about it–which indicates that it is a serious matter about which they personally feel to be powerless.

However complex and contentious the processes that animate the culture of the public world in the Philippines, the overall image it evokes is that of a market, a place to bargain and to earn a living that is kept at a safe distance from private concerns. Of course, this is not really possible. State and economy penetrate ordinary lives. Yet, in the absence of a developed civic tradition of the public world–transparent politics, representative democracy, human rights –demands for justice, rule of law, or economic fairness remain weak and do not connect with obvious practice. This reinforces the private realm, the family as the moral bastion in the unruly world of wider society. This bifurcation between the moral and the market, between intimacy and "connections," between family and politics, weakens demands on the public sphere, and considerably reduces the part civil society can play.

In spite of a clamorous press, and any quantity of social-critical writings, there is little consistency in demands, while the personalistic style of politics contributes to the nebulous perception of the public world. Society becomes an agglomerate of individuals and families presided over by self-serving politics that inspire little personal identification. Citizens appear to be members of families most of all.

The question that remains is to evaluate the invidious image of the publ world of the Philippines by comparing it with other images and other states of affairs within Southeast Asia. In that region, it may be argued that an active civil society arose in the Philippines, as a result of economic development and western education, well before it emerged in Indonesia and Thailand. In the latter countries, civil society–the modern component of a fully fledged public world–came into existence, mainly through modern schooling, in the first decades of the twentieth century only. Be that as it may, efforts at nation-building and the formulation of a national doctrine have been much more vigorous and effective in these neighboring countries than ever in the Philippines. So, although there can be no doubt that politics is important anywhere, among the neighbors it is not the quasi-monolithic occupant of the public sphere that marginalizes the nationalist discourse. On the contrary, the nationalistic discussions there are rather lively.

This combines with an orientation that is far less outward-directed than in Philippine society. In comparison, the role of English in the educational systems of Thailand and Indonesia is negligible. External labor migration is recent and slight. The effective propagation of national doctrines and myths results in an inward focus. In school, history is made much of. The state is represented by strong centralized bureaucracies that are prestigious and highly visible. Yet, although all this puts its stamp on the respective cultures of the public worlds, it also suppresses an active civil society. In Indonesia, it was, until recently, practically nonexistent. In Thailand, it is only newly arising after the setbacks of the 1970s and 1991-1992.

These differences notwithstanding, the diverse cultures of the public world appear to have much in common at present. They are, as may be expected, urban-centered; derive their contents from local modern education and global ideational and material inputs; are generated by intelligentsia, media, and organized civil society ; are subject to the pushes and pulls of economy, politics and state. Especially since the time that economic development became the buzz word, the cultures of the public world began converging. There are older similarities, too. Whatever its economic basis, early civil society in the region originated from modern western education and incipient anti-imperialism. As a result, ideas about socialism, humanism, democracy and nationalism began to circulate. This led to questions on: "We *versus* the Other"; "western *versus* eastern"; "right *versus* injustice"; and the desired direction of national development. The intellectual outcome of the discussions has been written in the constitutions of the nations concerned. The high hopes so formulated have a distinct (western) idealistic flavor, reminding of the utopian socialism of the 1920s: people can make their environment; society can be constructed and improved.

The primacy of the economy changed all this. Of course, the constitutional ideas–often rewritten–remained in place, but generations emerged who were less exposed to idealism and more to practical experience and technocracy. They were produced in quantity as from the late 1960s. The people concerned are essentially new people who are highly (upwardly) mobile, mass educated–and who live in a world filled with consumer culture. They are less impressed by lofty ideas, including nationalism, than by career prospects. Their leaders talk less about humanism and egalitarianism, and more about the "Asian values" of hierarchy, harmony, and hard work. Certainly, most members of the intelligentsia will dismiss these "values" as opportunistic humbug, but it has some influence among the middle classes who fear the specter of extreme individualization–probably demonstrated by the example of their own children.

The Southeast Asian societies in focus experienced extremely rapid change. This means that the parental world, let alone the grandparental, has lost much of its relevance for the conduct of life of the young. We have noted that during their education, Philippine schools failed in connecting the confusing present to a meaningful past. They did not hand over intellectual tools for comprehending actual society either. This holds for Thai and Indonesian formal education, too. The approach school takes is based on ideas about community, about the idealized nation that, practically, is in the care of a state run by rapacious politicians. As a result, the new generations shrug at nationalistic propaganda–although the Thais, with their king, are doing better on that count. All the same, though, the anonymous urban environment invites consumerism and self-centeredness rather than identification with society or nation.

School recognizes this as a problem. It counters with plenty of moralistic advice. Yet, such advice is family-based, and not conducive to guide life in the big world. Even if it were, ideas like legality, representative democracy, citizens' and human rights make little sense in an environment where the practice of privilege, inequality, and patronage spell the order of the day. For the better educated this often results in global perspectives and comparisons (we should be democratic!). Irrespective of education, we see that more locally focused and personal commitments flourish. Religion, cults, and sectarianism are booming. Regional identities are reviving. Small-familism is convincing. These tendencies hint at a separation of the public and the private spheres the constitution-writing older generation hoped to overcome. This means that the hoped-for citizen, who feels responsible for the common weal, is scarcely forthcoming–which is reflected in the underdevelopment of civil society.

Another way of putting this is the idea that the experience of society is, in itself, new. The social imagination is, of old, preoccupied with community. The confrontation with urban society, with the persistent pursuit of money, with a businesslike attitude and anonymity is, therefore, new in the sense that little or no positive culture to deal with that situation has ever developed (unlike in the West or other places with old traditions of urban life and citizenship). This moral void, this absence of commitment, fuels the powerful appeals of consumerism, particularism, religion and individualism. In society, one is on one's own. Enjoy it. Make the best of it.

This is born out by the state of the state. The state is run by business; politics is business. As far as the Philippines goes, this is an old situation that has been institutionalized by the regime of the first Commonwealth President Quezon. Gradually, business penetrated the state in Thailand, too. So, whereas of old, the bureaucracy lorded it over those who made money, in the 1960s, when development began, things begin to turn. In the 1980s and 1990s this change had matured, and resulted in the money politics of "business" or "buffet" cabinets. In Indonesia, crony capitalism as a system of state has grown so blatant as to discredit and delegitimize the government. With this state of affairs, it can only be expected that feelings of nationalism and identification with country grow weaker. In combination with individualization and consumer culture, this results in urban indifference and cynicism, or a disinterested attitude towards civic action.

In the absence of a firm economic basis, civil society would anyhow be weak. In Indonesia, the middle classes are largely state-dependent, or ethnically Chinese–which practically means to be at the margin of society. In the Philippines, these classes seem to develop on the basis of advanced education, while business is intimately allied with patronage and power politics. In Thailand the mainly ethnic-Chinese middle classes are now part of mainstream society, and have recently given rise to the promise of a more vigorous civil society. It is too early, however, to predict that even where a more vibrant public opinion and activism have come to life that civil society will develop into a serious opponent of state and politics, and the big-business interests allied with these.

Considering these relative similarities, the culture of the public world seems to be dominated by business and consumerism, mass media–national and international, urban lifestyles, anonymity and individualization. The view of the nation, of the common good, and even civic activism are evaporating; the likeness with living in the market is increasing. Looking across borders is becoming more common.

This globalizing perspective seems to stimulate, not so much national identification, but identification with more particularistic, more primordial bonds, such as those offered by the family, region of origin, religion and sects. It appears, therefore, that the three societies under consideration all have come to suffer from a gradually growing deficit in nationalism and civic commitment. In the final analysis, their cultures of the public world appear to be subject to the same impulsions of modernity.

Bibliographic Note

THE IMAGES of the public world presented were self-evident. They were visible in the urban landscape, written down in newspapers, schoolbooks and other documents, and reflected in fiction. These images, therefore, needed little footnoting. Nonetheless, certain readers might want to know what to consult to advance their understanding of the Philippines, and of the specific subject matter put forward in this text. To these purposes, a few titles will here be suggested.

The standard introduction to country, culture and society is Steinberg's *The Philippines: A Singular and a Plural Place*. The currently available third edition has been revised and updated to 1994. Apart from touching upon a wide range of subjects of interest, the book should also be commended for its lavish list of bibliographic references. Mulder, in his *Inside Philippine Society,* takes a historical-anthropological approach to life in the urban Christian lowlands, explaining religious practice, interpersonal relationships, and the evolution of the public world. These are then placed in a comparative, Southeast

Asian perspective that results in making the Philippines far less exceptional to that part of the world than it is often held to be.

Most literature on urban space deals with specific problems, and spends little attention to the images cities convey, or the mentality of their inhabitants. Often such matters are best treated in books written for visitors and in certain, critical or chauvinistic, newspaper columns. Still, for the history and appearance of public space, the following titles may be useful: Doeppers, *Manila: 1900-1941;* Hart, *The Philippine Plaza Complex;* Caoili, *The Origins of Metropolitan Manila.*

There is a considerable amount of literature on the media, including movies and television. Much of this is published in the form of articles that are not always easy to find. About the press, it is worth one's while to be attentive to the publications of the National Press Club. Not too hard to find should be: Pinedo-Ofreneo, *The Manipulated Press;* del Mundo, *Philippine Mass Media;* Reyes, *Press Freedom: The People's Right.*

In our considerations of school materials we have noted that the teaching of history, educational practice, and the question of nationhood are often thought to be interconnected. For exposing the colonial nature of Philippine education, Constantino's "The Miseducation of the Filipino," first published in 1966, is the pioneering text. Constantino also is the father of writing "history with a purpose" such as, for instance, demonstrated in his influential *The Philippines: A Past Revisited.* Scott was perplexed by what he found to be quasi-perennial myths in standard school texts. His subsequent research, *Prehispanic Source Materials,* is most revealing. He also published a positive picture of life and conditions upon colonial contact through his adept use of early Spanish sources in *Looking for the Prehispanic Filipino.* Anyway, it will certainly take a fair amount of time before schooling induces the sense of nationhood. Of interest in this respect are Ma. Luisa C. Doronila's investigations, such as "The Nature, Organization and Sources of Students' National Identity Orientations."

With politics, we arrive at the economy and the national power elite. The interrelatedness of these institutions has been explored by Wurfel in his *Filipino Politics: Development and Decay* (which contains an excellent section on "suggested readings"), and have further been founded by Yoshihara in his *Philippine Industrialization.* Whereas many of the facts in these two studies are dated now, the system as such has not changed. What it looked like late in the Aquino administration has been brought together by Dahm in *Economy and Politics.* How the polity operates at the level of power brokerage has been documented by McCoy in the collection, *An Anarchy of Families*. In this work, the interface of the state on the one side, and of the influential families on the other, has been authoritatively explored. How things were, and often still are, when seen from below has been researched by Kerkvliet in *The Huk Rebellion: A Study of Peasant Revolt.*

Fiction offers a rich field of insights into Filipino life. A standard work–updated from time to time–is Lumbera's *Philippine Literature*. For somewhat different views, Francia's *Brown River, White Ocean* is interesting, too, although this anthology is restricted to Philippine literature in English. Eventually, it may be of interest to know a book everybody at high school has to read, namely the *Noli Me Tangere* by the national hero Jose Rizal. Of its many editions and translations, I hold those by Charles E. Derbyshire (*The Social Cancer*) and Jorge Bocobo to be the best.

In a few places, explicit comparisons have been made with Thailand and Indonesia. These were based on parallel investigations into the culture of the public world of these countries. The results have been published as Niels Mulder, *Thai Images* and *Mysticism in Java. Ideology in Indonesia* (Chapters 7-9).

Notes

Chapter 1

[1] See discussion in Chapter 4.

Chapter 3

[1] Fr. Leo James English, op. cit., vi.

Chapter 3 - Excursion One

[1] DECS, op. cit., 2.

[2] Ibid., 70.

[3] Ibid., 270.

Chapter 4

[1] This rewording of the intention of the Educational Development Decree of 1972 has been quoted from the Preface of the series, "Our Country and its People" (Manila: Bookmark, 1987).

[2] F.T. Leogardo et al., *Challenges in Philippine Community Life* (Manila: Philippine Book Company, 1974), 127, 130-32.

[3] DECS, 1989, 27.

[4] Ibid., 29.

[5] Ibid., 33.

[6] Ibid., 34-37.

[7] Ibid., 38.

[8] DECS, op. cit., 1989, 55.

[9] Ibid., 56.

[10] Ibid., 60.

[11] Ibid., 63.

[12] Ibid., 69.

[13] Ibid., 71.

[14] Ibid., 70.

[15] Ibid., 71-77.

[16] Ibid., 92-114.

[17] Ibid., 102-03.

[18] Ibid., 112.

[19] Ibid., 114.

[20] Ibid., 116.

[21] Ibid.

[22] Ibid., 143.

[23] Ibid., 149-58.

[24] Ibid., 182.

[25] Ibid.

[26] Ibid., 186.

[27] Ibid., 187-200.

[28] Ibid., 227.

[29] Andrew Gonzalez, F.S.C. et al., *Kasaysayan at Pamahalaang Pilipino: Unang Antas, Araling Panlipunan para sa Mataas na Paaralan* (Quezon City: Phoenix Publishing House, 1989).

[30] Gonzalez., op. cit., 46.

[31] Ibid., 51.

[32] Ibid., 54.

[33] Ibid.

[34] Ibid., 57.

[35] Ibid., 60.

[36] Ibid., 64-65.

[37] Ibid., 67.

[38] Ibid., 70-71.

[39] Ibid., 72-79.

[40] Ibid., 80-86.

[41] Ibid., 87-91.

[42] Ibid., 94-100.

[43] Ibid., 116-52.

[44] Ibid., 132.

[45] Ibid., 133.

[46] Ibid., 169.

[47] Ibid., passim, 70-75.

[48] Ibid., 174-82.

[49] Ibid., 183-84.

[50] Ibid., 184-87.

[51] Ibid., 191-93.

[52] Ibid., 195-96.

[53] Ibid., 212-30.

[54] Ibid., 232-82.

[55] Ibid., 284-94.

[56] Ibid., 284-312.

[57] Ibid., 313-18.

[58] Ibid., 321-27.

[59] Ibid., 327-37.

[60] Ibid., 340-43.

[61] Ibid., 344-54.

[62] Ibid.

[63] Hector S. de Leon, *Textbook on the Philippine Constitution* (Manila: Rex Book Store, 1996).

[64] Ibid., 40-41.

[65] DECS, op cit., 1986, 31-50.

[66] Ibid., 122.

[67] Ibid., 120-24.

[68] Ibid., 149-62.

[69] Ibid., 162-68.

[70] Ibid., 168-75.

[71] DECS, op. cit., 1989, 202-05.

[72] Ibid., 207-19.

[73] Ibid., 220-27.

[74] Ibid., 226.

[75] DECS, op. cit., 1992, 65.

[76] Ibid., 67-68.

[77] Ibid., 232.

[78] Ibid., 232-33.

[79] Ibid., 288-92.

[80] Ibid., 292.

[81] Hector de Leon, op. cit., iii.

[82] Ibid., 159.

[83] Ibid., 159-60.

[84] Ibid., 161.

[85] Ibid., 163.

[86] Ibid., 172.

[87] Ibid., 395.

[88] Ibid., 538-39.

[89] Ibid., 558.

Chapter 5

[1] Veneracion., op. cit., iii-iv.

[2] Ibid., iv.

[3] Ibid., 1.

[4] Ibid., 4.

[5] Ibid., 5.

[6] Ibid., 7.

[7] Ibid., 10.

[8] Ibid., 13.

[9] Ibid., 29.

[10] Ibid., 43-47.

[11] Ibid., 41.

[12] Ibid., 49.

[13] Ibid., 50.

[14] Ibid., 51-52.

[15] Ibid., 52-53.

[16] Ibid., 53-54.

[17] Ibid., 56.

[18] Ibid., 66-68.

[19] Ibid., 68-69.

[20] Ibid., 69-72.

[21] Ibid., 73-75.

[22] Ibid., 75.

[23] Ibid., 79.

[24] Ibid., 79-82.

[25] Ibid., 84-86.

[26] Ibid., 86-87.

[27] Ibid., 88.

[28] Ibid., 93-96.

[29] Ibid., 105-10.

[30] Ibid., 119-23.

[31] Ibid., 125-29.

[32] Ibid., 129-32.

[33] Ibid., 134.

[34] Ibid., 139-40.

[35] Ibid., 141-43.

[36] Ibid., 143-44.

[37] Ibid., 118.

[38] Ibid., 144-46.

[39] Ibid., 151-54.

[40] Ibid., 163-64.

[41] Ibid., 165-67.

[42] Ibid., 154-58.

[43] Ibid., 168-69.

[44] Ibid., 170-72.

[45] Ibid., 172-76.

[46] Ibid., 176.

[47] Ibid., 176-77.

[48] Ibid., 178-80.

[49] Ibid., 180-88.

[50] Ibid., 194-95.

[51] Ibid., 188-90.

[52] Ibid., 193.

[53] Ibid., 196-97.

[54] Ibid., 198-99.

[55] Ibid., 200-03.

[56] Ibid., 203-04.

[57] Ibid., 206-10.

[58] Ibid., 212-21.

[59] Ibid., 221-22.

[60] Ibid., 226-39.

[61] Ibid., 239-40.

Chapter 6

[1] Domingo Landicho, *Bulaklak ng Maynila* (Quezon City: Ateneo de Manila University Press, 1995).

[2] Irah Borinaga, *Shifting Sands* (Quezon City: Giraffe Books, 1997).

[3] Published by the Quezon City Center for Migrant Workers (Kanlungan Center Foundation, Inc.), 1994.

[4] Comment of Conrad de Quiros, back cover.

[5] Irah B. Borinaga, *Distant Echoes: A Modern-day Novella* (Quezon City: New Day Publishers, 1993).

[6] Crescenciano Gonzaga, *The Yawning Gap* (Quezon City: New Day Publishers, 1991).

[7] Josefina Protacio, *Fiesta People* (Quezon City: New Day Publishers, 1994).

[8] Protacio, op. cit., 8.

[9] Ibid., 10-11.

[10] Ibid., 12.

[11] Ibid., 34.

[12] Ibid., 32.

[13] Ibid., 33.

[14] Ibid., 54.

[15] Ibid., 82.

[16] Ibid., 99.

[17] Quentin Reynolds and Geoffrey Bocca, *Macapagal: The Incorruptible* (New York: David McKay Co. Inc., 1965).

[18] Protacio, op. cit., 107.

[19] Ibid., 116-17.

[20] Ibid., 146.

[21] Ibid., 146-47.

[22] Ibid., 149.

[23] Ibid., 198.

[24] Ibid., 193.

[25] Paulino Lim, Jr., *Requiem for a Rebel Priest* (Quezon City: New Day Publishers, 1996).

[26] Ibid., 41.

[27] Ibid., 108.

[28] Ibid., 188.

[29] F. Sionil Jose, *Sin: A Novel* (Manila: Solidaridad Publishing House, 1994).

[30] Ibid., 167.

[31] F. Sionil Jose., op. cit., 13.

[32] Ibid.

[33] Ibid., 38.

[34] Ibid., 97.

[35] Roland B. Tolentino, *Alibangbang* (Manila: Anvil Publishing Inc., 1994).

[36] Ibid., v.

[37] Ibid., vi.

[38] Ibid., 66.

[39] Ibid., 16.

[40] Ibid., ix.

[41] Eli R. Guieb III, *Pitada* (Metro Manila: Anvil Publishing Inc., 1994).

Chapter 7

[1] de Leon, op. cit., 558.

Bibliography

Abante, 11 December 1997.

Agoncillo, Teodoro A. *The Revolt of the Masses: The Story of Bonifacio and the Katipunan.* Quezon City: University of the Philippines, 1956.

Azurin, Arnold M. *Reinventing the Filipino: Sense of Being and Becoming.* Quezon City: University of the Philippines Press, 1993.

Caoili, Manuel A. *The Origins of Metropolitan Manila: A Political and Social Analysis.* Quezon City: New Day Publishers, 1988.

Constantino, Renato. "The Miseducation of the Filipino." *The Filipinos in The Philippines and Other Essays.* Quezon City: Malaya Books, 1966.

________________. *The Philippines: A Past Revisited.* Metro Manila: Tala Publishing Corporation, 1975.

Corpuz, Onofre D. *The Roots of the Filipino Nation.* Vol. I, II. Quezon City: Aklahi Foundation, Inc., 1989.

Covar, Prospero R. "Tatlong Sanaysay: Pagkatao at Paniniwala." In *Reading Popular Culture.* Edited by Soledad Reyes. Quezon City: Ateneo de Manila University, Office of Research and Publications, 1991: 182-97.

Dahm, Bernhard, ed. *Economy and Politics in the Philippines Under Corazon Aquino.* Hamburg: Institut fur Asienkunde, 1991.

De Leon, Hector S. *Textbook on the Philippine Constitution.* Manila: Rex Book Store, 1996.

DECS

Agap at Sikap: Batayang Aklat sa Edukasyon Pantahanan at Pangkabuhayan para sa Ikaanim na Baitang. Quezon City: Instructional Materials Development Center, 1988. (Textbook printed annually until 1997.)

"Araling Panlipunan I." *Pagtatag ng Bansang Pilipino. Batayang Aklat para sa Unang Taon ng Mataas na Paaralan.* Quezon City: Instructional Materials Corporation, 1989.

"Araling Panlipunan IV." *Ang Kasaysayan ng Daigdig. Ikaapat na Taon ng Mataas na Paaralan.* Quezon City: Instructional Materials Corporation, 1992.

Pilipinas: Heograpiya at Kasaysayan; Ang Pilipinas sa Iba't-Ibang Panahon; Ang Pilipino sa Pagbuo ng Bansa. Quezon City: Instructional Materials Corporation, 1986. (Textbook series reprinted annually until 1995.)

Sibika at Kultura I, II, III. Quezon City: Instructional Materials Corporation, 1991. (Textbook series reprinted annually until 1992.)

Del Mundo, Clodualdo, ed. *Philippine Mass Media: A Book of Readings.* Manila: CA Publishers, 1986.

Doeppers, Daniel F. *Manila, 1900-1941: Social Change in the Late Colonial Metropolis.* New Haven, Connecticut: Yale University Southeast Asian Studies, 1984.

Doronila, Ma. Luisa C. "The Nature, Organization and Sources of Students' National Identity Orientations." Education Forum (ed.), *Towards Relevant Education.* Quezon City: Association of Major Religious Superiors in the Philippines, 1986.

English, Leo James. *Tagalog-English Dictionary.* Metro Manila: Congregation of The Most Holy Redeemer and National Book Store, 1989.

Enriquez, Virgilio E. *From Colonial to Liberation Psychology: The Philippine Experience.* Quezon City: University of the Philippines Press, 1992.

Francia, Luis H. *Brown River, White Ocean: An Anthology of Twentieth-Century Philippine Literature in English.* New Brunswick, NJ: Rutgers University Press, 1993.

Gonzalez, Andrew, et al. *Kasaysayan at Pamahalaang Pilipino. Unang Antas, Araling Panlipunan Para Sa Mataas Na Paaralan.* Quezon City: Phoenix Publishing House, 1989.

Guerrero, Amado. *Philippine Society and Revolution.* Oakland, California: International Association of Filipino Patriots, 1979.

Hart, Donn V. *The Philippine Plaza Complex: A Focal Point in Culture Change.* New Haven, Connecticut: Yale University Southeast Asian Studies, 1955.

Hidalgo, C. P. and P. Patajo-Legasto. *Philippine Post-Colonial Studies: Essays on Language and Literature.* Quezon City: University of the Philippines Press, 1993.

Joaquin, Nick. *Culture and History: Occasional Notes on The Process of Philippine Becoming.* Metro Manila: Solar Publishing Corporation, 1988.

Jose, Vivencio R. "The Profession of Literature and The Road to Excellence: A Foreword." *Philippine Humanities Review I/1-2,* 1984a, i-vii.

_______________. "Folk Literature and Social Movements." *Philippine Humanities Review I/3-4,* 1984b, 38-65.

Kerkvliet, Benedict J. *The Huk Rebellion: A Study of Peasant Revolt in the Philippines.* Berkeley (etc.): University of California Press, 1977.

Leogardo, F. T. and J. R. Navarro. *Challenges in Philippine Community Life.* Manila: Philippine Book Company, 1974.

Lumbera, Bienvenido. *Philippine Literature: A History and Anthology.* Metro Manila: National Book Store, 1982.

Manila Bulletin, 11 December 1997.

Manila Standard, 11 December 1997; 23 February 1998.

The Manila Times, 6, 7, 8, January 1998.

McCoy, Alfred W. *An Anarchy of Families: State and Family in the Philippines.* Madison, Wisconsin: University of Wisconsin, Center for Southeast Asian Studies, 1993.

Mulder, Niels. "Philippine Textbooks and The National Self-Image." *Philippine Studies 38/1*, 1990, 84-102.

______________. *Inside Southeast Asia: Religion, Everyday Life, Cultural Change.* Amsterdam, Kuala Lumpur: The Pepin Press, 1996.

______________. *Inside Philippine Society: Interpretations of Everyday Life.* Quezon City: New Day Publishers, 1997a.

______________. *Thai Images: The Culture of the Public World.* Chiang Mai: Silkworm Books, 1997b.

______________. *Mysticism in Java. Ideology in Indonesia.* Amsterdam, Singapore: The Pepin Press, 1998, Chapters 7-9.

Navarro, Atoy, et al., eds. *Pantayong Pananaw: Ugat at Kabuluhan.* Lunsod Mandaluyong: Palimbagang Kalawakan, 1997.

Philippine Daily Inquirer, 1, 13, 24 December 1997; 1, 16, 27 January 1998; 4, 5, 8, 12, 23 February 1998.

The Philippine Journal, 6 December 1997.

The Philippine Star, 11, 19 December 1997; 10, 18 January 1998.

Pilipino Star Ngayon, 11 December 1997.

Pinedo-Ofreneo, Rosalinda. *The Manipulated Press: A History of Philippine Journalism since 1945.* Metro Manila: Solar Publishing Corporation, 1986.

Reid, Anthony. *Southeast Asia in the Age of Commerce, 1450-1680.* New Haven, London: Yale University Press, 1988.

Reyes, Ed. *Press Freedom: The People's Right-Assertion and Repression in the Philippines.* Manila: Philippine Movement for Press Freedom, 1992.

Reyes, Soledad, ed. *Reading Popular Culture.* Quezon City: Ateneo de Manila University, Office of Research and Publications, 1991.

Rizal, Jose. *Noli Me Tangere.* Berlin, 1887.

Salazar, Zeus A., et al., "Philippine Studies and Pilipinolohiya: Two Heuristic Views in the Study of Matters Filipino." Draft paper, European Conference on Philippine Studies, Amsterdam, 1991.

______________. *Pantayong Pananaw: Ugat at Kabuluhan.* Lunsod Mandaluyong: Palimbagang Kalawakan, 1997.

Scott, William H. "Boat-building and Seamanship in Classic Philippine Society." In *Cracks in the Parchment Curtain.* Quezon City: New Day Publishers, 1982.

______________. *Prehispanic Source Materials for the Study of Philippine History.* Quezon City: New Day Publishers, 1984. (Originally published in 1968 by the University of Santo Tomas.)

______________. *Looking for the Prehispanic Filipino.* Quezon City: New Day Publishers, 1992.

Steinberg, David J. *The Philippines: A Singular and A Plural Place.* Boulder, Col.: Westview Press, 1994.

Taliba, 11 December 1997.

Today, 7 February 1998.

Veneracion, Jaime B. *Agos ng Dugong Kayumanggi.* Quezon City: Abiva Publishing House, 1990.

Wurfel, David. *Filipino Politics: Development and Decay.* Ithaca: Cornell University Press, 1988.

Yoshihara Kunio. *Philippine Industrialization: Foreign and Domestic Capital.* Quezon City: Ateneo de Manila University Press, 1985.

Index